LA FRANCE GASTRONOMIQUE

London
Nov. 1996.

LA FRANCE
GASTRONOMIQUE

ANNE WILLAN

PAVILION

This edition published in Great Britain in 1995 by
PAVILION BOOKS LIMITED
26, Upper Ground, London SE1 9PD
Originally published in paperback in 1991
Text copyright © Anne Willan Inc. 1991
Photographs copyright © Michael Boys 1991

Designed by Bernard Higton
Cover photograph by John Miller

A CIP catalogue record for this book is available from the
British Library.

ISBN 1 85793 715 5

10 9 8 7 6 5 4 3 2 1

Printed and bound in Spain

This book may be ordered by post direct from the publisher.
Please contact the Marketing Department.
But try your bookshop first.

Title page photograph Papeton d'Aubergines
Right: Landscape in Burgundy

Acknowledgements

In writing *La France Gastronomique* I've been fortunate to have
had the generous assistance of my friend and fellow francophile,
Elisabeth Evans. Her research and guidance informs so much of
this book, particularly the chapters on Brittany, Gascony,
Périgord and the Loire, where we shared the footwork and
itinerant tastings. I am also indebted to Linda Sonntag for her
painstaking review of each chapter as the work progressed. As
always, in compiling this book I have relied on trainees at La
Varenne Cooking School for fact-finding and, most importantly,
for developing and testing the recipes and it is my pleasure to
thank Mary Bunten, Michele Gentile, Martha Holmberg, Kate
Krader, Lauren McGreal, Cynthia Nims and Kelly Worth for
their help. Nor could I forget my husband, Mark Cherniavsky,
invaluable witness to all that I saw, heard and scented as we
travelled around France. *Testis unus, testis nullus.*

Anne Willan

CONTENTS

INTRODUCTION

Maurice Sailland, better known as Curnonsky, Prince des Gastronomes, was the first person to write a book called *La France Gastronomique*. That was seventy years ago, when motoring around France involved lots of tyre changes and radiators on the boil. It must have been quite an effort for a Dion-Bouton to haul Curnonsky up a hill, for he not only looked like Mr Bibendum, the portly man composed of tyres, but was actually cast in that role by the Michelin Tyre Company.

Town by town, if not village by village, Curnonsky documented the rich gastronomic heritage of rural France. 'Good food is when things have the flavour of what they are,' he said. Any habitation, anywhere, that could boast a fine table or lay claim to an indigenous cooking method or recipe, was entered in the book – or rather whole series of books that eventually saw the light of day as 21 small paperbacks.

In this new *La France Gastronomique* I make no claim to such encyclopedic coverage. Rather I have explored 10 very different regions, focussing on their gastronomic makeup, on their geography, on their history, and most importantly on their people, who make them what they are – the fish farmer in the Pays de Dombes who never eats fish, the farmer's wife for whom the food of Provence is 'like the light, red, yellow and explosive'. Each chapter traces an itinerary, though often it wanders quite indirectly from point to point, or traces an uneven circle. In general I've kept to the countryside, though a few great gastronomic cities are included, such as Lyon and Strasbourg.

Much has disappeared, of course, since Curnonsky did his rounds, but France still describes itself as 'profondément rurale' with 85 per cent of the landmass and 27 per cent of the population so classified. Little more than an hour from Notre Dame you'll still find peasants living off the land, growing their own fruit and vegetables, raising rabbits, poultry and eggs, brewing wine or cider and 'eau-de-vie', the water of life.

I am happy to report that things still do have the flavour of what they are, summed up I hope in the 100 recipes of this book. Long concerned with quality, the French are preoccupied with good ingredients. They are the only nation in the world to apply not just hygiene controls, but also quality controls – 'appellation contrôlée' – to their food as well as their wine. Where else would you find an 'Association de Croqueurs de Pommes', a group of apple eaters (not growers, you notice) on the Loire, devoted to saving ancient, tasty varieties of the fruit. As for cooking, here too standards are exacting: apprentices start at age sixteen, and the village 'boulanger' is at work by 4 a.m. to give his dough the long, slow rising needed for flavour.

That the French outdo us all in appreciation of good things is still true, and I've had a wonderful time putting it to the test!

Anne Willan
Château du Feÿ, 89300 Villecien

RULES OF THE ROAD

3 ASK THE LOCALS for advice, whether in a shop or café. A packed restaurant or charcuterie overflowing with customers speaks for itself.

4 CLOSING TIMES CAN BE A TRAP. Villages and provincial towns start early and close from midday until 2 p.m. In the Mediterranean this may extend to 4 p.m. with late closing at 7 to 8 p.m. So that lunch and dinner can be purchased on the way home from work, many food shops open from 9 a.m. to 1 p.m., then from 4 to 8 p.m. Sunday morning is most important of all for charcuteries and pâtisseries, but they close all day Monday in compensation, as does commerce in general in most of the country. Tuesday is standard closing day for museums.

5 PUBLIC HOLIDAYS or 'jours fériés' are observed with enthusiasm. If they fall on a weekend, a Friday or Monday may be taken instead. If they fall on a Tuesday or Thursday, the intervening 'pont' to bridge with the weekend may be thrown in, especially by banks.

6 DON'T TRAVEL WITHOUT AT LEAST ONE GUIDEBOOK. The three major hotel and restaurant guides are the Michelin red guide, Gault Millau and Bottin Gourmand. Gault Millau is informative and lively, but can be opinionated, and many people prefer Michelin, despite its conservatism. These guides also tell you each restaurant's weekly closing day and annual holidays, which may catch you unawares. If you are a buff of weekly markets, antique fairs ('brocantes'), and local festivals, there's an obscure but useful annual, *Indicateur Lahure*, issued by Publications Mandel in Paris.

7 FOR GENERAL BACKGROUND INFORMATION on history, geography and cultural matters, the green *Guides Michelins* are without equal, and most are available in English. For the inveterate traveller, the *Guides Bleus* provide exhaustive information.

8 BEWARE OF THE HIGH TOURIST SEASON, in summer in the south and on the coasts, and in winter on the ski slopes. Accommodation is full, facilities overstretched and expensive. May/June and September/October in those same resorts can be delightful, and you can risk travelling without reservations. Out of season, however, many resort hotels and cultural attractions are shut.

1 CHOOSE YOUR ROAD CAREFULLY. Less frequented N roads ('routes nationales') or better still D roads ('routes départementales') provide much the best view of the countryside. However, to travel long distances and reach your destination quickly, the autoroute is best. Some double-track N roads are also fast-moving but many are three-lane, clogged with traffic and with impatient drivers.

2 MAKE GOOD USE OF TOURIST OFFICES or 'syndicats d'initiatives'. They supply free maps, list hotels and events and local attractions and, if you encounter the right person behind the counter, offer lots of lively advice.

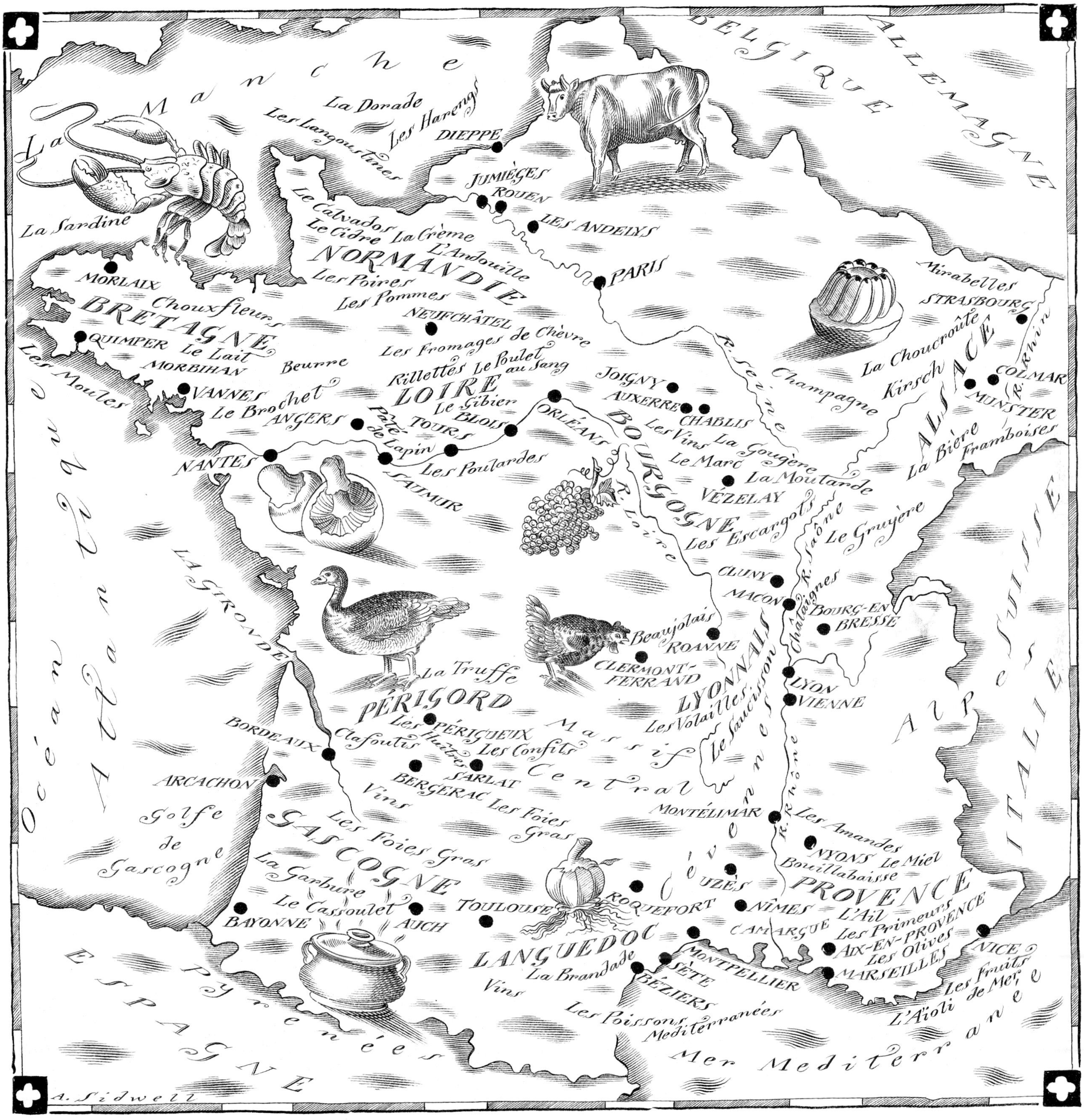

La Manche

BELGIQUE

ALLEMAGNE

La Dorade
Les Langoustines
Les Harengs
DIEPPE

JUMIÈGES
ROUEN
LES ANDELYS

PARIS

La Sardine
Le Calvados
Le Cidre La Crème
L'Andouille
NORMANDIE
Les Poires
Les Pommes

MORLAIX
Chouxfleurs
BRETAGNE
QUIMPER Le Lait
MORBIHAN   Beurre
VANNES Le Brochet
ANGERS
NANTES

NEUFCHÂTEL
Les Fromages de Chèvre

Rillettes Le Poulet au Sang
LOIRE
Le Gibier
TOURS BLOIS
Pâté de Lapin
SAUMUR
Les Poulardes

ORLÉANS

Mirabelles
STRASBOURG
La Choucroûte
Kirsch
COLMAR
MUNSTER
La Bière
Framboises
ALSACE

JOIGNY
AUXERRE CHABLIS
Les Vins La Gougère
Le Marc La Moutarde
VÉZELAY
BOURGOGNE
Les Escargots
Le Gruyère

CLUNY
MÂCON
BOURG-EN-BRESSE
Beaujolais
ROANNE
CLERMONT-FERRAND

Les Moules
Les Fromages

Champagne
R. Seine
R. Loire
R. Saône
R. Rhône
Chataignes

LA GIRONDE

La Truffe
PÉRIGORD
Les Huîtres PÉRIGUEUX
Clafoutis Les Confits
BERGERAC Les Foies Gras
SARLAT

BORDEAUX
ARCACHON
Golfe de Gascogne
Les Foies Gras
GASCOGNE
La Garbure
Le Cassoulet
BAYONNE AUCH

Massif Central

Les Volailles
LYONNAIS
Le Saucisson
LYON
VIENNE

Les Amandes
MONTÉLIMAR
NYONS Le Miel
Bouillabaisse
UZES
PROVENCE
L'Ail
CAMARGUE Les Primeurs
AIX-EN-PROVENCE
Les Olives
NÎMES
ROQUEFORT
TOULOUSE
LANGUEDOC
La Brandade
MONTPELLIER
SÈTE
BÉZIERS
Vins
Les Poissons Méditerranés

MARSEILLES
NICE
Les Fruits de Mer
L'Aïoli

Océan Atlantique
ESPAGNE
Pyrénées

SUISSE
Alpes
ITALIE

Mer Méditerranée

A. Sidwell

9

BURGUNDY

*Hearty country cooking in the lush valleys of
the Yonne, land of cherries, Chablis and fine cheeses, and
vegetable gardening at the Château du Feÿ*

To find Burgundy at its best only two hours' drive from Paris comes as a surprise. Or it did to us when first we moved to the Yonne valley, the lush, sunlit northern point of this most coveted province of France. The department of the Yonne embraces two of France's finest restaurants, while from Chablis comes a world-class wine. The churches at Sens, Auxerre, and Vézelay reflect a millenium of wealth, as do the neighbouring châteaux and manors, some equal to those of the Loire.

To reach the Yonne, take the Autoroute du Soleil to the southern exit at Auxerre, then branch east to Tonnerre. At once you are plunged into Burgundy proper – gentle rolling fields of grain, grazing herds of the brooding, buff Charolais cattle that are so renowned for their tasty lean meat. Within

minutes vines appear, their ordered rows swooping down from the horizon: you have reached Chablis. Soon they crowd on every hand as the ground upgrades from ordinary 'appellation contrôlée' territory to Chablis Premier Cru and finally to the Grand Cru slopes just outside the town. Above the town, at the lookout point to the north, you'll find a map which delineates the areas.

The town of Chablis is modest, with none of the tourist hype that the fame of its name might imply. Chablis has been through bad times: the climate is marginal for the Chardonnay grape and the technology for protecting budding vines from springtime frost is quite recent. In the cold winter of 1956 there were no vines on the 'grand cru' slopes of Les Clos and it became a toboggan run. The Chablisien vignerons maintain a low profile and to find the bourgeois houses normally associated with a wine town you must wander the back streets. Behind one of the honeyed stone façades is hidden the Hostellerie des Clos, a well-furbished hotel installed in an old hospice. The kitchen is inventive, adding a touch of modern lightness to dishes like fricassée of snails with garlic and basil, and young duck with cherries. Around the corner, you can taste the full range of local wines at 'La Chablisienne', one of the better-run French cooperative wineries to which small-scale producers sell their grapes. In the main square the Maison de L'Andouillette stocks not just sausages approved by the AAAAA (Association Amicale d'Amateurs d'Authentiques Andouillettes), but rarer vintages of Chablis together with decanters, glasses and bottles of Burgundian marc. Next door the charcuterie sells 'gougères', cheese choux puffs as big as your fist, the perfect accompaniment to a glass of Chablis in the café opposite. On the last Sunday in November, Chablis mounts a wine fair to celebrate the harvest.

Head northwest from Chablis and you'll come to the little-known Cistercian abbey of Pontigny. Within the tranquil purity of its walls Thomas à Becket passed most of his six years of exile before his martyrdom in 1170. It was after a visit to Pontigny that I made the acquaintance of Madame Fournillon, farmer, vintner, cook and mother of three. 'Force de la nature' is the only way to describe her smiling dynamism. The property at Bernouil near Tonnerre has been in the family since 1763 and includes, thanks to an accident of nature, three hectares of prerevolutionary vines growing on their original root stock. The soil is so sandy that the deadly phylloxera louse which attacks most ungrafted French roots cannot take hold. The 200-year-old vines still yield a pleasant, 'appellation Bourgogne contrôlée' white wine which sells for a third the price of Chablis.

If you call past to buy a case or two, Madame will give you a tour of the farm, with its orchards, vegetable garden, barns sheltering piglets by the dozen, 50 milking cows (she makes fresh cheese for the family table), flocks of turkeys, chicken and guineafowl/hen. The ducks and geese are herded separately, for they need more water. Last time I was there five mongrel puppies were gambolling in the yard, spared drowning at birth by Madame's kind heart. 'We always have babies of some kind here,' she laughs.

Back in the kitchen, Madame Fournillon 'mère' is in charge. The musky scent of simmering plums fills the air, while jars for the finished jam are waiting on the table. Already 'cornichon' gherkin pickles, apricot preserves, and peaches in syrup are stocked in the cupboard, with jelly to come once the red 'pinot noir' grapes are ripe. Soon the treats of autumn will appear: wild rabbit and perhaps the occasional hare; golden 'girolles', wild mushrooms which the Fournillon family top with a snail butter of garlic and herbs; and geese with chestnuts simmered in milk until almost tender, then roasted with the bird. All come from the property, together with 'marc' distilled from the lees of their own wine. Marc is the cousin of Italian 'grappa' and, as you might expect, has the dank, musty taste of grape seeds; it is little used in cooking though it makes a heady sorbet. Madame can truthfully claim as a matter of record as well as of pride that for the Fournillon family, living off the land is a reality.

There are many 'routes des châteaux' in France, but the one which winds south from Tonnerre along the lush blooming valley of the little Armançon river must be one of the most attractive. Tanlay and Ancy-le-Franc are the two star attractions. At Ancy the village baker sells fantasy loaves of 'pain d'épices' spice bread, baked in beehive or snail shapes, a speciality that dates back centuries to the height of Burgundian power when the Dukes ruled as far north as Flanders, key to the spice trade. In the late 1500s, spice bread bakers were so numerous that they formed a corporation to protect quality. Aromatic and moist but not heavy, spice bread is laden with honey – often you'll find beekeepers offer it in local markets as part of their stock in trade.

From Ancy the destination is Vézelay, with a detour via the Abbaye de Fontenay, founded by St Bernard in the 12th century. As you head west you will pass the fortified town of Semur-en-Auxois, with its pepperpot towers, and then Epoisses, an evocative name for the gastronome. Epoisses is one of France's great cheeses, its orange crust rinsed with a mixture of marc and water, until after two months the curd within is mellowed to a redolent golden cream. So tricky is the ageing process that one artisan producer advises ordering three weeks ahead to be sure the cheese is 'à point', when its odour is detectable at several yards!

Opposite: Chablis is an ancient wine centre. The cultivation of the Chardonnay grape in this northernmost point of Burgundy is not easy since vines are vulnerable to late spring frosts.

Above: Winter often brings snow to Northern Burgundy.

Left: For sausages approved by the AAAAA, visit the Maison de L'Andouillette in Chablis.

One of the most unusual wine counters in France is deep inside the caverns at Bailly, just south of Auxerre. It opens on weekends and does a brisk trade in crémant de Bourgogne.

Vézelay itself, once a departure point for the Crusades, is now a focus of gastronomic pilgrimage to L'Espérance in the valley at St Père-sous-Vézelay. Here the ambience is up-to-the-minute and the cuisine superb. Marc and Françoise Meneau form the classic husband and wife team, he in the kitchen, she in the dining room. Meneau is one of the chefs whose creations inspire imitators throughout France. It is here you should taste the originals of dishes like his astonishing fritters filled with a morsel of melted foie gras, his broth of kidney with vegetables, and his sea bass with anise in a crust of salt. Once a year Marc Meneau invites friends to a 'Fête de Cochon', when he serves such dishes as fresh 'boudin' blood sausage, tiny, light-as-a-feather pork pies, and the ancient Burgundian 'couée', a stew of lungs, liver and heart laced with red wine, onion, and the blood of the pig – potent stuff!

Any meal at L'Espérance must be accompanied by a visit to Vézelay, set on a spur of rock and riding like an ocean liner above the village of St Père. Ascending the narrow main street, you pass several studios selling the work of local artisans including Les Arts Régionaux, which stocks the pastel-tinted pottery of nearby Clamecy. Collectors pick up charms called 'fèves' – literally beans – in the shape of a fleur-de-lys or perhaps a bee. A fève is baked in the 'galette

des rois' on 6 January, and he who receives it is king for the day. The great basilica itself dates from the 12th century, the open, unadorned nave with Romanesque arches emphasized by a decoration of black and white stone. So successful is Viollet-le-Duc's 19th-century restoration that it is difficult to imagine that the abbey was in ruins even before the French Revolution.

From Vézelay, Auxerre beckons some 43 miles/70 kilometres to the north up the attractive valley of the rivers Cure and Yonne. Shortly before Auxerre come the wine villages of the Auxerrois Irancy, Coulanges-la-Vineuse, St Bris-le-Vineux and Chitry. This is the nearest wine-growing area to Paris, a short barge trip away, and Auxerrois wines were well known until a century ago when railways made the bolder wines from the south competitive in price. After decades of obscurity, the reputation of Auxerrois wines – mainly Chardonnay and Aligoté, but including some unusual reds from Irancy – is improving again. Best appreciated is the sparkling 'crémant de Bourgogne', which rivals a modest Champagne – look out especially for the pink version.

If you happen to hit a weekend, a treat awaits you at Bailly, a charming hamlet on the Yonne, where the local cooperative, SICAV, makes its crémant. Taking your car, you drive hundreds of yards inside the riverbank, deep into the quarry which provided the stone for the Panthéon in Paris. A huge spotlit cavern opens out, lined with a counter fringed with genial travellers sampling a glass before stocking up with bargain-price bubbly. Liqueurs are available too – 'mûre' (blackberry), 'framboise' (raspberry), and perfumed

'pêche de vigne' or wild peach, which is my favourite. Any of them can be substituted in 'kir', traditionally made of a tablespoon or two of 'cassis' blackcurrant liqueur topped with dry aligoté wine (the addition of crémant makes a 'kir royale'). Kir is named for Canon Kir, World War II resistance hero and mayor of Dijon, the capital of Burgundy.

Just a few miles downriver stands the ancient city of Auxerre, built along the curve of the Yonne in a majestic panaroma that has scarcely changed in 600 years. Set on the riverbank in the heart of the old town, the cozy Hôtel Le Maxime provides a good base for exploring the cathedral, the abbey church of St Germain, the Friday market in the central square, and shops like Chocolaterie Goussard on Place Charles Surugue, with its specialities of chocolate snails and grape truffles. As you wander, look upwards for lovebirds, caryatids, angels and Adam and Eve – you'll find them all on the carved wooden lintels that are a feature of Auxerre.

West from the city along the route B5, you enter the Puisaye region. The landscape loses its rolling Burgundian contours and becomes more intimate, dotted with smallholdings and artisan enterprises. I came across one of them quite by chance when shopping in the market. 'Ow are you today?' enquired the cheese-seller in fluent English learned, it transpired, in my obscure hometown of Northallerton in Yorkshire. Such coincidence was too good to miss and now Maurice Ravillard is our regular supplier of the well-aged 'crottins de Chavignol' goat cheeses that we like best – Sancerre, their place of origin, borders the Puisaye. Maurice has plenty of scope, for he works in an area well supplied with cheese. Soft yellow-skinned Soumaintrain and St Florentin cow cheeses come from near Tonnerre, the world-famous soft paste Brie and Coulommiers are made just to the north, with the tart cylindrical Chaource from nearby. The region of Vézelay also makes its own goat cheese, shaped as a truncated cone.

Maurice was once in the transport business, and his family were deeply disapproving when he changed career to deal in cheese. Unable to afford a cellar, he has airconditioned an old produce truck, lining the metal walls with shelves to hold the hundreds of cheeses bought locally or at Rungis wholesale market in Paris, to age or 'refine' at home. Each day they must be reversed; humidity is more critical than temperature in ensuring a cheese does not 'turn', becoming rancid before it is ripe. 'Buying is as important as selling,'

Real snails, chocolate snails, carved wooden snails – all are to be found in Auxerre.

remarks Maurice. He must carefully estimate demand so a cheese is sold at its peak, which may only last a day or two for delicate cheeses like Brie. 'I survive supermarket competition by offering service,' he says, 'by advising clients and explaining what to choose at a particular season.' Maurice points out that milk is at its best in spring and summer when cows are out at pasture. Since Brie, Coulommiers, Camembert, and the soft paste cheeses need about two months' ageing time, they are at their peak in summer and early autumn, as are Roquefort and other sheep cheeses. Goats do not lactate naturally in winter, so goat cheese almost disappears. Least seasonal of all are the hard cheeses such as Gruyère; as they are aged a year or more, a few months either way makes little difference.

The huge wine press at Champvallon, just south of Joigny, is wheeled into action once a year at a ceremonial pressing on a Sunday in late September or early October, depending on the harvest.

The Puisaye was the beloved home country of novelist Colette, who wrote: 'Not far from my village they made Soumaintrains, the red St Florentins, which came to our market dressed in beet leaves. I remember that the butter reserved for itself the long, elegant chestnut leaf with its serrated edges.' Colette was born at Toucy near the church in the rue des Vignes, a street which fills with basket-laden, jostling crowds during the Saturday market. Tastings of fresh peaches and bits of cheese are pressed into your hand: 'Just look at this! What quality! What a bargain!' cry the merchants. As always I am unable to resist. Last time we came away with a jar of limeflower honey, two basil plants, a selection of farmhouse goat cheeses, an antique cruet stand, a box of the biggest blackcurrants I've ever seen, and a pair of live doves for the pigeonhouse. Lunch at the Lion d'Or provided much-needed refreshment and honest country cooking: snails Bourguignonne, 'confit' of rabbit, a hefty steak and the local 'jambon Chablisienne' were on offer, the latter a piquant mix of ham baked in a sauce of juniper berries, shallots, and white wine, brilliant with paprika and tomato.

To explore this pretty country further, cut across to Champignelles and the farm of Madame Gilet who raises foie gras geese. Madame Gilet belongs to the Fermes Auberges group of more than 500 farmers throughout France who pledge to offer guests a family welcome and the best of homegrown produce at the table. Lunch or dinner taken in the Gilet farmhouse will include hearty dishes such as pumpkin soup, duck rillettes, and apple and apricot pie, the perfect end to a dinner of duck confit.

From here our route heads back northeast towards Joigny via the D14, but distractions lie along the way. In Champvallon, just south of Joigny, a huge winepress has been in almost continuous use since medieval times. In the half-light of the barn, the looming beam and primitive capstan mechanism resemble nothing so much as a siege engine of war. Champvallon wine is vinegary stuff but they make unexpectedly good ratafia, a common rural liqueur consisting of spirits (often marc or Calvados) mixed with the juice of grapes or apples. To make it at home, simply mix one part spirit with two parts of juice, seal it tightly in bottles and leave in a cool dark place. The high alcohol content prevents the fruit juice from fermenting, and after six months you'll have a serviceable liqueur which improves with further storage. (Ignore the sediment which will gather at the bottom of the bottle.)

Between Champvallon and Joigny, you can see our own Château du Feÿ, set commandingly on the skyline for maximum effect. The main house is 17th-century, its panelled rooms an old-world blend of opulence and country comfort. The students who come for cooking classes each summer are intrigued to glimpse how a great agricultural property was run. Over 2,000 hectares (5,000 acres) once surrounded the house, a sizeable proportion planted in vines. The barn shelters an 18th-century winepress, as well as a stone wheel for extracting walnut oil. In one corner stands the turreted pigeonhouse, crowned by a bird fashioned in lead, and we often fire up the old brick oven, for the crisp-crusted bread it produces is incomparable.

Our great pride is the walled vegetable garden, marked on the map of 1751. This is the domain of 70-year-old Monsieur Milbert, who plants according to phases of the moon and despises chemical fertilizer. The sheltered hectare of ground burgeons with fruit, from raspberries, strawberries and half a dozen plums to more esoteric quince, kiwi, medlar, and little wild peaches of incomparable sweetness. Red, white and blackcurrants (the foundation of cassis liqueur) flourish hereabouts, as do black and red cherries, both sweet and tart. Single-handed, Monsieur Milbert marshals the regimented lines of leeks, onions, garlic and tomatoes, the froth-leaved carrots, bulbous cabbages, bushy green beans, and crawling vines of cucumber and squash. He has even been persuaded to grow sweetcorn, though it never reaches his own table. 'Cattlefood!' he growls.

Following tradition, Madame Milbert looks after the poultry yard, raising a flock of chickens and seething hutches of rabbits, each more endearingly fluffy than the last. Her rabbit terrine is a perfect blend of gamey richness. Most nights she simmers a pared-down version of 'potée bourguignonne' which traditionally consists of diced shin of beef, a bit of salt pork, a garlic sausage, cabbage heart, potatoes, leeks, celery and turnip. The broth is poured over sliced bread, and the meat and vegetables eaten separately. In spring Madame Milbert dries lime flowers for herb tea, in summer she sits in the shade, shelling beans and peas by the hour, while in autumn it is the turn of wild chestnuts, gathered from the avenue outside the gate. Each Christmas we are presented with a bottle of homebrewed cassis liqueur, and of excruciatingly fiery Calvados distilled from Monsieur Milbert's cider.

Joigny just nearby brings a return to today's world, though even here the paved pedestrian streets wind steeply in medieval style around the venerable churches and bourgeois 'maisons de maître'. They cluster on the Côte St Jacques, an escarpment which has given its name to what is now one of France's top hostelries. Comparisons between the Côte St Jacques and L'Espérance, only an hour to the south, are inevitable. The Côte St Jacques premises have the advantage of bordering the Yonne river, and the installations are more luxurious, including a pool and private tunnel under the RN6. The atmosphere is perhaps more relaxed – it is certainly family-style, for Chef Michel Lorrain is ably seconded in the kitchen by his son Jean-Michel, while their wives share the dining room.

I have to confess to prejudice, for we live only 2 miles up the hill and have come to know this charming family well. Our students are welcomed in the kitchen and our son when aged 16 spent three memorable weeks there as a trainee, carrying bags and washing up. Each evening we eagerly awaited his reports of the food. This was the year of Chef Lorrain's gazpacho, a piquant cream garnished with langoustine tails and zucchini quenelles. Fresh cod was lightly salted to serve with a caviar and cream sauce, the duck came spiced with nutmeg, cloves and anise, and raw oysters were trapped 'en terrine' in a delicate jelly of red wine and shallots. It is great cooks like Michel Lorrain who bear testimony to the Burgundian motto 'Better a good meal than fine clothes'.

Roger Milbert with his beloved leeks in his domain, the vegetable garden at the Château du Feÿ.

RECIPES FROM
BURGUNDY

Potage de Potiron
—— PUMPKIN SOUP ——

In 1766, when Tobias Smollet travelled through Burgundy, he observed 'a vast quantity of very large pompions, with the contents of which [the Burgundians] thicken their soups and ragoûts'.

Serves 10–12
1 medium-large pumpkin, about 17 lb/7.5 kg
1⅔ pint/1 quart/1 litre milk
2 tbsp butter
1 medium onion, chopped finely
2 cloves garlic, chopped finely
2 tbsp flour
1⅔ pint/1 quart/1 litre chicken stock (p. 186)
1 tbsp curry powder
¼ tsp ground cinnamon
¼ tsp cayenne
salt and peper
8 fl oz/1 cup/250 ml crème fraîche (p. 183)
or double/heavy cream
8 fl oz/1 cup/250 ml double/heavy cream
8–10 tbsp crème fraîche (p. 183) or double/heavy cream
(to finish)
8 quart/10 quart/10 litre round ovenproof pot

Heat the oven to No 2/300°F/150°C. Cut a hole in the stem end of the pumpkin, retaining it as a lid. Scoop out the seeds and fibres and discard. Put the pumpkin in an ovenproof pot large enough to contain it. Add the milk to the centre of the pumpkin and replace the lid. Bake it in the heated oven until the flesh is tender, 2–2½ hours.

Remove the pumpkin from the oven, take off the lid, and with a large spoon, scrape as much flesh as possible from the hard outer skin, taking care not to puncture the bottom. Purée the flesh and milk mixture in a food processor or blender or work it through a sieve. There should be about 4⅔ pints/3 quarts/3 litres of pumpkin purée.

Heat the butter in a large pan, add the onion and garlic, and cook them over low heat until they are transparent but not brown. Stir in the flour and cook for one minute without browning. Whisk in the chicken stock and bring to the boil, stirring constantly until the soup thickens. Add the pumpkin purée, curry powder, cinnamon, cayenne, salt and pepper, and taste the soup for seasoning. Simmer it 5–10 minutes, stirring occasionally. It can be refrigerated up to 2 days.

To finish, bring the soup to the boil, whisk in the crème fraîche and double/heavy cream, bring just back to the boil and taste for seasoning. Spoon the soup into bowls, and stir in a spoonful of crème fraîche or double/heavy cream to marble it.

Gougères
—— CHEESE PUFFS ——

In Burgundy 'gougères' come the size of your fist, a perfect accompaniment to a glass of red or white wine. They should be crisp on the outside but slightly soft in the centre.

Makes 9–10 large gougères
pâte à choux (p. 185) made with 6 fl oz/¾ cup/175 ml water,
½ tsp salt, 2½ oz/⅓ cup/75 g unsalted butter,
4 oz/1 cup/125 g flour and 3–4 eggs
4 oz/125 g finely diced Gruyère cheese
1 egg, beaten to mix with ½ tsp salt (for glaze)
1 oz/30 g grated Gruyère cheese (for sprinkling)
Pastry bag and ¾ inch/2 cm plain tube (optional)

Heat the oven to No 5/375°F/190°C. Butter a baking sheet. Make the choux pastry. Once the pastry has reached the desired consistency, beat in the diced Gruyère.

Transfer the dough to the pastry bag and pipe 2½ inch/6 cm large mounds on the prepared baking sheet. Alternatively, shape the dough with two spoons. Brush the puffs with egg glaze and sprinkle with the grated cheese. Bake in the oven until the gougères are puffed and brown but still slightly soft inside, 30–40 minutes. Gougères are best eaten while still warm, but they can be baked up to 8 hours ahead. Keep them in an airtight container and warm them in a low oven before serving.

Opposite: Gougères.

Terrine de Lapin de Madame Milbert
—————— MADAME MILBERT'S RABBIT TERRINE ——————

Gherkin pickles are a mandatory accompaniment to this game terrine, with black olives too, if you like them. Chicken can be substituted for the rabbit.

Serves 10–12
3 lb/1.4 kg rabbit, cut in pieces (p. 186), with the liver
1 tbsp butter
2 tbsp brandy
2 tbsp madeira or sherry
½ tsp ground allspice
pinch of ground cloves
pinch of ground nutmeg
2–3 chicken livers
8 oz/250 g thinly sliced barding fat (p. 182)
1½ lb/750 g belly pork, minced/ground
1 tbsp salt, or to taste
1½ tsp black pepper, or to taste
sprig of thyme
1 bay leaf
3¹/₄ pint/2 quart/2 litre terrine mould

With a sharp-pointed knife, cut the meat from the legs of the rabbit, discarding the sinews. Cut the saddle meat from the backbone, and then remove the fillets from under the ribs. Slice the fillets and half the saddle meat lengthwise into long thick strips. Reserve the remaining saddle meat for the stuffing. Heat the butter in a frying pan and cook the strips gently until firm and white, 2–3 minutes. Note: this prevents the meat from shrinking and making hollows in the terrine.

Put the strips in a bowl with the brandy, Madeira or sherry, allspice, cloves and nutmeg, and mix well. Cover and leave to marinate for about an hour. Trim the rabbit and chicken livers of membrane, sprinkle them with salt and pepper and roll them in a sheet of barding fat to form a cylinder as long as the terrine. Line the terrine with the remaining barding fat, reserving a piece for the top.

For the stuffing, work the remaining uncooked rabbit meat, including the meat from the thigh, through the fine blade of a mincer/grinder with the pork. Drain the marinated strips, and beat the marinade into the pork with the salt and pepper. Fry a small piece of the mixture and taste: it should be highly seasoned.

Heat the oven to No 4/350°F/175°C. Spread a quarter of the minced/ground mixture in the lined mould, arrange half the rabbit strips on top, cover with a quarter more mixture, and set the cylinder of livers down the centre. Cover with half the remaining mixture, add the remaining rabbit strips and top with the remaining mixture. Cut the reserved barding fat in strips and arrange in a lattice on top of the meat. Add the thyme and bay leaf.

Set the mould in a water bath (p. 187) and bring to the boil on top of the stove. Cook the terrine, uncovered, in the oven until firm, 1½–2 hours. A skewer inserted in the centre should be hot to the touch when withdrawn and the juices should run clear. Let the terrine cool to tepid and then press it overnight with a 2 lb/1 kg weight on top. Cover the terrine and refrigerate it for at least two days and up to a week to allow the flavour to mellow. Unmould the terrine for serving, or serve it in the mould, cutting it in thick slices.

Oeufs en Meurette

—————— POACHED EGGS IN RED WINE SAUCE ——————

'Sauce meurette' is a Burgundian classic, a robust mixture of red wine, bacon, mushrooms and baby onions. It is always paired with eggs or fish, rivalling any of the more usual sauces with white wine. A fairly light red wine such as a Beaujolais is best for 'meurette' and it must be thoroughly reduced so the sauce is mellow. In France the dish would form a first course, but to my mind two poached eggs 'en meurette' as a main course must surely satisfy all but the heartiest of appetites.

Serves 4 as a main course
8 eggs
1 bottle (3 cups/750 ml) red burgundy wine
16 fl oz/2 cups/500 ml brown stock (p. 183)
For the sauce
1 tbsp butter
1 onion, thinly sliced
1 carrot, thinly sliced
1 stick of celery, thinly sliced
1 clove of garlic, crushed
bouquet garni (p. 183)
6 peppercorns
kneaded butter (p. 184) made with 2 tbsp butter and
2 tbsp flour
For the garnish
2 tbsp unsalted butter
3 oz/90 g mushrooms, quartered
16–20 baby onions, peeled
3 oz/90 g streaky bacon, cut in lardons (p. 184)
salt and pepper
8 round fried croûtes (p. 183), 2½ inches/6 cm in diameter

Poach (p. 184) the eggs, using the wine and stock in place of water and vinegar. Strain the cooking liquid and reserve it.

For the sauce: melt the butter, add the onion, carrot and celery and cook them gently until they are soft but not brown. Add the poaching liquid, garlic, bouquet garni and peppercorns and simmer for 20–25 minutes until the liquid is reduced by half.

Meanwhile, cook the garnish. Melt half the butter in a frying pan and sauté the mushrooms until tender and their moisture has evaporated. Remove them, add the remaining butter and sauté the onions for 10–15 minutes until they are tender and lightly browned, shaking the pan so they colour evenly. Add them to the mushrooms. Finally fry the bacon until it has browned and add it to the mushrooms and onions, discarding the fat from the pan.

To thicken the sauce, first reheat it if necessary and then whisk in the kneaded butter, a piece at a time, until the sauce is thick enough to lightly coat a spoon. Strain it over the garnish and season to taste with salt and pepper. The eggs, sauce and garnish can be kept for up to 2 days in the refrigerator.

To finish: fry the croûtes. Reheat the sauce and garnish on

top of the stove if necessary. Reheat the eggs by putting them in hot water for 1 minute, then drain them on paper towels. Set the eggs on the croûtes and put them on a serving dish or on individual plates, allowing two per person. Coat the eggs completely with the sauce.

Oie Rotie aux Marrons et Champignons Sauvages
—— ROAST GOOSE WITH CHESTNUTS AND WILD MUSHROOMS ——

Madame Fournillon's method of cooking wild mushrooms in their own juices, then topping them with a garlic and herb butter, concentrates their flavour wonderfully. Any type of wild mushroom may be used.

Serves 6–8
a 10 lb/4.5 kg goose, with giblets
2 tbsp softened butter
salt and pepper
1 onion, sliced
1 carrot, sliced
2 pints/1¼ quarts/1.25 litres water
2 lb/1 kg fresh chestnuts, peeled (p. 183)
16 fl oz/2 cups/500 ml milk, more if needed
1 tbsp butter
2 lb/1 kg wild mushrooms, cleaned (p. 187) and sliced
For the herb butter
4 oz/½ cup/125 g butter
2 shallots, very finely chopped
1 garlic clove, very finely chopped
2 tbsp finely chopped parsley
trussing needle and string

Heat the oven to No 8/450°F/230°C. Truss (p. 186) the goose. Spread the softened butter on the goose, sprinkle with salt and pepper and set the bird on its back on a rack in a roasting pan. Roast it in the oven, basting occasionally, until brown, about 40 minutes. Lower the oven heat to No 4/350°F/175°C and continue roasting, basting and pouring off excess fat, allowing 15 minutes' cooking time per pound (about 30 minutes per kilo). When the bird is done, the juices will run clear when the thigh is pricked with a skewer.

Meanwhile, make stock with the giblets: in a heavy saucepan, fry the giblets in a tablespoon of fat from the goose until

very brown. Add the onion and carrot and brown them also. Pour in the water, season with salt and pepper and simmer for 1–1½ hours until the stock has reduced by about half and is concentrated. Put the peeled chestnuts in a pan with enough milk to cover and add the lid. Bring them to the boil and simmer until almost tender, 15–20 minutes. Drain them. Spread the chestnuts around the goose about 20 minutes before it is done, and stir to coat them with the goose fat. Bake them until glazed, 15–20 minutes.

Geese at the Saturday market in Toucy.

Melt the tablespoon of butter in a frying pan, add the sliced mushrooms with salt and pepper and cook, tightly covered, over very low heat until the juices run. Remove the lid, raise the heat and cook until the liquid evaporates, stirring occasionally. Cooking time varies with the type of mushroom. Make the herb butter by creaming the ingredients together with salt and pepper.

When the goose is cooked, remove it from the oven and keep it warm on a serving dish, with the chestnuts. To make the gravy, reduce the pan juices to a dark-brown glaze (p. 184) and pour off the fat. Strain in the stock and bring to the boil, stirring to deglaze (p. 184) the pan juices. Strain the gravy into a saucepan, bring it back to the boil and taste.

Meanwhile, warm the mushrooms over low heat. Toss them with the herb butter and taste for seasoning. Discard trussing strings from the goose, and carve the bird at the table, surrounded by the glazed chestnuts. Serve the gravy and the mushrooms separately.

Ragoût de Porc aux Poireaux
—————————— PORK STEW WITH LEEKS ——————————

Leeks are among the prize denizens of our garden at the Château du Feÿ, tended with care by Monsieur Milbert. They are at their best in this ragoût with pork.

Serves 6
2 lb/1 kg boned pork loin
salt and pepper
3 tbsp olive oil
2 cloves of garlic, finely chopped
8 fl oz/1 cup/250 ml full-bodied white wine
1 lb/500 g tomatoes, peeled, seeded and chopped (p. 186)
2 lb/1 kg leeks
1 tbsp chopped parsley

Preheat the oven to No 4/350°F/175°C. Cut the pork into six thick steaks, discarding any string, and sprinkle them with salt and pepper. Heat the oil in a flameproof casserole with the garlic. Add the pork steaks and brown them thoroughly, allowing 4–5 minutes on each side. Add the wine and tomatoes, cover and simmer for 15 minutes. Meanwhile, trim the leeks, leaving some green top. Split them, wash them very well and slice them.

Take the pork steaks from the casserole, add the leeks with salt and pepper and stir to mix. Cover the casserole and cook gently for 5 minutes. Put the pork on top of the leeks, cover and cook in the oven for 40–50 minutes until the pork is very tender. The ragoût can be kept for up to 3 days in the refrigerator. Reheat it gently on top of the stove and serve it in the casserole, sprinkled with chopped parsley.

Jambon Chablisienne
————— BAKED HAM WITH WHITE CHEESE AND CREAM —————

A re-creation from lunch at the Lion d'Or in Toucy.

Serves 4
2 tbsp butter
1 oz/¼ cup/30 g flour
12 fl oz/1½ cups/375 ml dry white Chablis wine
12 fl oz/1½ cups/375 ml brown stock (p. 183)
5 juniper berries, crushed
5 black peppercorns, crushed
1 tbsp tomato purée/paste
4 shallots, finely chopped
2½ fl oz/⅓ cup/75 ml white wine vinegar
4 fl oz/½ cup/125 ml crème fraîche (p. 183)
or double/heavy cream
salt (optional)
4 thick slices mild cooked country ham, weighing about
1½ lb/750 g
1 tbsp mixed chopped tarragon and parsley

In a saucepan, melt the butter, whisk in the flour and cook until foaming. Whisk in the wine, stock, juniper berries, peppercorns, tomato purée/paste, and half the shallots. Bring to the boil, stirring until the sauce thickens. Simmer for 10 minutes.

In a heavy pan, boil the vinegar with the remaining shallots until reduced to 1 tablespoon. Whisk in the wine sauce and simmer until the sauce is well flavoured and lightly coats a spoon, 5–10 minutes. Strain, whisk in the crème fraîche and add salt to taste. Note: the ham may be salty, so salt may not need to be added. The sauce can be kept in the refrigerator for up to 2 days.

To finish, preheat the oven to No 4/350°F/175°C. Arrange the ham in a shallow, heatproof dish and pour over the sauce to coat it completely. Cover with foil and bake in the oven until hot and bubbling, 15–20 minutes. Sprinkle with the herbs and serve.

Pain d'Épices
HONEY SPICE BREAD

'Pain d'épices' is akin to English gingerbread, but anise predominates in the blend of spices and much more honey is added. Be sure to keep the bread at least 3 days before you try it, so the flavours mellow.

Makes two medium loaves to serve 10–12
½ pint / 1¼ cups / 300 ml milk
6½ oz / 1 cup / 200 g sugar
1 lb / 1½ cups / 500 g honey
12 oz / 3 cups / 375 g rye flour
6½ oz / 1⅔ cups / 200 g plain flour
2 egg yolks
1 oz / 2 tbsp / 30 g chopped, candied orange peel (p. 180)
2 tsp baking soda
½ tsp ground anise
½ tsp ground cinnamon
½ tsp ground cloves
For the icing
1 egg white
3 oz / ⅔ cup / 90 g icing / confectioners' sugar
two 10×4×3 inch / 25×10×7.5 cm loaf pans / tins

Heat the milk, sugar and honey in a saucepan, stirring until the sugar dissolves. Bring just to the boil, then remove from the heat and cool to tepid. Stir the two flours together in a bowl, make a well in the centre and add three-quarters of the cooled honey mixture and the egg yolks. Stir with a wooden spoon, gradually drawing in the flour to make a smooth batter. In a small bowl, mix the candied peel, baking soda and spices. Stir in the remaining honey mixture and stir this mixture into the flour batter. Cover and leave the batter to stand 8 hours in the refrigerator. Allow the batter to return to room temperature before baking.

Preheat the oven to No 3/325°F/160°C. Butter the loaf pans / tins, line them with greaseproof / wax paper and butter the paper. Spoon the batter into the pans / tins and bake in the oven until a skewer inserted 2 inches / 5 cm from the end of

The baker at Ancy-le-France is faithful to the Burgundian spice bread tradition.

the mould comes out clean, 1–1½ hours. Note: spice bread should be slightly underbaked, so it is soft in the centre and has not started to shrink from the sides of the pan. Let the breads cool until tepid, then turn them out on to a rack, removing the paper.

While the loaves are still warm, make the icing. Whisk the egg white until frothy. Gradually whisk in the icing / confectioners' sugar to make an icing that pours easily. Pour it over the warm breads so that it thinly coats the top and drips down the sides. Pain d'épices can be stored for up to a month in an airtight container and the flavour will mellow. It can also be frozen.

Opposite: Tartouillats.

Tartouillats

———————— FRUIT FLANS IN CABBAGE LEAVES ————————

Long before the vines are in bud, the hillsides of the Auxer-rois are in blossom, for this region is the second largest producer of cherries in France. A tattered old local cookbook includes a curious recipe for 'tartouillats', which proves to be a kind of cherry pie with cabbage leaves replacing the pastry – a thoroughly modern conceit! When cherries are out of season, chunks of ripe pear can be substituted.

Serves 8
4 oz/1 cup/125 g flour
½ tsp salt
8 oz/1¼ cups/250 g sugar
4 eggs
8 fl oz/1 cup/250 ml milk
8 large rounded cabbage leaves, with no holes
1 lb/500 g black cherries or pears
2 tbsp marc or kirsch
8 ramekins of 6 fl oz/³/₄ cup/175 ml capacity each

Sift the flour into a bowl with the salt. Stir in the sugar and make a well in the centre. Add the eggs and half the milk and whisk just until the mixture is smooth. Stir in the remaining milk to form a batter. Cover the bowl and leave the batter to stand for about half an hour so the starch grains in the flour swell and thicken it. Preheat the oven to No 6/400°F/200°C.

Bring a large pan of water to boil and blanch (p. 182) the cabbage leaves, then drain them. If the stem ends of the cabbage leaves are large, cut them out. Butter the ramekins and line them with the drained cabbage leaves.

Stone/pit the cherries or peel, core and dice the pears. Stir the fruit and marc or kirsch into the batter and spoon the mixture into the cabbage leaves. Trim the edges of the leaves with scissors to leave a generous border above the ramekins. Set them on a baking sheet and bake in the oven until the filling is firm and the cabbage leaves are slightly brown, 25–35 minutes. The filling will puff up, but shrink again as it cools.

Let the tartouillats cool slightly and then unmould them onto a serving dish or individual plates. Serve them warm or at room temperature. They can be cooked a few hours ahead, but are best eaten on the day of baking.

Cassis

———————— BLACKCURRANT LIQUEUR ————————

This basic method of making liqueur by soaking fruits in sugar syrup and alcohol can be applied to almost any fruit, but juicy berries, particularly blackcurrants, result naturally in a full-flavoured, glowing cordial. In France, 60% alcohol is routinely available in supermarkets in the summer; here I suggest substituting vodka as its flavour will not override that of the blackcurrants.

Makes about 3¼ pints/2 quarts/2 litres
2 lb/1 kg blackcurrants
13 oz/2 cups/400 g sugar, or to taste
8 fl oz/1 cup/250 ml water
1²/₃ pint/1 quart/1 litre vodka
3¼ pint/2 quart/2 litre preserving jar

Pick over the blackcurrants, discarding the stems, rinse them and put them in a bowl. Mash them with a fork or potato masher. Make a syrup by heating the sugar and water in a medium saucepan until dissolved. Bring it to the boil and simmer for 5 minutes. Remove from the heat and allow to cool.

Put the fruit into the preserving jar, pour over the syrup and add the vodka. Cover tightly and leave in a cool place for at least 2 and up to 6 months.

Strain the liqueur through a cloth, pour into a bottle and cork or seal it tightly. The liqueur mellows on keeping.

Colmar is a busy commercial town but its old centre still retains a Hansel and Gretel charm.

ALSACE

Sweet breads, choucroûte and dark stews from the city of Strasbourg to the depths of the Vosges mountains, glimpses of an ancient culinary tradition respected throughout the world

Alsace is a gourmand's delight – note I say gourmand rather than gourmet. The combination of German gusto and French flair leads to a flamboyant cuisine which never loses sight of its ancestry. Yes, you'll find sauerkraut, but baked with Riesling wine and kirsch; fruit tarts may be spiced in German style with cinnamon but they are lightened with a cream topping. Breads are fluffy with eggs, sweet with dried fruits, and the pâtés, entrapped in a pastry crust, bring a new dimension to the concept of the sausage.

Further clues to the cooking of Alsace lie in its geography. The key strip of territory stretches about 40 miles south from Strasbourg to Colmar, bordered to the east by the river Rhine and to the West by the savage mass of the Vosges mountains. The rectangle thus formed, at its largest scarcely

Alsace's food shops are second to none in provincial France. The best are signalled by a continuous queue six days of the week.

with a bunch of grapes and white bread is slashed to resemble an ear of wheat, convenient for tearing into individual rolls. Wholewheat, rye and barley flavour the bread in German style, a habit less common in France than you might think.

The sweet breads, pride of Alsace, are braided, moulded and puffed, studded with dried fruits and nuts. Breakfast is – or should be – a slice of fluffy 'kougelhopf' baked in a fluted earthenware mould to achieve the authentic golden crust. 'Birnewecke' is so rich it contains almost no flour, but is based on pears, raisins, and nuts simmered together with kirsch, then pressed into a mould and baked. An Easter crown is shaped from a cylinder of dough stuffed with raisins and almond paste, twisted in a circle then slashed to show spirals of filling. At Christmas, the favourite egg bread is 'Christstollen', rich with candied fruits and almonds, shaped as a turnover. Finishes are important: Easter crown is topped with shiny glacé icing, while Christstollen is brushed with butter when still warm to soften the crust, then rolled thickly in icing sugar for a frosting of snow.

Souvenir shops cluster doggedly around the rose-pink cathedral which dominates the old city centre, but among them you'll find more than one respectable pâtisserie selling the traditional gingerbread cut in hearts and stars, topped with white icing. Hansel and Gretel would have felt quite at home. At the Musée Alsacien overlooking the river Ill on the quai St Nicholas, you'll find a quaint collection of moulds for cakes and wafers, fish for New Year, lambs for Easter, and crayfish, a symbol of fertility, for wedding cakes.

On the rue des Orfèvre, a two-minute stroll from the cathedral, the window of charcutier Frick-Lutz beckons with a dozen game, meat and fish terrines, patterned in a cheerful mosaic of pink ham, beige liver and green pistachios. Peer through the window and you'll see a forest of hams suspended from the ceiling – five types of raw ham alone are on display for slicing. Many of the dozen or more sausages are made on the premises – white veal 'boudin blanc' to be consumed within hours of making; 'boudin noir' blood sausages for serving with a contrasting purée of snowy potato; 'knackwurst' sausages of pork and beef seasoned with cumin; 'mettwurst', a soft liver sausage for spreading on a crusty baguette; and native Strasbourg sausages – fat and golden brown, resembling an overgrown frankfurter. Frick-Lutz is also a butcher specializing in veal. The provenance

16 miles wide, is some of the richest land in France, ideal for grain (hence the breads) and fruit trees (hence white alcohol and fruit liqueurs). Once salmon, eel, pike and other fresh-water fish were plentiful in the Rhine; some still survive in the Ill and other tributaries, making possible traditional dishes like 'matelote à l'alsacienne', a stew of eel, pike, perch, tench and trout with Riesling white wine and cream. (In local dialect Alsace becomes 'Illsass', meaning the country of the Ill.) And into the folds of the Vosges, looking eastwards towards the Rhine, are tucked the medieval wine villages which make of Alsace a Breughel painting come disconcertingly to life.

Where better to start a visit to the region than with the capital, Strasbourg? Flourishing medieval city and still a major river port, Strasbourg has found new prosperity in the last 10 years as home to the European parliament and the Council of Europe. The Strasbourg of today is cosmopolitan, the ancient pedestrian streets around the cathedral thronged with a multilingual crowd roaming the antique shops and glossy boutiques. The food shops provide stiff competition for the couturiers, I am glad to say. At Woerlé on the rue Division-Leclerc, crusty round loaves are adorned

Strasbourg – a cathedral town with fine museums, fine restaurants and an extraordinary array of bakeries and charcuteries.

Pigs are a common sight in Alsace where charcuterie is a major industry.

to have invented a pâté de foie gras in which he baked the liver in a pork stuffing packed in a heavy pastry crust. When his master sent such a pâté to Louis XVI, the Clause fortune was made. Nowadays connoisseurs insist that foie gras be baked in a terrine or pâté for maximum bouquet; the alternative method of wrapping foie gras in a cloth and poaching it keeps it moist and yields a higher weight per gram of raw liver, but the flavour is less intense. In Strasbourg not one, but half a dozen shops deal exclusively in foie gras, selling the liver raw, 'mi-cuit' or vacuum-packed and lightly cooked so it keeps a month or more, as well as offering canned foie gras in a variety of guises. The choice between duck foie gras, with its winey flavour, or the richer foie gras of goose presents a further dilemma. Unfortunately there are no short cuts – the more expensive the foie gras, the more meltingly luscious it is likely to be.

For a serious meal, repair just around the corner to Chez Yvonne on the promising rue du Sanglier (Wild Boar Lane). 'If Yvonne doesn't like the colour of your eyes, she won't take you,' we were warned, but we passed muster. This is the classic Alsatian 'winstüb' or bistro offering the best of local wine and food with an emphasis on generous portions rather than decor. As well as homemade 'choucroûte', with luck you'll find specialities like 'totelots', a hot noodle salad piquant with vinegar and shallot, and 'carpe à la juive' in which carp is served cold in its jelled juices on a bed of onions. Since the dish must be made ahead, it is ideal for serving on the Sabbath when cooking is forbidden. Strasbourg has long had a sizeable Jewish population – the Alsatian language shares some of the same eighth–century German roots as Yiddish.

At Chez Yvonne the couple sitting next to us were chatting in Alsatian until they broke into French for our benefit to explain the Tuesday special of 'baekoffe'. 'Baekoffe is our national dish,' they confided: 'you make a layer of sliced potatoes, then of leeks or baby turnips, then add beef, pork and lamb and cover them with more potatoes. Be sure to use an earthenware dish so the ingredients cook gently, and seal it with flour and water paste so no juices escape.' 'Baekoffe' means 'baker's oven' and in the old days it was cooked in the communal village oven after the bread was baked, so the housewife was freed on washday.

Further distractions lurk in and around Strasbourg in the form of half a dozen top restaurants, including Le Crocodile

and pedigree of each superb, milk-fed animal can be traced and their winning rosettes are displayed in the shop window.

Across the street, the pastry and chocolate shop, Naegel, tempts with a dizzy array of gâteaux, charlottes, tartes and petits fours, each more fantastic than the last. Black Forest cake is striped black with chocolate cake, white with cream and stuffed with moist kirsch-flavoured cherries. The raspberry charlotte is encircled with spiral walls of cake, the top laden with the outsize berries for which Alsace is famous. The shop is a dreamworld, a storybook evocation in chocolate, spongecake and whipped cream. To move on to sandwiches might seem banal, but in Alsace even a snack is taken seriously. At Burgard, towers of sliced loaves interleaved with every conceivable variety of sliced ham, sausage, cheese, vegetables and pickles bar the window, as if to protect the white-coated servers preparing bulging giant submarine rolls to order.

Fine wine is on sale next door, foie gras and truffles a door or two down. The Romans are recorded as fattening geese for gourmet delectation, but it is an Alsatian, Jean-Pierre Clause, who while chef to the governor in the 1780s, claims in central Strasbourg, and the illustrious Auberge de l'Ill to the south at Illhausern. The menus of both are a roll call of luxury – fresh foie gras with meat glaze, potato cake with truffles, ragoût of frog's legs with little sausages, morels from the forests of the Rhine. Such is the standard of cooking in Alsace that these two restaurants scarcely stand out as one of a kind, as they would almost anywhere else in France, but rank more modestly as being first among equals.

Escaping from the city, villages along the 'route des vins' are scarcely half an hour away. Many of them boast good eateries like the Hôtel du Cerf in Marlenheim, just west of Strasbourg, run by four generations of the family Husser. It was here I had salmon, larded with bacon as in the old days, served with lentils and horseradish cream sauce – horseradish is a Germanic flavouring which, like caraway and juniper, you'll find often in Alsace. Take your time to meander further south, for the little towns – Molsheim, Obernai, Bergheim – become ever more scenic. Many are walled, their remparts and the fortresses perched on the mountain peaks above them a witness to the centuries-old struggle for the wealth of Alsace. In all of them you will find bierstübe for a modest meal, or the makings of a picnic to eat with the fragrant white wines offered everywhere for tasting and sale along the road. Gertwiller is the gingerbread capital, while Alsatian tablelinens, commonly available in traditional red, green and blue patterns, are at their finest in Ribeauvillé, where the old firm of Steiner has revived the glowing 19th-century designs.

Side-by-side with the vineyards in Alsace you'll see tall poles entwined with fluffy hop plants, for this is beer country too. Twice as much beer per head is drunk in Alsace than in the rest of France, and the producers centred on Strasbourg and Obernai are in fierce competition with Germany. Beer soup, strongly laced with onions, goes down well on a cold day, while a 'coq à la bière', might be held to rival a bird simmered in local Riesling wine. Alsatians have a passion for onion dishes, from 'zewelwaï' onion quiche, to onion fondue, and onion 'pizza' – a flat bread base topped with onion, bacon and cream. 'Suri rüewe', a pot au feu of smoked ham, onions and white turnips with white wine, is a speciality of Colmar.

On autumn weekends, busloads of tourists descend on the hillside villages to sample first the new beer, then the new wine, to the accompaniment of sauerkraut and sausages. The

The pigeon loft at Riquewihr.

first crunchy, slightly acid sauerkraut traditionally appears in Strasbourg on 25 September. Each village has its festival to celebrate sauerkraut or some other local product – at the festival of Ribeauvillé the renaissance fountain flows with wine. It was in the charcuterie of Riquewihr, with its sloping, cobbled street lined with winstübe and bierstübe, that I talked about sauerkraut to Madame Fischer. 'The right proportions are 45 g/1½ oz of salt for every 10 kg/22 lb of shredded cabbage,' she explained. 'It will take about a month to finish fermenting, and after three days, the liquid produced by the cabbage should be exchanged for fresh water. Keep the cabbage weighed down under water with a plate, and of course don't let it come in contact with metal. In the old days we used wooden barrels, as crocks broke so easily, but now plastic is common.'

Contemporary chefs like to use sauerkraut in creative ways, but when I mentioned to Madame Fischer the delicious oysters in butter sauce with sauerkraut I had tasted the previous evening, she looked appalled. 'Oh no, only pork is right!' she said. In her book, an authentic 'choucroûte Alsacienne' should include Strasbourg smoked sausages, together with a piece of smoked lean pork, preferably loin, a chunk of smoked fat bacon, a ham hock, and often lean fresh little sausages as well, all flavoured with juniper, coriander, garlic and wine. This habit of mixing different meats, or fish, in a single dish was spotted in the 16th century by Montaigne, who added approvingly of Alsatians: 'They are excellent cooks, particularly of fish, and they never water their wine.'

It was in a valley near Riquewihr that I talked to René Legoll, a distiller of white alcohols from fruits such as 'quetsche', a purple plum, and 'poire Williams', a pear often sold trapped in a bottle of its own alcohol. White alcohol is the common local pick-me-up, both before and after a meal, and Alsatians scoff at suggestions of its potency. It's even used for cleaning windows! For the cook, these white alcohols are invaluable, for small quantities add a concentrated kick to fruit soufflés, sorbets, and cream desserts. The day I visited Monsieur Legoll, mirabelle plums were being distilled, filling the warehouse with sharp perfume. He brings in wild raspberries and bilberries from Romania, but does not pass up rosehips and serviceberries from just up the road, or even holly berries for making a white alcohol called 'houx'.

When the fruit arrives, it is lightly crushed, then piled in vats and left to ferment a week, a month, or even more depending on the type of fruit and its ripeness. 'We leave it to nature,' says René Legoll. As the sugar slowly converts to alcohol, juice from the base of the vat is constantly siphoned on top to keep the fruit moist. 'That's what assures the quality.' The fermentation over, René distils the pulp at his leisure. The best white alcohol is distilled twice to remove maximum impurities, following the same methods as for cognac. Ageing, however, has less influence on the final product as steel vats are used rather than the oak casks of cognac. 'I'm a bit of a dreamer,' grins René – he likes to experiment and has hidden a whole vat of 10-year-old 'mirabelle' from his father, who does not approve of such quixotic extravagance.

It is but a few kilometres from Riquewihr to Colmar at the end of the most scenic stretch of the 'route des vins'. In contrast to Strasbourg, Colmar is an intimate country town rather than a city, with one of the finest medieval centres in Europe. Wandering the twisted streets under the overhanging beams and wrought iron signs, it comes as a surprise to find hardware stores and photocopy centres installed behind 12th-century façades. But it's reassuring, too. These streets are for real, not a stage set. The Alsatian talent for sensitive restoration, for exluding cars as well as neon signs, is notable not just here but throughout the region.

To find restaurants in such a setting seems more natural. In a house of rustic charm in the old town, Le Fer Rouge proposes local dishes like pot au feu of snails and baekoffe of quail and sweetbreads beside the contemporary fish with sauerkraut. The popularity of snails dates at least from the days when the Church decreed up to three fish days a week, thoughtfully allowing frogs and snails to creep in under the wire. In the rue des Boulangers – bakers' alley – you will find, strangely enough, three outstanding charcuteries, their windows a mesmerising display of creations 'en bellevue'. I watched in amusement one Sunday morning (the big day for French family dining) as the chef stood outside in his whites directing minions how best to show off his display behind the plate glass. A visit to the Unterlinden museum with the brilliant, mystic Grünewald altarpiece with its folding panels, painted in the early 16th century, puts such material matters in perspective.

You will sleep soundly at Le Maréchal in central Colmar, a magnificent mansion on the river Lauch. A stop of at least one night is indicated, for Colmar forms a golden gastronomic triangle with the hillside fortress of Kaysersberg and the town of Munster, of cheese fame. The D417 road through Munster, first side of the triangle, is deceptively placid. Then just beyond the town you branch north to Orbey, and at once start to negotiate tortuous roads with ever more precipitous hillsides. Chalet-like farms cling alpine-style to the slopes. As in Switzerland, the staple industry is cheese – soft paste Munster cheese, produced in small shallow discs famous for their pungency. A lesser-known variant is Geromé from further west near Gerardmer, one of the several spas in the Vosges.

Officially Munster should be made only of milk from the tough little Vosgienne cattle, black with a lateral white stripe. If you stop at one of the many 'fromage fermier' signs, you will see the dairy in action, for the milk must be clabbered and the curds drained each day. As with all soft cheese, only raw milk is used for Munster because pasteurization kills some of the cultures essential for it to ripen to its creamy, oozing best. The curd for Munster may be flavoured with anise or cumin and it is turned each day and washed with brine during ageing. Locally the cheese is available at varying stages of maturity from fresh up to the full four-week bloom, when the rind is soft and yellowish-brown and the inside a melting gold. The cheese should never smell ammoniac, but is pungent indeed – at Huglin, the best charcutier on the Grande rue in Munster, vacuum-wrapping is offered as an extra with the reassuring slogan 'travel without odour'.

When in Munster, don't miss Pâtisserie Gilg, also on the Grande rue, which bakes some of the finest fruit tarts in the region. I asked Marie-Claire behind the counter which flavour she preferred and without a moment's hesitation she exclaimed 'mirabelles!', the little golden plums that are universal in tarts, jams, and 'alcohols blancs'. Other popular fruits include cherries, apricots, plums, blackberries, and tiny purple mountain bilberries, and all are cooked directly in the pastry shell rather than being arranged in it after baking. This conserves their flavour, but is tricky as all good fruit exudes juice, so the dough must be rolled thickly to absorb it. A dexterous hand is needed to keep it light and some cooks prefer to use a raised yeast dough. Opinions vary on the arrangement of the fruit: 'Halve them and put them cut side up after you've removed the stone,' instructs Marie-Claire. 'No, no,' chimes in her sister Jeanne, 'cut side down!' However both unite in condemning 'migaine', the custard of egg yolk and cream often added to fruit tarts in Alsace. The sisters come from Lorraine, where migaine is customary only in savoury quiches.

In folkloric Kaysersberg, stop for coffee and kugelhopf at Au Pêché Mignon, where the locals gather to gossip. If lunchtime approaches, try a slice of their unusual bacon kugelhopf, excellent with a glass of white wine. On the third side of the triangle which returns you to Colmar, the landscape changes quickly from forests dotted with little green fields to fruit orchards, and finally to the vineyards of the plain.

For the last night in Alsace, the choice is wide. You might wish to head back into the mountains to the Grand Hôtel in

For sheer variety, Alsace can claim title as bread capital of France.

Les Trois Epis, with its sweeping views across the Rhine to the Black Forest. In the winstüb you'll find a traditional 'choucroûte gourmande', and excellent salmon en croûte, with grander cooking in the dining room. Down-valley in Ammerschwir, the luxurious Aux Armes de France sums up all things Alsatian, with timbered beams, geranium-clad windows and an open cobbled courtyard. Here in winter you will find the best of deer as well as the wild boar which inhabits the Vosges in such abundance that it is classed as 'nuisible' (a pest). You'll be offered 'civet' of pigeon in a dark blood sauce, or perhaps a veal kidney with calf's foot in a sauce of sweet Tokay wine – the cellar at Aux Armes is one of the finest in Alsace.

Alsace is a fantasy world, a promotor's dream. With its medieval ramparts, stork nests, and wild boar it escapes the kitsch by a hair's breadth. Its strategic location on the Rhine, almost closer to Prague than to Paris, positions it for an international future. Ask a Frenchman where the best cooks come from and the chances are he'll say Alsace. Gastronomically, it is already world class.

RECIPES FROM
ALSACE

Pâté en Croûte Strasbourgeoise
—— VEAL PÂTÉ IN PASTRY ——

This veal pâté, shaped as a freestanding, long loaf, is studded with black morel mushrooms and green pistachios. Serve it warm with Madeira sauce, or bake it ahead to serve cold.

Serves 10–12 as main course
12 oz/375 g veal escalope
6 oz/175 g pork fat
2 tbsp white wine
2 tbsp brandy
2 tbsp Madeira
salt and pepper
pâte à pâté dough (p. 185) made with 1 lb/4 cups/500 g flour,
8 oz/1 cup/250 g unsalted butter, or
3 oz/6 tbsp/90 g lard
and 5 oz/⅔ cup/150 g butter, 2 eggs, 2 tbsp oil, 2 tsp salt
and 2–3 tbsp water
5 oz/150 g morel mushrooms, cleaned (p. 187)
2 tbsp butter
1 egg, beaten to mix with ½ tsp salt (for glaze)
For the stuffing
1 lb/500 g lean veal, minced/ground
1½ lb/750 g pork (half fat, half lean) minced/ground
8 oz/250 g lean cooked ham, minced/ground
4 oz/¾ cup/125 g pistachios, shelled
2 eggs, beaten to mix
1 tsp ground nutmeg
1 tsp ground allspice
For the Madeira sauce
16 fl oz/2 cups/500 ml brown stock (p. 183)
3 tbsp Madeira, more if needed
1 tbsp arrowroot, dissolved (p. 182) in 3–4 tbsp water
salt and pepper

Cut the veal escalope and pork fat into ¼ inch/6 mm strips. Put them in a bowl, add the wine, brandy and Madeira, salt and pepper and mix well. Cover and leave to marinate for 30–45 minutes. Make the pâte à pâté dough and chill 30 minutes. Sauté the mushrooms in the butter with salt and pepper until tender, 3–5 minutes. Butter a baking sheet.

For the stuffing: mix together the veal, pork, ham, pistachios, eggs, nutmeg, allspice, salt and pepper and the marinade drained from the veal. Beat with a wooden spoon or your hand until the stuffing holds together. Cook a piece of the mixture in a frying pan or in the oven, taste, and adjust the seasoning if necessary.

Roll out the dough and trim to a 14×20 inch/35×50 cm rectangle. Divide the stuffing into 3 portions. Spread one portion lengthwise on the dough in a 4×14 inch/10×35 cm strip. Top with a lengthwise layer of half the strips of marinated veal and half the strips of pork fat, setting half of the morel mushrooms between them. Cover with another portion of stuffing and top with the remaining veal strips, pork fat strips, and mushrooms. Cover with the last portion of stuffing and smooth to make an even layer. Mould the meat with your hands so that the rectangle is compact and tall.

Cut a square of excess dough from each corner and brush the edges of the rectangle with the egg glaze. Lift one long edge of the dough on top of the filling and fold over the opposite edge, pulling tightly to enclose it. Press gently to seal the dough and fold over the ends to make a neat parcel, being sure that the meat is thoroughly enclosed in the dough. Roll the parcel over on to the baking sheet so that the seam is underneath. Brush the pâté with egg glaze.

To decorate the pâté, roll out the dough trimmings, cut a long strip, and set it around the edge of the pâté. Decorate the top with any remaining dough cut in the shapes of leaves or whatever your fancy dictates. Brush the decorations with beaten egg. Make a hole near each end of the pâté and insert a cone of foil as a chimney so that steam can escape. Chill for 30 minutes. Heat the oven to No 6/400°F/200°C.

Bake the pâté in the heated oven until the pastry is set and starts to brown, about 15 minutes. Turn the heat down to No 4/350°F/175°C and continue baking until a skewer inserted in the centre of the pâté for half a minute is hot to the touch when withdrawn, about 1 hour. If the pastry browns too much during cooking, cover it loosely with aluminium foil.

For the Madeira sauce, bring the stock to the boil and reduce by one half. Stir in the Madeira and enough dissolved arrowroot to thicken the sauce so it coats the back of a spoon. Taste the sauce for seasoning, adding salt, pepper and more Madeira to taste. The pâté and sauce can be made up to 2 days ahead and refrigerated.

If necessary, reheat the pâté in a moderate (No 4/350°F/175°C) oven and serve it hot with Madeira sauce. If serving cold, leave the pâté plain and pass gherkin pickles separately.

Opposite: Pâté en Croûte Strasbourgeoise.

Dos de Saumon Lardé au Raifort
— SADDLE OF SALMON WITH BACON AND HORSERADISH CREAM —

This is my recreation of a dish from the Hôtel du Cerf in Marlenheim. Fresh ginger can be used in place of the horse-radish if you prefer. The mix of rosy pink salmon with earthy lentils and creamy sauce makes for a stunning presentation of texture and colour.

Serves 8 as a main course
2 lb/1 kg piece of centre cut salmon on the bone,
scales removed
4 oz/125 g piece of bacon, cut in thin lardons (p. 184)
1½ oz/3 tbsp/45 g butter
salt and pepper
12 fl oz/1½ cups/375 ml crème fraîche (p. 183) or
double/heavy cream
2 tbsp grated fresh horseradish, or 3–4 tbsp
bottled horseradish
2 shallots, finely chopped
For the lentils
8 oz/250 g lentils
1 onion, studded with a clove
1 clove garlic
bouquet garni (p. 183)
16 fl oz/2 cups/500 ml water, more if needed

To cook the lentils, pick them over, discarding any stones, and wash them well. Put them in a saucepan with the onion, garlic, bouquet garni, some pepper, and enough water to cover generously. Add the lid, bring to the boil and simmer the lentils for 30 minutes, stirring occasionally. Add salt with more water if the lentils seem dry, and continue simmering until they are tender, 20–30 minutes longer. The lentils should be soupy, but most of the water should be absorbed; if necessary remove the lid towards the end of cooking so water evaporates. Discard the onion, bouquet garni and garlic and taste the lentils for seasoning. They can be refrigerated for up to 3 days.

To cook the salmon, heat the oven to No 3/325°F/160°C. With the point of a knife, poke holes in both sides of the salmon and insert a lardon of bacon in each one. Spread the salmon with butter, sprinkle it with pepper and set it in a flameproof baking dish. Bake it in the heated oven, basting often until a skewer inserted in the centre is hot to the touch when withdrawn after half a minute, 30–40 minutes.

To finish, reheat the lentils if necessary on top of the stove. Transfer the salmon to a serving platter, cover loosely with foil and keep it warm. Discard the fat from the baking dish, add the cream and bring it to the boil, stirring to dissolve the pan juices. Strain the cream into a separate pan, add the horseradish and shallots with salt and pepper to taste, bring back to the boil and simmer for 2 minutes. Spoon the lentils around the salmon and serve the sauce separately.

Choucroûte Alsacienne
—————— SAUERKRAUT WITH PORK AND SAUSAGES ——————

Little baked potatoes in their jackets, not the more usual boiled ones, are the best accompaniment for this supremely Alsatian dish.

Serves 6
3 lb/1.4 kg uncooked sauerkraut
1½ lb/750 g salted or smoked shoulder or loin of pork
1 lb/500 g piece of bacon
1 bay leaf
2 cloves
8 juniper berries
4–5 coriander seeds
2 cloves garlic
5 oz/⅔ cup/150 g goose fat or lard
2 onions, sliced
2 lb/1 kg pork shank
salt and pepper
¾ pint/1¾ cup/400 ml dry white wine, more if needed,
preferably Alsatian Riesling
12–18 small potatoes
6 Strasbourg sausages or frankfurters (1 lb/500 g total)
muslin/cheesecloth

Wash the sauerkraut under cold running water and squeeze out the excess moisture; rinse and squeeze again. Put the salted (but not the smoked) pork in a pot with the bacon, cover with water and bring to the boil. Simmer for 5 minutes and taste the water; if it is very salty, repeat the blanching process. Drain thoroughly. Cut the bacon into 6 slices. Tie the bay leaf, cloves, juniper berries, coriander and garlic in a piece of muslin/cheesecloth.

Melt all but 2 tablespoons of the goose fat in a large casserole, add the onions and cook over low heat, stirring occasionally, until they just begin to brown. Spread half of the sauerkraut over the onions; then put in the salt pork, smoked shoulder or loin, with the pork shank, bacon and spice bag on top. Season it very lightly. Cover the meat with the rest of the sauerkraut and enough wine to moisten without covering it with liquid. Spread the remaining goose fat over the top. Cut a piece of greaseproof/wax paper to fit inside the pot and place it directly on top of the sauerkraut.

Cover and simmer on top of the stove or cook in a low oven (No 2/300°F/150°C), allowing 3 hours for crunchy sauerkraut, or 5–6 hours if you like it tender. If cooking for the longer time, remove the meat from the pan after 2–2½ hours of cooking, then replace it to reheat 30 minutes before serving.

About an hour before the end of cooking, put the potatoes in the oven with the sauerkraut. Poach the sausages in water for 10–12 minutes. The sauerkraut can be prepared ahead and refrigerated for up to 3 days.

To finish, reheat the sauerkraut if necessary in a low oven. Discard the spice bag and taste the sauerkraut for seasoning. Carve the meat in slices. Pile the sauerkraut on a platter with the meat, sausages and potatoes on top.

Baekoffe
MEAT AND POTATO CASSEROLE

Following my conversation on 'baekoffe' at Chez Yvonne in Strasbourg, I searched a half-dozen Alsatian cookbooks for their views on the authentic recipe. Some authors suggest adding a pig's foot, others include carrots, but the basic ingredients are the same – pork, lamb, beef, potatoes and onion.

Serves 6–8

1½ lb/750 g boned pork loin, cut in 2 inch/5 cm cubes
1½ lb/750 g boned shoulder of lamb,
cut in 2 inch/5 cm cubes
1½ lb/750 g lean stewing beef, cut in 2 inch/5 cm cubes
2 tbsp lard or oil
3 large leeks, sliced
5 lb/2.3 kg potatoes, thickly sliced
salt and pepper
¾ pint/1¾ cups/400 ml water, more if needed
For the luting paste
8 oz/2 cups/250 g flour
5 fl oz/⅔ cup/150 ml water, more if needed
For the marinade
2 carrots, thinly sliced
2 onions, thinly sliced
1 sprig of thyme
1 bay leaf
3 cloves garlic, peeled and crushed
1 sprig of parsley
5 whole cloves
1⅓ pints/3 cups/750 ml sweet white wine, preferably
Alsatian Sylvaner or Riesling
salt and pepper

Put the pork, lamb and beef in a large non-aluminium bowl with the marinade ingredients, cover and leave to marinate overnight in the refrigerator. Remove the meat from the liquid, reserving the marinade.

Heat the lard in a large casserole, add the leeks and cook over a low fire, stirring occasionally, until they begin to brown; remove the pot from the heat. Put half of the sliced potatoes in a layer over the leeks, then put the marinated meat on top; season with salt and pepper. Cover the meat with the remaining potato slices and season again. Strain the

it is well done. The twisted, chewy Alsatian pasta called 'spaetzle' is ideal with venison, as is a purée of chestnuts or root celery.

Serves 4
a leg of venison (7–8 lb/3.5–4 kg)
8 oz/250 g fresh or frozen cranberries
4 fl oz/½ cup/125 ml water
8 oz/1¼ cups/250 g sugar
1½ oz/3 tbsp/45 g lard or oil
8 fl oz/1 cup/250 ml brown stock (p. 186), or water
4–5 tbsp 'quetsche' plum brandy, or kirsch
8–10 fried croûtes (p. 183), in 2½ inch/6 cm rounds
For the marinade
1 bottle (750 ml) red wine
white part of 2 leeks, sliced
4 carrots, sliced
2 onions, sliced
2 stalks celery, sliced
head of garlic, halved crosswise
2 tbsp vegetable oil
bouquet garni (p. 183)
salt and white pepper

In a saucepan, combine the marinade ingredients, bring to the boil, simmer for 5 minutes and let cool completely. Put the venison in a deep dish just large enough to hold it and pour the cold marinade over it. Cover and leave to marinate for 1–3 days in the refrigerator, turning the meat occasionally. Lift the haunch out and pat dry with paper towels, reserving the marinade. Strain the marinade. With a cleaver trim off the shank bone and chop it in pieces.

To cook the cranberries: in a saucepan, mix the berries, water and sugar. Simmer uncovered, stirring occasionally, until the berries soften and begin to burst, 8–10 minutes. Taste, adding more sugar if necessary. The cranberries can be cooked up to 24 hours ahead.

Heat the oven to No 6/400°F/200°C. In a roasting pan, heat the lard, add the venison and baste with the hot fat. Add the chopped bones, 8 fl oz/1 cup/250 ml of the marinade and half the stock. Roast in the heated oven until medium rare and a meat thermometer registers 125°F/51°C, ¾–1 hour. Baste often during roasting and add more marinade if the pan gets dry. Heat the plum brandy or cognac in a small saucepan, flame it and pour it while still flaming over the venison.

marinade over the meat and vegetables and add enough water to come halfway up them. Heat the oven to No 3/325°F/160°C.

For the luting paste, put the flour in a bowl, add the water and stir to make a soft paste, adding more water if necessary. Note: do not overwork the paste or it will become elastic. Seal the gap between the casserole and lid with luting paste. Heat the casserole gently on top of the stove for 10–15 minutes, then cook in the oven for 3 hours. Do not try to open the casserole once it has been sealed; the meat should cook slowly and in an even heat. When done, break the seal and discard the luting paste. Taste the cooking liquid. The meat should be very tender and falling apart. If still firm, continue cooking it. Serve the meat and vegetables directly from the casserole.

Gigot de Chevreuil à l'Alsacienne
——— LEG OF VENISON WITH CRANBERRIES ———

The Vosges mountains are famous for berries as well as game. In this recipe cranberries have been substituted for bilberries/huckleberries ('myrtilles'), acting as both a garnish and a thickening for the rich wine sauce. Venison should be served rare or pink as the meat is tough and dry if

Transfer the venison to a serving dish and keep warm.

Meanwhile, boil the remaining marinade in a pan, skimming off the foam, until reduced to 8 fl oz/1 cup/250 ml. Fry the croûtes. When the venison is done, reduce the pan juices to a glaze (p. 184). Add the reduced marinade and the remaining stock and reduce to about 8 fl oz/1 cup/250 ml. Strain, stir in a quarter of the cranberries and purée the sauce in a food processor, or work it through a sieve. Taste, adding more brandy, sugar, salt or pepper if needed.

To serve: arrange the croûtes around the venison on the serving platter and top them with the remaining cranberries. Spoon a little sauce over the venison and serve the rest separately.

Leckerli

HAZELNUT GINGERBREAD COOKIES

I find regular gingerbread recipes a bit dry, but the following hazelnut version is superb. Do not overbake the cookies as they should be chewy rather than crisp.

Makes 3 dozen bars
5 oz/1 cup/150 g shelled hazelnuts
10 oz/2½ cups/300 g flour
3 tbsp baking powder
½ tsp ground cinnamon
½ tsp ground cloves
pinch of anise, crushed
pinch of ground cardamom
pinch of salt
3 oz/⅓ cup/85 g honey
6 oz/¾ cup/175 g sugar
3 oz/6 tbsp/90 g unsalted butter
2 tbsp fresh lemon juice
2 tbsp candied orange peel (p. 180), finely chopped
2 eggs, beaten to mix
For the icing
1 egg white
4½ oz/1 cup/135 g icing/confectioners' sugar, more if needed
11×17 inch/28×44 cm shallow baking tin/pan

Butter the tin/pan, line the bottom with greaseproof/wax paper and butter the paper. Heat the oven to No 5/375°F/190°C. Put the hazelnuts on a baking sheet and

Riquewihr is one of many Alsatian wine villages that somehow retain their charm despite wave upon wave of tourists from both sides of the Rhine.

toast them until brown, 12–15 minutes. Let them cool slightly, then rub them if necessary in a coarse cloth to remove the skins. Then chop the nuts finely by hand or in a food processor.

Sift the flour with the baking powder, cinnamon, cloves, anise, cardamom and salt. In a saucepan, heat the honey, sugar and butter, stirring until the sugar is dissolved and the butter melted. Take from the heat, mix in the lemon juice and candied orange peel, and let cool. Beat in half of the flour mixture and the chopped nuts, add the eggs, and then beat in the remaining flour. Beat for 2 minutes until the dough is smooth, pliable and still slightly sticky. Alternatively, mix and knead with the dough hook of an electric mixer.

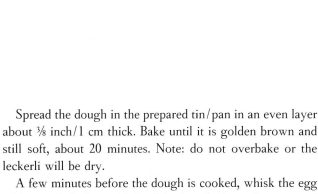

Spread the dough in the prepared tin/pan in an even layer about ⅜ inch/1 cm thick. Bake until it is golden brown and still soft, about 20 minutes. Note: do not overbake or the leckerli will be dry.

A few minutes before the dough is cooked, whisk the egg white until frothy, add the icing/confectioners' sugar and whisk until smooth; the icing should pour easily but if it is thin, add more sugar. As soon as the cookies are done, brush on a light coating of icing. Allow to cool for 5 minutes, then cut into 3×1½ inch/7.5×3.75 cm bars, discarding the dry edges. The leckerli will keep for a month or more in an airtight container.

Kugelhopf aux Lardons et aux Herbes
—— KUGELHOPF WITH BACON AND HERBS ——

This savoury kugelhopf, a variation on the traditional sweet raisin and nut bread, makes a welcome afternoon snack, perfect complement to a glass of white Riesling.

Serves 6–8
8 fl oz/1 cup/250 ml milk
5 oz/⅔ cup/150 g unsalted butter
1 tbsp sugar
⅔ oz/20 g compressed yeast, or ⅓ oz/10 g dry yeast
6 oz/1½ cups/175 g walnut halves
1 lb/4 cups/500 g flour
1 tsp salt
3 eggs
4 oz/½ cup/125 g lean smoked ham, finely chopped
1½ tsp dried sage
1½ tsp dried thyme
two 1⅔ pint/1 quart/1 litre kugelhopf moulds

Scald the milk in a small saucepan, pour about half into a small bowl and let cool to tepid. Meanwhile add the butter and sugar to the remaining milk and continue heating, stirring until the butter is melted and the sugar dissolved, 2–3 minutes. Crumble or sprinkle the yeast over the tepid milk and leave until dissolved, about 5 minutes. Coarsely chop the walnuts, reserving 20 halves for decoration.

Sift the flour with the salt into a large bowl and make a well in the centre. Add the butter and yeast mixtures, and the eggs. With your hand, stir the central ingredients, gradually

Left: Kugelhopf.

drawing in the flour to make a smooth dough. It should be very soft. Using your cupped hand, knead the dough in a slapping motion against the side of the bowl. Knead the dough until shiny and very smooth, about 5 minutes. Alternatively, mix and knead the dough in an electric mixer with a dough hook.

Transfer the dough to an oiled bowl, cover it with a damp cloth and leave to rise in a warm place until doubled in bulk, 1–1½ hours. Butter the kugelhopf moulds and set the reserved walnut halves in the bottom.

When risen, knead the dough lightly to knock out air and gently stir in the chopped walnuts, ham, sage and thyme. Drop the dough by spoonfuls into the moulds. Cover with a damp cloth and leave the dough to rise to the top of the mould, 30–45 minutes. Heat the oven to No 5/375°F/190°C.

Bake the kugelhopf in the heated oven until puffed and golden brown, 40–50 minutes. Turn it out on to a rack to cool. It is best eaten on the day of baking, but can be stored in an airtight container up to 3 days.

Soufflé aux Poires Williams
PEAR BRANDY SOUFFLÉ

The flavour of ripe pears emerges clearly in this feather-light soufflé flavoured with pear brandy. Be sure to reduce the pear purée thoroughly so the whipped egg whites are not softened by too much juice.

Serves 4
4 ripe dessert pears (about 1½ lb/750 g)
juice of ½ lemon
3 tbsp 'Poire Williams' pear brandy
8 egg whites
1½ oz/3 tbsp/45 g sugar
icing/confectioner's sugar (for sprinkling)
For thick pastry cream
6 fl oz/¾ cup/175 ml milk
3 egg yolks
2 oz/⅓ cup/60 g sugar
½ oz/2 tbsp/15 g flour
1 tbsp cornstarch
3¼ pint/2 quart/2 litre soufflé dish

Make the pastry cream: scald the milk. Beat the egg yolks with the sugar until thick and light. Stir in the flour and cornstarch. Stir in half the hot milk and add the mixture to the remaining hot milk in the pan. Bring to the boil, whisking until the pastry cream thickens, and simmer for 2 minutes. To prevent a skin from forming, rub the surface of the hot cream with butter.

Peel and core the pears and purée them in a blender or food processor with the lemon juice. Cook the purée in a small suacepan, stirring until it is thick enough to hold a shape, 10–15 minutes. Let cool, then stir it into the pastry cream with the pear brandy. Press a piece of plastic wrap tightly on top to seal out the air. The pear cream can be refrigerated 2–3 hours.

To finish: heat the oven to No 7/425°F/220°C. Thoroughly butter the soufflé dish. Whip the egg whites until stiff, beat in the sugar and continue beating until glossy, about 30 seconds. Meanwhile, reheat the pear cream until the mixture is hot to the touch. Fold a quarter of the meringue into the warm pear cream, mixing thoroughly, then add the mixture to the remaining meringue. Gently fold them together and pour into the prepared soufflé dish.

Bake the soufflé in the heated oven until puffed and brown, 20–25 minutes. Sprinkle the top with icing/confectioner's sugar and serve at once.

Christstollen
CHRISTMAS FRUIT BREAD

Christstollen is delicious toasted, and because of its high fruit content it keeps so well that one old book advises hiding away a slice or two until Easter.

Makes 1 medium loaf
3½ oz /¾ cup/100 g raisins
1¾ oz/½ cup/50 g candied orange peel (p. 180), finely chopped
¾ oz/¼ cup/25 g candied cherries, chopped
grated zest of 1 orange
3 tbsp rum
8 fl oz/1 cup/250 ml milk
½ oz/15 g compressed yeast, or ¼ oz/7 g dry yeast
12 oz/3 cups/375 g flour, more if needed

1½ oz/¼ cup/50 g sugar
¾ tsp salt
1 egg, beaten to mix
2 oz/¼ cup/60 g unsalted butter, melted
3 oz/½ cup/75 g blanched almonds, finely chopped
For the coating
3 tbsp unsalted butter, melted
8 oz/1¼ cups/250 g icing/confectioners' sugar

Macerate the raisins, candied fruits and orange zest in the rum until well saturated, 1–2 hours. Butter a baking sheet.

Scald the milk and let it cool to tepid. Crumble or sprinkle the yeast on top and leave until dissolved, about 5 minutes. Sift the flour with the sugar and salt on to a work surface and form a well in the centre. Put in the yeast mixture with the egg and melted butter. Mix with your fingers, slowly drawing in the flour to form a dough; it should be soft but not sticky – if necessary, add more flour. Sprinkle the work surface with flour and knead the dough until very smooth and elastic, about 5 minutes. Alternatively mix and knead the dough in an electric mixer with the dough hook.

Press the dough flat, sprinkle it with the fruits and almonds and roll it into a cylinder. Knead the dough again until the fruits are evenly distributed, about 1 minute. Shape the dough into a ball, transfer it to an oiled bowl, and flip so the top is oiled. Cover the bowl with a damp cloth and leave in a warm place until the dough is well risen and almost doubled in bulk, 1½–2 hours.

Knead the dough lightly to knock out the air. Shape it into a ball on a floured work surface, then press out with your fist to an oval. With the rolling pin, roll one end of the oval flatter than the other. Fold the thick side on to the flatter one and press the top to seal the layers. Set the bread on the prepared baking sheet, cover with a cloth and leave in a warm place to rise until well puffed. Heat the oven to No 6/400°F/200°C.

Bake the bread in the heated oven for 15 minutes, then turn the oven down to No 2/300°F/150°C and continue baking until browned and the bottom sounds hollow when tapped with your fist, 25–35 minutes longer. Transfer it to a rack. While still hot, brush the top with melted butter and sprinkle thickly with icing/confectioners' sugar.

Tarte aux Mirabelles
GOLDEN PLUM TART

Stone fruits such as apricots and purple plums can take the place of mirabelle plums, and should be prepared in the same way. Cherries are good too and should be stoned/pitted and left whole.

Serves 6–8
pâte brisée (p. 184) made with 8 oz/2 cups/250 g flour,
4 oz/½ cup/125 g unsalted butter, 1 egg, 1 tsp salt and
5–6 tbsp water
2 lb/1 kg mirabelle plums
3 tbsp dry breadcrumbs
2 eggs, beaten to mix
2 fl oz/¼ cup/60 ml double/heavy cream
2 oz/⅓ cup/60 g sugar
icing/confectioners' sugar, or ground cinnamon
(for sprinkling)
12 inch/30 cm tart tin/pan

Make the pâte brisée dough and chill 30 minutes. Halve the plums, discarding the pits. Heat the oven to No 7/425°F/220°C. Butter the tart tin/pan.

Roll out the pâte brisée and line the tin/pan. Sprinkle the breadcrumbs in the pie shell and arrange the plums on top, cut side up. Bake in the heated oven for 10 minutes. Whisk together the eggs, cream and sugar and pour the mixture over the plums. Lower the oven to No 4/350°F/175°C and bake the pie until the dough is browned, the fruit is tender and the cream mixture is set, 40–45 minutes. Do not overbake or the custard will curdle. Serve the tart warm or cold, sprinkled with icing/confectioners' sugar or cinnamon. It is best eaten the day of baking.

In Brittany one is never far from the sea nor from fishing tackle for catching crustaceans. Inland, the region is equally rich in vegetable crops.

BRITTANY

To the jagged shores and fishing towns of the most westerly tip of France, for fresh Breton tuna and sardines, butter cakes and buckwheat crêpes

The French have never understood why the Bretons have preserved their language and traditions for so long, as well as a loyalty to the saints who first gave the scattered population such a sense of identity. Brittany is certainly isolated by geography, but it has never been an insular province. From Roman times, Breton ships have carried wealth in and out of the region's sheltered harbours, starting with salt, timber, and garum (a piquant fish sauce used for seasoning) and expanding in the Middle Ages to spices, sailcloth and canvas. Later came a succession of new foods such as sugar, tea, coffee and ship's biscuit.

Trade not only maintained Brittany's links with the outside world, it also provided the wherewithal for ambitious town plans. Today one of the most important of these

Marie-Madeleine Gisquiaud is a 'paludier' or gatherer of Guérande salt, prized by chefs and bakers throughout France for its natural mineral flavour.

see. As for fish, the display is a triumph. The northwesterly currents of the Atlantic Gulf Stream bring tuna and shark close to Brittany's shores, with sardines, anchovy, and mullet in season. Halibut, sea bass, and Dover sole jostle the common cod and hake ('line-caught' adds to the price, for the fish are fresher caught close to shore) beside several unknowns – local specialities are tantalizingly delicious, I was told.

The poultry stand features Nantais duck – delicate, tender little birds about half the size of the more common meaty Barbary (also known as Muscovy). Nantais ducks are white, with none of the unattractive Barbary black pin feathers. A plump young female 'canette' is just right for roasting to serve two people and is preferable (say perfectionists) to the more bony male 'caneton'. A full-grown 'canard' is more versatile, equally good braised to serve with green peas, or cooked classically 'en ragoût' with turnips.

In fact, Brittany not only produces much of France's best food, but also processes it. Nantes was the cradle of the French food industry, the first to exploit the canning of vegetables, tuna and sardines. Fish is now frozen as sticks and fingers, or sauced and vacuum packed. The old ship's biscuit trade, which expanded during the last century into sweet confections, now turns out cakes for the popup toaster and microwave. In Nantes the best selection of biscuits – and the best are very good – are to be found at La Friande near the Marché Talensac. Try their 'cigarettes' and 'biscuits mouzillons' for dipping in sweet wine.

From Paris to Nantes is only two hours on the TGV high-speed train, and the centre of Nantes is only an hour away from the marshes of the Grand Brière, one of the wildest areas on Brittany's long coastline. It seems a miracle that an ancient network of canals and reed-thatched cottages has survived here virtually into the 21st century, within sight of the oil refineries of St Nazaire. The inhabitants still live by turf-cutting, basket-making and fishing, based on a system of common ownership, self-regulation, and even self-taxation. At the restored village of Kérinhet you can stay the night and enjoy dishes like eel, caught perhaps with the traditional long forks, or roast leg of 'pré-salé' lamb raised on the salt marshes and served 'à la bretonne' with dried white beans in tomato sauce.

La Grande Brière is even more astonishing when you look at nearby La Baule, a seaside resort rivalling Deauville and Cannes in social pretention. Reclaimed from sand dunes a

historic towns is Nantes, gateway to Brittany from the sea and the south. Grand 18th-century merchants' houses on the Ile Feydeau recall the days of sailing ships and the slave trade, when city life was centred around the waterfront. The international atmosphere of a great port remains – you'll find evidence at once in the thriving Marché Talensac where the fishmonger shouts in Breton, and the herb and spice man is Arab. Nantes has the privilege of drawing on the finest ingredients from three very different regions of France. From the east along the Loire come fine fruits, mushrooms, baby vegetables and asparagus. Charentes, to the south, is famous for its butter – you'll see great mountains on the dairy stands, one of sweet butter and one salted (Breton cooks are unique in France in preferring salted butter). To the west lies Brittany proper. It vies with both the Loire and Charentes for all the above products, while reigning supreme as the source of the best fish and shellfish in France.

On Friday at the fish stand there's no time to gossip: three sizes of live 'langouste' (spiny lobster) are on offer beside 'homard' (clawed lobster) at a bargain price. A French lobster is worth almost double a Canadian import, I was amused to hundred years ago, the beach at La Baule is now dominated by highrises, though some large and curious villas still survive among the pines, together with one or two palace hotels. For less expensive eating, you'll do best to head for the Guérande peninsula and le Croisic to see the salt pans gleaming white in the marshes on one side, and the wave-battered shore on the other.

Stopping on the road to buy a bag of the renowned Guérande salt, I fell into conversation with Marie-Madeleine Gisquiaud, one of the 'paludiers' who gather the salt following methods at least 500 years old. The brine is evaporated in a complex series of pans (the system is explained in the salt museum at Batz) until the white 'fleur de sel' crystallizes on the surface and is skimmed – a woman's job. The men are left to rake up the much greater yield of inferior grey salt which falls to the bottom. Harvest continues from mid June to September, depending on the weather – the yield in a hot dry year such as 1989 or 1990 can be double the average.

Not surprisingly, in a temperate climate such artisan methods cannot compete with the great Salins du Midi on the Mediterranean at the mouth of the Rhône. But Guérande salt is full of minerals and prized by chefs and bakers for its flavour. Use it for grilled meats, to bake fish in a salt crust as they do locally, and for pickles. As an alternative to piquant 'cornichon' cucumbers, Madame Gisquiaud bottles the samphire, or sea fennel, which grows in the salt pans. She also recommends salt as fertilizer on her fields of garlic and shallot, particularly as it kills slugs. 'It's good in a footbath, too,' grins a toothless neighbour who has wandered up as we talk.

Continuing on our route from Nantes to Roscoff, the tranquil estuaries of Brittany's south coast shelter some prosperous settlements. The walled town of Vannes is the place to catch a boat to historic Belle Ile, off the Gulf of Morbihan. The waters of this great inland sea are so rich in organic matter and oxygen that more than 100 species of sea creatures are found. At low tide in spring and autumn, armies of locals wade out with baskets, combing the mudflats and rocks for mussels, winkles, periwinkles, cockles, Venus clams, and a few 'pétoncles', 'palourdes', 'praires' and 'amandes', which have no English equivalents.

Such fecundity has its problems. Enclosed waters like this gulf are plagued with pollution and disease. Until the 1970s, Morbihan flat oysters were famous, but now all are dead of a wasting disease. Growers have been forced to turn to the

hardy, but inferior, hollow or Portuguese oyster. Immature oysters (called spat) are raised away from the diseased beds, then sent for two to three months to fatten and take on local flavour in river estuaries such as the Belon or the Penerf. But they do not rival the 'plates' or flat oysters. When I enquired from a group of garrulous fisherman, faces fell. 'We once had so many "plates", tonnes and tonnes of the best, raised in deep sea water – it's a tragedy.' Further west in the village of Ile-Tudy, Ronan Cariou fattens oysters and raises a dozen other varieties of shellfish. 'We are lucky here to be on the ocean,' he remarks. 'Our parks are washed clean every day by the tide and we have less trouble with pollution.'

Food in Brittany is a history of the struggle with nature, bread being another example. The rocky terrain and thin topsoil of lower (western) Brittany does not support wheat. Yet only wheat contains gluten in sufficient quantity for yeast to raise a loaf. So cooks have had to find substitutes – hence the Breton tradition of buckwheat crêpes. Modern Breton bakers love to mix several grains in breads like 'Le Floron', a combination of wheat, rye and buckwheat flour, marked with an 'hermine', the Breton fleur-de-lys. At La

In the village of Ile-Tudy, Ronan Cariou fattens oysters and raises other varieties of shellfish, notably mussels.

Sunflowers in full glory.

Opposite: The 'hermine' sketched on this Breton loaf is the local version of a fleur-de-lys.

Hûche à Pain on the medieval Place des Lices in Vannes, half a dozen such breads are baked, including a six-grain loaf with barley, rye, wheat, oats, maize and millet. But surely 'L'essentiel', with cotton, linen and sunflower seeds carries a good thing too far!

A town bakery cannot afford the labour-intensive luxury of a wood-fired oven, but you might be lucky enough to find one out in the countryside. In the hamlet of Ty-Glas, I talked to Michel Helias, who for 45 years, six days a week, has timed his day around his rising dough, working from midnight to 2.00 a.m., then from 5.00 a.m. onwards. His great cast-iron oven dates from 1905 and is still in working order, fired with faggots which burn to ash before being raked out when the dough is ready for baking. 'That's the natural way,' he insists, 'oil fuel gives a bad taste.' His rye bread is renowned in the area, made with stone-ground flour from

local mills. Each batch varies – autumn flour, ground from the new season's grain, is particularly tricky. Only when the flour has had time to age and dry, towards Christmas, does the dough become predictable.

Driving westwards from Vannes, jagged fingers of the sea creep deeper and deeper inland to towns like Auray, Hennebont, Riec, Pont-Aven, Concarneau and Quimper. Around Carnac are scattered groups of dolmens – prehistoric stone monuments whose origin has never been explained. Travelling west the wind gets stronger, the salt air more pervasive (in spring it carries the perfume of yellow gorse). You can eat in the sheltered calm of waterfront restaurants near the famous oyster parks of the Belon river, or in the quaint mill-house at Pont-Aven, 'town of 14 mills and 15 houses', where Gauguin painted a century ago. Maurice Sailland, better known as Curnonsky or the 'Prince des

Gastronomes', passed World War II in Riec-sur-Belon at Chez Mélanie, where he was 'more friend than client' of the innkeeper, Mélanie Rouet. The original Bibendum for the Michelin company, Curnonsky did his sponsors a service by encouraging motor travel and hence a faster turnover in car tyres. His effusive writings on French cooking helped make France into what he called 'the paradise of gastronomic tourism'. It still is.

Brittany profits from holiday visitors, but suffers too. The season is painfully short, lasting scarcely two months from July until early September. The weather is fickle, but in a hot year be warned that resorts are almost as swamped with tourists as the Riviera. You need to leave the beaten track (no hardship as every sideroad is a temptation) to discover oases like Hotel Belle Etoile at le Cabellou near Concarneau. To stay there, overlooking the bay to Concarneau's attractive 'ville close' or old town, is to step back into the unpretentious comfort and service of 30 years ago.

Concarneau itself is the third largest fishing port in France, handling a bulk catch processed at sea on ocean-going ships which depart for weeks at a time. Weekday mornings the bustling auction, called a 'criée' because of the shouted bidding, starts at 5.00 a.m. More picturesque 'criées' are held at lesser ports like Plovannelec and Guilvinec towards evening, when local boats come in with the variegated catch of the day. This is where chefs like Guy Diquelou like to buy. Guy is a native of Sainte Marine, a coastal village in the Pays Bigoudin to the south of Quimper. After eight years cooking in Paris, he has come home to run his own little restaurant on the port, serving the freshest of 'plateaux de fruits de mer', and fish with butter sauce.

He describes his favourite recipe for whole fish, baked on a bed of potato with tomato and vegetables, and his fish soup, based on tasty 'poissons de roches', fish which feed around the rocks rather than in open water. Most are full of bones, so Guy thoroughly simmers the fish with plenty of vegetables and garlic, then sieves it to a purée. When I mention 'cotriade', a fish stew with chunks of fish, potatoes, cream and topped with mussels, supposedly a Breton speciality, Guy snorts in derision. 'Cotriade is an invention of the super-chefs who have invaded Brittany – far too many of them, charging high prices. They are in for a hard time.'

He talks of his parents' grocery store up the road, where the daily special may be 'far Breton', a batter pudding with a

Plateau de Fruits de Mer at Guy Diquelou's restaurant in Sainte Marine.

golden crisp crust from baking in earthenware. 'Customers buy that for supper, and with a bowl of soup it's all they need.' He talks also of crêpes and crêperies: 'Some are for tourists, some are for us. Most of us eat crêpes on Friday, we are religious around here, you know.' La Cremaillière a hundred yards away is definitely for 'us'. Savoury crêpes are based on nutty dark buckwheat flour; the composition of the batter is the cook's secret. Here in the Pays Bigoudin, it is made with milk and the crêpes are golden; elsewhere water is used so the crêpes tend to be greyish, if slightly crisper. Be under no illusion that you can recreate them at home. An agile turn of the wrist – an acquired skill – is needed to spread the batter in a wafer-thin, even layer on the hot griddle (called a 'pillig'). I've known Parisian chefs try to manipulate the small wooden rake or 'rozell' for hours without success.

For savoury crêpes, the most popular filling is a 'complète' of ham and egg. You'll be asked if you prefer the egg 'brouillé', briskly scrambled on the hot crêpe, or 'miroir', left untouched to bake on top of the crêpe on the griddle. When folded, the golden egg yolk peeps out of the centre of the crêpe. Sweet crêpes are more delicate, made with wheat flour (to add a savoury filling is taboo). Often they are simply rolled around a sprinkling of sugar or a spoonful of honey or jam, made at La Cremaillère with figs from the garden. Drinks are equally *du pays*: farm-brewed sweet or dry cider (the best in Brittany is said to come from Fouesnant, only a dozen miles away), milk, buttermilk ('lait ribot'), or 'gros lait', a local speciality that resembles soft yoghurt. Bretons have always preferred such fresh dairy products to the complex, aged cheeses found in the rest of France.

The grey stone streets of Quimper are good for shopping, retaining a certain charm despite the number of visitors. At the Musée Breton there are superb rooms with carved antique furniture fitted around the walls – the modular concept is nothing new. Nor is the familiar Quimper pottery, with its kitsch figures of women in coiffes and men in clogs (modes of dress you may still see occasionally on feast days), for Quimper has been a centre of artisan potters since the 17th century. You can see their work in the Musée de Faïence as well as in souvenir stores, or at the factory near the centre of the town.

The orange, blue, and green of the pottery is echoed in the designer napkins and tablecloths at François Le Villec on the rue du Roi Gradlon (King Gradlon is a legendary figure, the sixth-century founder of Quimper). Around the corner on the rue du Parc, Bijoux Bretons carries handmade gold and silver jewellery, Celtic crosses, serpent earrings and bracelets with a double-headed ram. Artisanat Vêtements on the rue Renée Madec is even more old-world, a dusty repository of unbleached linen shirts, embroidered Breton waistcoats and slippers called 'lutins', and genuine needlepoint lace coifs.

Quimper is the capital of the most westerly French department – Finistère, literally 'the end of the earth'. It is here that Breton separatism takes on real meaning. The language of friendship around the café table is Breton, not French. Place names bear prefixes like 'kemper' for 'crossing' and 'plou'

meaning 'parish'. The parish churches, with their splendid 15th-century Flemish carvings and curious 'closes' or walled burial grounds, remain lively cultural centres – the finest lie between Morlaix and Pleyben. Calvaries and crosses abound, said to recall the menhirs (single standing stones) of prehistory, and religious festivals or 'pardons' are very much alive, occasions for processions in regional costume.

From Quimper every road holds an invitation provided you avoid the autoroute which roughly divides 'armor', the land of the sea, from 'argoat', the inner land of the woods. Westwards is Cap Sizun, heart of the medieval kingdom of Cornouaille. (The name reflects the close links between Breton culture and the Cornish peninsula across the water.) You quickly reach the coast, lined with rocks, lighthouses and hardy little ports crouched down behind the headlands. Wind, not cold, is the enemy, for sea and land are warmed by the Gulf stream drift from the Gulf of Mexico. In areas like the Plougastel peninsula, strawberries can be raised in the sandy soil from April through October, thanks to greenhouses of plastic and the shelter of trees and fern-clad walls so high you have to climb them to glimpse the crop.

To the east stretch the Montagnes Noires, rocky black granite outcrops called 'kêrs', surrounded by a patchwork of woods and fields as green as Ireland. To the north stretch the Monts d'Arhée, less rugged hills where you may see some white-flowered buckwheat, somewhat like a bushy sunflower. (Botanically, buckwheat is not a cereal grain but a fruit closely related to rhubarb.) Finally, north of Morlaix, the ground relaxes to the 'golden belt' stretching from Roscoff to St Malo. Here flourish potatoes, cabbages, green peas, and the artichokes and cauliflowers that symbolize Brittany in the world of wholesale produce. Like most farmers, Jean-Marie Legathu is full of gloom. 'We've had two mild winters, too many artichokes, so many I had to throw them away. You English are the worst, you take only my cauliflowers.'

Recent interest in seaweed as a food has spawned a shop in Roscoff called Thalado, which sells bread made with bright green stringy laver weed, high in minerals. Piquant samphire, sometimes called sea asparagus, is delicious boiled – it makes a change from green beans and, like them, just needs tossing in butter. The familiar brown bladderwrack seaweed forms a good bed on which to steam fish, though it is too tough to eat. Most chefs remain sceptical about the potential

La Cremaillière at Sainte Marine – popular with the locals for all kinds of Breton crêpes.

of seaweed. Not so local farmers, who have used it as fertilizer for centuries.

It is tempting to imagine Brittany as a rural retreat, though in fact only 15 per cent of the population is employed in agriculture and their number is falling, lured away by higher-tech industries. However, the region still produces more than half of France's milk, pork, chicken, eggs, onions, cabbages, and almost all the cauliflowers and artichokes. The small fields are easily diversified, so farmers are branching out into luxury products like oyster mushrooms, snails, foie gras, hare, venison and game birds. So jump now on the cross-Channel ferry to Roscoff, or take a high-speed train to Brest, to plunge into a coast and countryside of bucolic charm, with a style of cooking to match.

RECIPES FROM
BRITTANY

Oeufs de Pêcheur
—— FISHERMAN'S EGGS ——

'Brittany is a paradise for conchyliophages [eaters of shell-fish],' declared gastronome Curnonsky with typical hyperbole. He spent part of World War II in Brittany and I like to think he might have eaten this recipe for poached eggs, perfectly complemented by piquant mussels in a light wine sauce.

Serves 8 as a starter / appetizer or 4 as a main course
3¼ pints / 2 quarts / 2 litres mussels
8 fl oz / 1 cup / 250 ml dry white wine, preferably Muscadet
3 shallots, very finely chopped
bouquet garni (p. 183)
1 clove garlic, chopped
freshly ground black pepper
8 eggs
2 tbsp vinegar
2 tbsp potato starch dissolved (p. 186) in 3–4 tbsp water
2½ fl oz / ⅓ cup / 75 ml heavy cream
2 egg yolks
2 tbsp parsley, chopped
8 round fried croûtes (p. 183)

Clean the mussels (p. 184). In a large saucepan combine the wine, shallots, bouquet garni, garlic and plenty of pepper; bring to the boil and simmer for 2 minutes. Add the mussels, cover and cook over high heat for 5–7 minutes until the mussels open, tossing occasionally. Shell the mussels, discarding any that do not open. Carefully pour the cooking liquid into another saucepan, leaving behind any sand or grit.

Meanwhile, poach the eggs. Bring a large shallow pan of water to the boil. Add the vinegar. Break 4 eggs, one by one, into places where the liquid bubbles. Lower the heat and poach the eggs for 3–4 minutes until the yolk is fairly firm but still soft to the touch. Transfer to a bowl of cold water and trim the stringy edges with scissors. Poach the remaining eggs in the same way.

To finish, reheat the eggs by soaking them in a bowl of hot water for 2 minutes and draining them. Fry the croûtes. Bring the mussel liquid to the boil and whisk in enough of the diluted potato starch to obtain a sauce the consistency of thin cream. Whisk together the cream and egg yolks and stir

in about 4 fl oz / ½ cup / 125 ml of the hot sauce. Return it to the remaining sauce and cook over low heat, whisking constantly until just slightly thickened. Note: do not boil the sauce or it will curdle. Add the mussels and chopped parsley and heat briefly. Set the eggs on the croûtes on individual plates, spoon over the mussels and sauce and serve immediately.

Tartare de Thon
—— TUNA TARTARE ——

This unusual recipe, good as an appetizer or with cocktails, is a light version of steak tartare. The tuna used must be very fresh.

Serves 4 as an appetizer
1 lb / 500 g piece of tuna
2–3 tbsp olive oil
2–3 tbsp salad oil
2 fl oz / ¼ cup / 60 ml white wine vinegar
3 shallots, very finely chopped
2 tbsp capers, drained and chopped
1 tbsp chopped chives
1 tbsp chopped parsley
salt and pepper

With a very sharp knife, clean the tuna fillets, removing all skin, bones and membrane. Chop the tuna finely with a knife and put it in a bowl. Add the oils, vinegar, shallots, capers, chives, and parsley and mix well. Season the tartare to taste, cover tightly with plastic wrap and leave to marinate 2–3 hours. Serve with crisp slices of toast.

Oeufs de Pêcheur.

Poisson au Four Chef Guy

BAKED FISH WITH TOMATO, POTATO
AND GARLIC

Fish baked with vegetables can be served hot or at room temperature – almost any well-flavoured fish can be used. Chef Guy Diqueliou is particularly fond of sea bass and salmon trout. He leaves the scales on the fish to retain moisture, so it should be skinned before serving.

Serves 4–6
6–8 tbsp olive oil
4 medium onions, thinly sliced
1½ lb/750 g tomatoes, peeled, seeded and chopped
4 shallots, thinly sliced
6 cloves garlic, thinly sliced
2 lb/1 kg potatoes, peeled and thinly sliced
salt and pepper
one 4½ lb/2 kg whole fish, or two 3 lb/1.25 kg fish,
cleaned but not scaled
6–8 sprigs fresh thyme
juice of 1 lemon
4 fl oz/½ cup/125 ml white wine
1 lemon, cut in wedges (for garnish)

In a frying pan heat 2 tablespoons of the olive oil and sauté the onions until soft but not brown. Oil a large baking dish and spread in it the tomatoes, sautéed onions, shallots, garlic, and finally the potatoes. Season with salt and pepper. The vegetables should form a bed about 1 inch/2.5 cm thick.

Wash the fish, trimming the tail and fins but leaving the head intact. Pat it dry with paper towels. Score the flesh deeply with 3 or 4 slashes on each side so that it cooks evenly. Set the fish on top of the vegetables in the gratin dish and tuck a sprig of fresh thyme into each of the slashes. Spoon the rest of the oil over the fish and sprinkle with salt, pepper, the juice of the lemon and the white wine. The fish can be prepared up to 3 hours ahead and kept in the refrigerator.

Heat the oven to No 3/325°F/160°C. Bake the fish uncovered, basting occasionally, until it just flakes easily, about ¾–1 hour for the larger fish and 30–45 minutes for the smaller fish.

If the vegetables are not tender, remove the fish, wrap it in foil and keep warm. Turn the oven heat to No

Left: The Brittany coastline is second to none for the yachtsman.

6/400°F/200°C and continue baking the vegetables until cooked and brown on top.

To serve, discard the foil, set the fish on the vegetables, add a garnish of lemon wedges and serve.

Sauté de Poulet à la Marinière
SAUTÉ OF CHICKEN WITH CLAMS AND SAMPHIRE

Shellfish and seaweed add salty emphasis to this classic chicken sauté. Mussels can be substituted for the clams, while green beans are a look-alike for samphire. A crisp potato cake is an excellent accompaniment.

Serves 4
3–3½ lb/1.5 kg chicken, cut into 8 pieces (p. 183)
3–4 tbsp flour, seasoned with salt and pepper
1 oz/2 tbsp/30 g butter
1 tbsp vegetable oil
2 tbsp white wine
2 tbsp dry vermouth
12 oz/375 g samphire
12 hardshell clams, cleaned as for mussels (p. 184)
4 fl oz/½ cup/125 ml chicken stock (p. 186), more if needed
1 tbsp chopped fresh chives
salt and pepper

Sprinkle the chicken pieces with seasoned flour, patting them until thoroughly coated. In a sauté pan or shallow casserole heat the butter and oil. Add the chicken pieces, skin side down, and sauté over medium heat until very well browned, 10–15 minutes. Turn and brown the other side. Add the wine and vermouth to the chicken. Cover and cook until the chicken is almost tender when pierced with a fork, 20–25 minutes. If some pieces cook before others, remove them. The chicken can be cooked up to 48 hours ahead and refrigerated. Undercook it slightly to allow for reheating.

To finish: cook the samphire in boiling salted water until just tender 3–4 minutes. Drain, rinse with cold water and drain thoroughly.

If necessary reheat the chicken on top of the stove. Set the clams on top of the chicken, cover and cook until they open, about 5 minutes. Remove the chicken and clams from the pan and keep them warm.

Discard any fat from the pan, add the chicken stock and bring to the boil, stirring to dissolve the juices. If necessary, continue boiling until concentrated and slightly syrupy. Stir in the chives, then add the chicken, clams and samphire and heat gently for 2–3 minutes. Season with salt and pepper. Serve on individual warm plates or in a serving dish.

Salade de Choufleur, Sauce Gribiche
CAULIFLOWER WITH PIQUANT MAYONNAISE

Gribiche is a light version of mayonnaise, good with cooked vegetables, particularly artichokes. To prepare and boil artichokes, see Artichauts à la Barigoule (p. 172).

Serves 6
a medium (about 2 lb/1 kg) cauliflower
salt and pepper
For the sauce gribiche
2 hardboiled eggs
1 raw egg yolk
12 fl oz/1½ cups/375 ml oil
2 tbsp white wine
1 tsp Dijon mustard
1 tbsp gherkin pickles, chopped
1 tbsp capers
2 tbsp chopped mixed herbs such as parsley,
chives and tarragon
herb sprigs (for garnish)
Six 6 fl oz/¾ cup/175 ml custard cups

For the sauce, separate the egg whites from the yolks and coarsely chop the whites. Pound or mash the hardboiled yolks in a small bowl with the raw yolk. Gradually whisk in the oil a few drops at a time until the mixture thickens, as for mayonnaise. When the mayonnaise is thick add the white wine, then whisk in the remaining oil in a steady stream. Finally, stir in the mustard, chopped gherkins, capers, herbs and chopped egg whites and mix well. Add salt and pepper to taste.

Trim and core the cauliflower, then separate it into florets. Put the florets in a large pan of boiling salted water and simmer until tender but still firm, 5–8 minutes. Drain the cauliflower, rinse it with cold water and drain it again thoroughly.

Generously butter the custard cups. Pack the cooked florets into the moulds with the stems inward. Fill the centre with more florets, then press each lightly with a saucer. The sauce and cauliflower can be stored separately in the refrigerator for up to 24 hours. Allow the cauliflower and sauce to come to room temperature before serving.

To finish, unmould the small cauliflowers on to a platter or individual plates. Spoon over the gribiche sauce to half coat the cauliflower and garnish the top with a herb sprig.

Gochtiale

DEMI BRIOCHE

'Gochtiale' has a pleasantly light texture, with less butter and eggs than a classic brioche. With its high sugar content, it toasts well.

Makes 2 medium loaves
½ oz/15 g compressed yeast, or ¼ oz/7 g dry yeast
4 fl oz/½ cup/125 ml lukewarm milk
9 oz/2½ cups/300 g unbleached flour, more if needed
2 oz/⅓ cup/60 g sugar
½ tsp salt
2 eggs, beaten to mix
3¼ oz/7 tbsp/100 g salted butter
1 egg beaten with ½ tsp salt (for glaze)
a 7 inch/18 cm round cake tin/pan

Crumble or sprinkle the yeast over the milk and let it stand for 5 minutes or until dissolved. Sift the flour on to a work surface and make a large well in the centre. Sprinkle the sugar and salt on to the flour. Add the yeast mixture with the beaten eggs to the well. With your hand, gradually work in the flour to form a smooth dough; it should be quite sticky. Knead the dough on the work surface, lifting it up and throwing it down until it is very elastic and resembles chamois leather, about 10 minutes. Work in more flour if necessary so that at the end of kneading, the dough is slightly sticky but peels easily from the work surface.

Transfer the dough to an oiled bowl, turn it over so the top is oiled and cover the bowl with a damp cloth. Leave it in a warm place for an hour or until doubled in bulk. Butter the cake tin/pan.

Work the dough lightly to knock out air. Squeeze the butter with your fist until it is pliable. Add it to the dough and knead, squeezing with your fist and throwing it down, until the butter is completely incorporated, 5–10 minutes. If you like, the dough can be kneaded and the butter added using an electric mixer with the dough hook.

On a floured board shape the dough into a ball, folding the edges to the centre. Flip the ball so the smooth side is upwards and drop gently into the prepared pan. Cover with a cloth and let rise in a warm place until the dough is almost doubled, ½–1 hour. Heat the oven to No 5/375°F/190°C.

Brush the brioche with the egg yolk mixture. With the point of a very sharp knife, slash a cross on the top of the loaf. Bake the brioche in the heated oven until the loaf starts to shrink away from the sides of the pan and sounds hollow when tapped on the bottom, 40–50 minutes. Unmould and cool on a rack. Brioche is best eaten the day of baking and it freezes well.

Le Floron

THREE-GRAIN BREAD

This loaf is typical of the multi-grain breads favoured by Breton bakers. In French, buckwheat is called 'sarrasin' because supposedly it was introduced to Europe by the Saracens who invaded in the 14th century, pushing north as far as Tours.

Makes 2 large loaves

½ oz/15 g compressed yeast, or ¼ oz/7 g dry yeast
16 fl oz/2 cups/500 ml lukewarm water
1 lb/4 cups/500 g plain/all-purpose flour, more as needed
3 oz/⅔ cup/90 g rye flour
3¼ oz/¾ cup/100 g buckwheat flour
1 tbsp salt
1 egg yolk mixed with 1 tbsp water, for glaze

Crumble or sprinkle the yeast over 6–8 tablespoonfuls of the warm water in a small bowl. Let stand until dissolved, about 5 minutes. Sift the flours and salt into a large, wide bowl, make a well in the centre and add the remaining water and the dissolved yeast. With your hand mix some of the flour with the water, drawing in enough flour to make a thick batter. Sprinkle more of the flour on top of the batter, cover and leave in a warm place until bubbles break the surface, 30–40 minutes.

Mix the batter with the remaining flour to make a smooth dough. It will be very sticky. Turn the dough on to a floured work surface and work in more flour until the dough no longer sticks to your fingers. Knead it until it is smooth and elastic, 5–8 minutes. Alternatively, knead the dough in an electric mixer with the dough hook.

Transfer the dough to an oiled bowl, turn it over so the top is oiled and cover the bowl with a damp cloth. Leave in a warm place to rise until doubled in bulk, 1–1½ hours. Butter the baking sheet.

Punch the air out of the dough. Divide it in half and on a floured board shape each half into a loose round ball. Fold the edges to the centre, turning to make a tight round ball. Flip the balls so the smooth side is uppermost and set them on the prepared baking sheet. Cover with a cloth and let them rise in a warm place until almost doubled, about 45 minutes. Cut a flexible stencil of card in the shape of the Breton 'ermine' (p. 48).

Heat the oven to No 6/400°F/200°C. Set the stencil on a loaf, thickly sift flour over the loaf and then carefully remove the stencil using a knife or metal spatula. With a small paint brush or the point of a teaspoon, glaze the 'ermine' shape left on the loaf with the egg yolk and water mixture. With the point of a very sharp knife, slash a continuous circle around the bread, about 1 inch/2.5 cm above the edge of the baking sheet. Repeat with the second loaf.

Bake the loaves in the heated oven for 15 minutes. Lower the heat to No 4/350°F/175°C and continue baking until the loaves are brown and sound hollow when tapped on the bottom, 30–40 minutes longer. They are best eaten the day of baking and they freeze well.

Petits Vacherins aux Fraises

STRAWBERRY MERINGUE BASKETS

This recipe combines everyone's favourite ingredients – strawberries, ice cream and whipped cream – in a snowy sandwich of meringue.

Serves 6

4 egg whites, at room temperature
6½ oz/1 cup/200 g sugar
1 tsp vanilla extract
1 lb/1 qt/500 g strawberries
Chantilly cream (p. 183) made with 8 fl oz/1 cup/250 ml
double/heavy cream, 2 tbsp sugar and 1 tsp vanilla
1 pint/2½ cups/600 ml vanilla ice cream
2 baking sheets; pastry bag with ⅜ inch/1 cm plain tube

Stiffly whip the egg whites. Whisk in 4 tablespoons of the sugar, one at a time. Continue beating until the egg whites are glossy and form short peaks when the whisk is lifted, about 30 seconds. With a spatula, fold in the remaining sugar and vanilla and continue folding until the meringue forms long peaks, ½–1 minute. Heat the oven to No ½/250°F/120°C. Grease and flour the baking sheets or line them with non-stick parchment paper. Mark twelve 4 inch/10 cm circles on the baking sheets.

Fill the meringue into the pastry bag with the plain tube. Pipe twelve 4 inch/10 cm rounds in a spiral inside the marked circles, or spread the meringue evenly in rounds with a metal spatula. Sprinkle with sugar and bake until crisp and dry, 1–1¼ hours. Leave to cool on the baking sheets. They can be stored in an airtight container for up to 2 weeks.

To finish: shortly before serving, hull the strawberries, washing them only if sandy. Make the Chantilly cream. Put a scoop of vanilla ice cream in the centre of 6 of the meringue rounds. Surround the ice cream with strawberries, cutting them in half if they are large. Top the ice cream and strawberries with a spoonful of Chantilly cream and add a second round of meringue, pressing it down lightly. Serve at once.

Tarte aux Figues
———— FIG TART ————

In the mild Breton climate, fig trees flourish. These individual tarts, made with thinly sliced figs on a wafer-thin layer of puff pastry, were on a menu in Roscoff. Serve them warm, with crème fraîche or whipped cream.

Makes 8 individual tarts
pâte feuilletée (p. 185) made with 8 oz/2 cups/250 g flour,
8 oz/1 cup/250 g butter, 1 tsp salt, and 4 fl oz/
½ cup/125 ml water
2 lb/1 kg fresh figs
6½ oz/1 cup/200 g sugar
2 oz/¼ cup/60 g butter

Make the pâte feuilletée dough and chill thoroughly. Roll the dough to an 8×16inch/20×40 cm rectangle, trim the edges and cut into 8 equal squares. Roll each square to a very thin 4 inch/10 cm diameter round. Prick the pastry rounds with a fork to prevent them from rising too much and chill them until firm, about 30 minutes. Heat the oven to No 7/425°F/220°C.

Cut the figs in ⅜ inch/1 cm slices, discarding stems. Arrange the slices slightly overlapping on the pastry rounds so that they just reach the edge of the pastry. Sprinkle 2 tablespoons sugar evenly over each tart and dot the top with butter. Bake until the pastry is thoroughly browned and the surface of the figs is lightly caramelized, 20–25 minutes.

Michel Helias' Gâteau Breton
———— MICHEL HELIAS' BUTTER CAKE ————

Once a week, Michel Helias bakes gâteau Breton, a golden crusty version of pound cake that highlights good butter. You'll see large and small gâteaux Bretons in all the pâtis-series, recognizable by their latticed tops, but the Helias version flavoured with rum is undeniably superior.

Makes 1 cake to serve 6 or about 6 individual cakes
6 egg yolks
9 oz/2¼ cups/275 g flour
8 oz/1 cup/250 g salted butter
6½ oz/1 cup/200 g sugar
1 fl oz/2 tbsp/30 ml rum
One 8 inch / 21 cm tart tin / pan or six 4 inch / 10 cm tartlet tins / pans

Heat the oven to No 3/325°F/160°C. Thoroughly butter the tart tin/pan. Set aside a tablespoonful of the egg yolks for glaze.

Sift the flour on to a work surface and make a large well in the centre. Cut the butter in small pieces and put it in the well with the sugar, egg yolks and rum. Work them together with your fingertips until smooth. Gradually incorporate the flour using the fingers and heel of your hand in a rocking motion, and then work the dough gently until smooth. It will be sticky at this point and must be mixed with the help of a pastry scraper or metal spatula.

Transfer the dough to the buttered tin/pan or individual tins/pans and smooth it with your fist to an even layer, wetting the back of your hand to prevent sticking. Brush the surface of the dough with the reserved egg yolk and mark a lattice design with the prongs of a fork.

Bake in the oven for 1–1¼ hours (35–45 minutes for smaller cakes) until the top is golden and firm to the touch. The inside should remain moist. Leave to cool, then unmould the cake or cakes carefully on to a rack. Gâteau Breton can be stored for up to a week in an airtight container.

Left: Château Roquetaillade,
a splendid fortress in the
Graves-Sauternes wine area.
Below: Auch — gastronomic
capital of the southwest.

GASCONY

*In the shadow of the Pyrenees, exploring rich
confits and cassoulet, prunes and Armagnac, ending with
a sweet Sauternes on the outskirts of Bordeaux*

The English have a special affection for Southwestern
France. In the 14th and 15th centuries they ruled huge tracts
of this beautiful land, the dowry of King Henry II's wife,
Eleanor of Aquitaine. Aquitaine then included Gascony, an
area known not only for its courageous and belligerent
soldiers, but also for good cooking and gourmandise. The
Gascons acquired such a reputation for bravado that 'gasconnade' came to denote an absurd boast. The story goes that
when a Gascon was asked what he thought of the Palais du
Louvre in Paris, he countered: 'Pretty good. It reminds me
of the back part of my father's stables.' Memories of the good
life in Gascony linger on, savoured by the many foreigners
who enthusiastically snap up old houses left vacant by the
French heading for the big towns.

The stained glass windows of the Cathedral at Auch display fruits of the region.

meringue cake (named after the spa of Dax), with cups of thick, cinnamon-flavoured hot chocolate, a local speciality dating from the 17th century when chocolate arrived from the New World. Spare a thought for the intrepid sailors who brought the precious cocoa beans to Bayonne and Bordeaux in their small ships, though don't be too sympathetic: one leg of their voyage often included Africa for a cargo of slaves.

For the night I would retreat to Montréjeau and the Hostellerie des Cèdres, with its views of the mountains, fine grounds, and menus 'mi-régionale et mi-traditionelle'. St Gaudens nearby is a market centre famous for its white cattle, for its charcuterie, and for its cheese. Traditional cheese-making survives here as almost nowhere else, a black skin denoting a cow's milk cheese and a red skin sheep's milk (the whey goes to feed the pig). In the market you'll see salt pork hocks called 'cambajous', plus a multitude of 'saucissons secs' (dried salami-type sausages), some rolled in cracked pepper, wood ash, or hot red 'espelette' pepper from the neighbouring Basque country.

Most famous of all is the excellent smoked ham of the Pyrenees, known as 'jambon de Bayonne' though the lengthy curing process generally takes place out of town in the mountains. The pigs themselves are fed with maize, swill, and acorns gathered from the forests. The pig-killing ceremony lasts two days, the first devoted to cleaning the intestines for sausages, making liver pâté and a blood pudding called 'sanquette'. By the end of the second day, the carcass has been dismembered, the trimmings reduced to sausages, the back salted for bacon.

Bayonne hams are salted for three days (local salt comes from Salies-de-Béarn), then pickled in brine with red wine and herbs for up to a month, then finally smoked in the fireplace. To ward off flies, coarse pepper is rubbed into the meat, particularly around the bone, then the hams are hung in a cool airy place to age three months or more. Jambon de Bayonne is moist and piquant, often thinly sliced to serve raw as a first course, or in a sandwich, as well as flavouring omelettes and chicken as part of the classic 'basquaise' mixture of red and green bell peppers with ham. So prized are the hams from local pigs that there are not enough to go around and the great majority are brought in for curing from elsewhere.

From St Gaudens all serious gastronomes head north up the D929, skirting Béarn and its 'poule au pot', to André

Gascony can be approached from the north at Bordeaux, from the south at Bayonne, or the east at Toulouse where this itinerary begins. It is an easy drive towards Luchon on the N117 southwest along the Pyrenees beside countless rivers and streams which cascade down from the mountains through pretty valleys with bright houses and well-kept gardens. Near St Bertrand de Comminges, southwest of Toulouse just beyond St Gaudens, the Romans founded one of their first spas, channelling the hot sulphur springs into baths which they regarded as second only to those at Naples.

The Romans would have approved of the self-indulgent tearooms and restaurants that abound in the spa towns today. At Luchon you'll find half a dozen pâtisseries packed with 'curistes' enjoying the 'dacquoise', buttercream

Daguin's famous restaurants at Auch, the capital of Gascony. A visit to the cathedral with its fine stained glass windows and carved choir stalls gives just the necessary appetite for Daguin's sumptuous variations on the regional theme. Lentil soup with confit of goose gizzard, boned pigeon wing with truffles and vinegar, lamb shanks 'en gasconnade' with vegetables and garlic, and outstanding country bread are just a beginning. Truffles perfume the 'ballotine de dinde' as well as the foie gras, which Daguin presents in four guises as appetizer: raw, as pâté, baked in salt, and baked in a scallop squash. The archetypal Gascon, André Daguin is a giant bull of a man with a personality to match, the only chef ever invited to address the illustrious Institut de France. 'For us, cooking is a celebration,' he declares. 'We undertake it with pleasure, we eat it with delight, and the enjoyment begins long before the first glass of wine.'

Daguin is one of many who like to hold forth on the preparation of 'cassoulet', that ultimate one-pot meal based on dried beans. All sorts of legends surround its preparation: the pot should be made of earthenware from Issel, near Castelnaudary: the oven should be heated with mountain brushwood; only if cooked in rainwater are the beans really tender; and for authentic depth of flavour, the crust on top should be broken and mixed half a dozen times into the beans. What nonsense! Cassoulet is no more nor less than a

The church at Bazas, a cattle centre of the region.

The Gascons have long been famed for rearing ducks and geese.

boiled maize, queuing up one by one to take their turn. They recognize who feeds them and are upset by strangers.' There is no guarantee of success: 'We have 600 or more birds at a time, and I count myself lucky if I lose only one in ten,' she continues. 'We use the rejects at home but I believe larger producers sell them as chicken livers.'

Foie gras is not just hard to produce – it is equally tricky to cook. 'I like to bake the whole liver at No ½/250°F/120°C in a terrine with just salt, pepper and a sprinkling of Armagnac,' says Madame Brisac. 'The heat and timing must be exactly right. But the biggest uncertainty is finding the best foie gras.' Colour is no indication of quality. The ideal liver weighs around 1½ lb/750 g – if outsize, it is more likely to dissolve to the soft, lemon yellow fat which is the sign of over-fattening. After years of watching professionals like Madame take the gamble, I thankfully buy my 'terrine de foie gras' already cooked by an expert.

Throughout the southwest a flourishing cottage industry centres around ducks and geese. Often whole families are involved. In the little village of St Martin d'Armagnac, Madame Sarran has achieved fame for her cooking at the Auberge du Bergerayre, while her son and daughter-in-law look after the rearing, processing, and selling of fattened birds. A rural drive along the N124 brings you to the gentle hills of Armagnac near Nogaro and the Sarran farmhouse, with its perfume of magnolia and wallflowers to greet the jaded traveller. Inside, one detects the whiff of 'garbure' vegetable soup and browning pastry, all overlaid with a healthy garlic tang.

Garbure is to Gascony what bouillabaisse is to Provence, but is much easier to reproduce. Recipes vary from cook to cook and day to day. The best are based on seasonal vegetables from the garden, with a handful of spinach or sorrel leaves in the spring, zucchini and tomatoes in summer. 'Winter is the best season for garbure,' says Madame Sarran. 'My recipe comes from my mother-in-law and uses green cabbage, potatoes and trimmings of confit, all slowly simmered and thick, as in the old days. Some people add dried beans, but not me.'

'Visitors come here to enjoy the local produce,' Madame Sarran adds. 'Duck features in three-quarters of the dishes I cook.' Her dinner that night was up to all expectations, opening with foie gras grilled over vine shoots, or served warm with grapes, and continuing to homemade confit with

casserole of baked white kidney beans, enriched with pork, pork sausages, and if you like a bit of lamb or game. One other ingredient is indispensable – 'confit' of goose or duck.

Although ducks and geese are now reared all over France to satisfy the new demand for foie gras, the actual production is concentrated in Périgord and the southwest, especially around the market centres of Dax, Aire-sur-l'Adour and Mont-de-Marsan. Traditionally the three-week 'gavage' or fattening of geese (four weeks for ducks) begins when the first maize is ripe and the countryside is awash with fizzy new wine which the Gascons call 'bourret'. However today you can witness the thrice-daily ritual of 'gavage' for most of the year. Many foie gras farms welcome visitors and you can see for yourself that the geese actually enjoy it. 'Fattening geese is a very personal matter,' explains one artisan producer, Madame Brisac. 'The birds are given a special mixture of a purée of spinach. Appropriately, the finale was punctuated with Armagnac, which infused the flaky apple 'tourtière' and the prune ice cream. For a send-off Madame Sarran offered Armagnac 'hors d'âge' – over 10 years old – but I opted for the lighter 'floc de Gascogne', made by combining white wine with distilled spirit.

St Martin lies in Bas-Armagnac, where the best distilleries are located. Armagnac differs from cognac in that it is distilled only once and at a much lower strength – 53 per cent as opposed to cognac's 70 per cent – so that the flavour is more complex, with a tang of the local black oak in which it is aged. The producers' cooperative in Nogaro welcomes visitors to its huge copper stills, named after the Three Musketeers, those archetypal Gascon creations of the novelist Alexandre Dumas. Dumas, by the way, would willingly have traded his quill pen for a cooking pot: 'I see with pleasure that my culinary reputation is growing and bids fair to eclipse before long my literary reputation. God be praised!' he exclaimed.

Continuing along the N124, 'production artisanale' of foie gras, confit, regional wines and liqueurs bids constantly for your attention. In autumn you may be offered homemade preserves of almost-forgotten fruits like quince and medlar; snap up any bilberry/huckleberry jelly if only to reward the back-breaking work involved in detaching tiny purple berries from the low bushes with a special comb. The cultivation of more conventional stone fruits – plums, peaches, nectarines and apricots – is a major Gascon industry. Try them macerated in Armagnac, or the famous prunes which hail from Agen, up north on the Garonne. Prunes soaked in tea before pickling in Armagnac are a 'digestif' more palatable than any medicine.

Just west of Aire-sur-l'Adour lies temptation at the spa of Eugénie-les-Bains. Here one of the finest chefs in France, Michel Guérard, and his wife Christine have created a sophisticated retreat offering two styles of cuisine – 'gourmande' and Guérard's own 'minceur', inspiration of so much of today's spa cuisine. The spa menu is limited to 'curistes' who stay for a week of massage and mud baths, and such is the genius of Guérard that without envy they eat side by side with gourmands feasting on such indulgences as hot goat cheese soufflé in a chilled vegetable cream sauce, fritters of langoustines on a salad of raw artichokes with olive oil, or 'drunken' pork with fruits and Armagnac – my favourite.

If all Gascon roads lead to Eugénie, all roads from Eugénie lead to Bordeaux. Soon you cross the Landes, that curious sandy expanse bordering the Atlantic. Once a desert of shifting dunes, in the 19th century the Landes was drained and planted with pines which now forest an interminable stretch of France's lower Atlantic coast. This is hunter's paradise, where the fever caused by the arrival of 'palombes', the migratory wild pigeons, is called 'le mal bleu', after the colour of their feathers. The birds are lured by spinning a white disc into the air; mistaking this for a predatory sparrow hawk, they come down to land and are trapped in nets.

The Armagnac Producers Cooperative at Nogaro, named after the Three Musketeers of Alexandre Dumas. This Lascaux bull (below left) is a roadside advertisement for one of the major producers.

The locals pursue other delicacies with excessive zeal. Tiny bunting ('ortolans') and pippets ('becs fins') are ensnared, then kept in a darkened cage and fed with Armagnac until their bones dissolve – not something I would care to try. Less esoteric game including pigeon, quail and woodcock is common on the menus of restaurants such as the rustic Relais de la Haute Lande in Luxey, along the D9 from Roquefort (not to be confused with the home of blue cheese, much further south). Here you can enjoy such seasonal specialities as 'gibelotte de garenne' (ragoût of wild rabbit) and lamprey 'bordelaise' in red wine sauce. Lamprey is serpent-like, a sucker which attaches itself to other bigger fish. The meat is rich and gelatinous, resembling eel, but the cartilagenous cord running down the spine is poisonous and must be removed with care. Perhaps it caused the English King Henry I to die of a surfeit of lampreys while in Normandy in 1135.

From Luxey minor roads will take you through the depths of the Landes to Bazas on the edge of the rich Garonne valley running up to Bordeaux. Bazas is famous for its cattle and for its ancient 'Fête des Boeufs Gras', held just before Shrove Tuesday, when the local livestock is decked in flowers and ribbons and paraded around the arcaded Place de la Cathédrale. This is as authentic a place as any for 'entrecôte bordelaise', with its classic brown sauce of red wine, shallots and bone marrow. I must say I prefer the simple version introduced to me by food writer Jane Grigson, who spent her summers in France: pan fry your steak, deglaze the pan with a little red wine, then top the meat with a generous layer of finely chopped, crunchy raw shallots. Best of all, so they say, is entrecôte bordelaise barbecued over vine prunings – centuries ago the original dish was made with the meat of vineyard rats!

In early autumn, the perfect accompaniment to both beef and game is a dish of 'cèpes' or king boletus wild mushrooms sautéed with oil and garlic. Cèpes sprout generously in the woods around Bordeaux, and should be cut off neatly at the base of the stem without pulling up the roots. The boletus family is relatively easy to recognize by its bulbous stem, green and gold earth tones, and the spongy underside to its cap which contrasts with the gills of most other mushrooms. The king boletus is beige, plump, and highly perfumed. If in doubt about any wild mushrooms, ask for advice at the nearest pharmacy as they routinely offer this service. Even

so, every year one or two people die of mushroom poisoning in France.

Just north of Bazas you can join the autoroute at Langon and speed to Bordeaux, but I would recommend a side trip to Sauternes and Barsac. The road winds through a labyrinth of neat vines and fine properties such as Château de Malle, Suduiraut, Climens, and the legendary Yquem, producer of the finest sweet wine in the world. My own taste for foie gras and Château d'Yquem, preferably slightly madeirized to moderate its sweetness, began when I first came to live in Paris with a family who had lined their cellar with a notable collection of bottles dating back to the 1900s. This pleasant custom has spread and with a liver pâté, many restaurants now offer a glass of Sauternes, or a well-rounded Jurançon from Béarn.

Good food naturally follows fine wine, and nowhere more than in the city of Bordeaux. The current 'numéro un' is the Restaurant Amat in St James across the river in Bouliac. Chef Jean-Louis Amat takes a highly original approach in dishes such as 'tartare' of raw lobster with chives, and eel sautéed with wild leeks, pine nuts and baby onions. You will find more traditional fare at one of the many Bordeaux bistros offering regional specialities like omelette with 'piballes' or baby eels, shad stuffed with sorrel, roast baby 'pré-salé' lamb from the salt marshes of the Gironde estuary, and 'hachis Parmentier' or shepherd's pie of goose. Don't miss the oysters from the nearby bay of Arcachon, or the green-tinged Marennes oysters from the head of the Gironde estuary. To find them at their best, go to Le Vieux Bordeaux, 27, rue Buhan, and eat them like the locals with spicy hot sausages – a provocative idea that is easy to copy at home.

Fine food stores there are aplenty in Bordeaux; go to Boulangerie Bastarac on the rue Fondaudège for the best of bread and brioche, to Charcuterie de Tours on the rue Michel Montaigne for artisan pâtés, sausages and superb foie gras; to Cerruti on the rue Voltaire for a grand range of delicacies from caviar to handmade chocolates, exotic spices to canned confit. Above all don't miss the daily display of produce under Les Halles aux Capucines, a traditional market which rivals any in France. For wines, you have your choice in 'vinothèques' or wine supermarkets like the one in the Maison de Bordeaux opposite the train station. With over 3,000 wine-making châteaux in the neighbourhood, there's plenty to choose from – but that's another story!

Opposite: 'Osier', or rushes, for basket-making.

RECIPES FROM
GASCONY

Garbure
GASCON VEGETABLE SOUP

'Garbure' is hearty, not a sophisticated cream soup. It may be served unstrained with the vegetables in slivers, or puréed to be quite thick. Croûtes of bread, sometimes topped with the puréed vegetables and grated cheese, then browned in the oven, are the accompaniment. In another variant, the soup is topped with croûtes, then sprinkled with cheese and gratinéed like French onion soup.

Serves 6
3 oz/6 tbsp/90 g butter
1 medium white turnip, thinly sliced
2 large carrots, thinly sliced
¼ medium head cabbage, shredded
white part of 3 leeks, thinly sliced
2–3 stalks celery, thinly sliced
2 medium potatoes, thinly sliced
2⅓ pints/1½ quarts/1.5 litres white veal or chicken stock
(p. 186) or water, more if needed
salt and pepper
2–3 long crusty rolls, fried or toasted in croûtes (p. 183)
1½ oz/½ cup/50 g grated Gruyère cheese
2 tbsp chopped parsley
For the dried beans
2 oz/⅓ cup/60 g dried white haricot beans or navy beans
1 onion studded with 2 cloves
1 small carrot
bouquet garni (p. 183)
salt and pepper

To cook the dried beans: bring the beans to the boil with enough water to cover by 2 inches/5 cm. Cover the pan, remove from the heat, and allow the beans to stand and soften for an hour. Drain the water and put the beans, onion studded with cloves, carrot and bouquet garni in a pan with water to cover. Simmer until the beans are tender, 2–3 hours. Add salt and pepper halfway through the cooking time. Drain the beans, discarding the onion, carrot and bouquet garni.

For the soup: in a large heavy-based saucepan, melt 2 tablespoons of the butter, add the turnip, carrot, cabbage, leek, celery and potato and press a piece of buttered foil on top. Add the lid and cook very gently, stirring occasionally, until the vegetables are fairly tender, about 15–20 minutes. Note: do not let them brown. Add the beans, stock or water, salt and pepper. Cover and simmer until the vegetables are very tender, 20–30 minutes.

Toast or fry the croûtes. Preheat the oven to No 5/375°F/190°C. Lift out about a quarter of the vegetables from the soup with a slotted spoon and purée them in a food processor or blender. In a small pan, melt a further tablespoon of butter, add the purée and cook, stirring constantly, until it thickens to the consistency of mashed potatoes. Spread the purée on the croûtes, mounding it well, and sprinkle with grated cheese. Bake the croûtes in the heated oven until well browned, 10–12 minutes.

Meanwhile, reheat the soup and add more stock or water if needed to thin it to the consistency of cream. Taste it for seasoning. The soup and croûtes can be made 48 hours ahead and kept covered in the refrigerator.

To finish: bring the soup to the boil and warm the croûtes in the oven. Take the soup from the heat, stir in the remaining butter in small pieces, spoon it into bowls and sprinkle with the chopped parsley. Serve the croûtes separately.

VARIATION
Follow the recipe, but purée all the vegetables together. Just before serving, add the butter and parsley to the soup and pour it into heatproof serving bowls. Cover the surface of each bowl with thin overlapping slices of crusty bread and sprinkle each bowl with 2–3 tablespoons grated Gruyère cheese. Sprinkle on a little melted butter. Bake at No 10/500°F/260°C until browned, or brown it under the grill/broiler.

Truite au Jambon de Bayonne
──── SAUTÉED TROUT WITH BAYONNE HAM ────

It was years ago in a little mountain restaurant that I first tasted trout with the piquant smoked ham of Gascony, and I've enjoyed it ever since. Prosciutto or any other raw smoked ham may be substituted.

Serves 4
4 trout each weighing about 8 oz/250 g
salt and pepper
1 oz/¼ cup/30 g flour
2 oz/¼ cup/60 g butter
2 shallots, chopped
2 cloves garlic, chopped
2 oz/¼ cup/60 g Bayonne, prosciutto,
or other raw smoked ham, diced
2 tbsp wine vinegar
2 tbsp chopped parsley

Cut the fins off the trout and trim the tails to a 'V'. If they are not already cleaned, clean them through the gills without slitting the stomach. Wash the fish thoroughly and pat dry. Sprinkle the trout with salt and pepper and coat with flour, patting off the excess.

Heat the butter in a large frying pan, add the trout and sauté them until golden brown and they just flake easily, 4–5 minutes on each side. Transfer them to a platter, cover and keep warm.

Add the shallot to the hot pan and sauté briefly until soft. Stir in the garlic and ham and cook 1 minute. Remove the pan from the heat, add the vinegar, and then the parsley, standing back as it will splutter. While still foaming, pour the vinegar and ham mixture over the fish and serve immediately.

Huitres aux Crépinettes
──── OYSTERS WITH SPICED SAUSAGES ────

Around Bordeaux little sausages, hot in both senses of the word, are the traditional accompaniment to oysters on the half shell. The bother of stuffing sausage casings is avoided if you make 'crépinettes' or little cakes of sausagemeat wrapped in caul fat. Eat them with your fingers, between mouth-

A fishing platform on the Garonne river.

fuls of oyster and chilled white wine. Lacy caul fat from the lining of cow's stomach is available at good butchers; otherwise, simply roll the patties in flour.

Serves 8
8 servings of shelled/shucked oysters on the half shell, on ice
For the crépinettes
about 4 oz/125 g piece of caul fat
2–3 tbsp melted lard
1 onion, chopped
2 cloves garlic, chopped
1½ lb/750 g lean pork, minced/ground
8 oz/250 g pork fat, minced/ground
3 tbsp chopped parsley
pinch of thyme
½ bay leaf, crumbled
pinch of grated nutmeg
¼ tsp ground hot pepper, or to taste
1 tsp peppercorns, coarsely crushed
1 tsp salt

Soak the caul fat in cold water for about 30 minutes to make it pliable. Heat 1 tablespoon of the lard in a frying pan, add the onion and cook gently until soft but not brown. Add the garlic and cook ½ minute. In a bowl mix the minced/ground pork and pork fat. Stir in the onion, garlic, parsley, thyme, bay leaf, nutmeg, hot pepper, pepper and salt. Beat the mixture with a wooden spoon until it holds together, 2–3 minutes. Sauté a small piece and taste for seasoning.

Drain the caul fat, spread it on a work surface and cut it into 24 rectangles. Divide the meat mixture into 24 balls, and shape each into a cylinder. Wrap each cylinder in caul fat. Put them in a greased baking dish and spoon over the remaining lard. The crépinettes can be refrigerated up to 24 hours.

To finish: preheat the oven to No 5/375°F/190°C. Bake the crépinettes, basting frequently, 15–20 minutes or until well browned. Serve very hot, with the chilled oysters.

Douillons de Pigeon aux Pommes
───────── PIGEON DUMPLINGS WITH APPLES ─────────

For this tasty dumpling, pigeon or quail are roasted until just rare and still juicy. (Use raised, not wild, birds otherwise they may not be tender.) Then the meat is taken off the bone, sliced and layered with apple before wrapping in puff pastry – a contemporary notion which echoes the fruit-flavoured meat pies of medieval days.

Serves 4
pâte feuilletée (p. 185) made with 8 oz/1 cup/250 g unsalted
butter, 8 oz/2 cups/250 g flour, 1 tsp salt,
and 4 fl oz/½ cup/125 ml water
2 pigeons
1½ oz/3 tbsp/45 g unsalted butter
salt and pepper
2 tart apples, peeled and cored and cut in
¼ inch/6 mm wedges
1 tbsp sugar
1 egg, beaten to mix with ½ tsp salt (for glaze)
For the sauce
16 fl oz/2 cups/500 ml brown stock (p. 186)
2 tbsp Armagnac
2 tsp arrowroot dissolved (p. 182) in 2 tbsp water

Make the pâte feuilletée and chill for at least 30 minutes. Preheat the oven to No 10/500°F/260°C. Spread the pigeons with 1 tablespoon of the butter, spinkle with salt and pepper and set them in a roasting pan. Roast them in the heated oven until browned but still pink when the breast is pierced with a skewer, 15–18 minutes. During roasting, baste them occasionally and turn them from one side on to the other and finally on to their backs. Let them cool. Remove from the pan. Discard the fat, add a few tablespoons of stock to the pan and boil, stirring to dissolve the pan juices. Return to the remaining stock.

Melt the remaining butter in a frying pan and add the apples. Sprinkle them with half the sugar and turn them over. Sprinkle with the remaining sugar and fry briskly until brown, about 5 minutes. Turn, brown the other side and let them cool.

Cut the legs from the pigeons and cut off the thigh meat. Cut the meat from each side of the breast in one piece and cut the breasts in 3–4 diagonal slices. With a cleaver chop the carcasses in pieces. Simmer the carcass and leg bones with the stock until well reduced, ¾–1 hour.

Roll the pâte feuilletée dough to a 16 inch/40 cm square. Trim the edges and cut into 4 equal squares. Arrange half the apple slices diagonally on each square, working from the centre so that 4 triangles of uncovered dough are left surrounding the apples. Top the apples with half the pigeon slices, then add remaining apples and pigeon on top, mounding them well. Sprinkle a little salt and pepper between each layer. Brush the edges of dough with egg glaze. Fold the dough over the filling, pinching the edges in the shape of a cardinal's hat. Pierce the top of each dumpling with a skewer and insert a foil chimney in each hole to allow the steam to escape during baking. Brush the dough with glaze and chill the dumplings until firm, at least 30 minutes. They can be refrigerated up to 8 hours.

To finish: heat the oven to No 7/425°F/220°C. Bake the dumplings on a baking sheet until puffed and brown and a skewer inserted in the centre is hot to the touch when withdrawn after 30 seconds, 30–40 minutes. If the dumplings brown too quickly, lower the oven heat to No 5/375°F/190°C and cover them loosely with foil. For the sauce, strain the stock into a small saucepan and bring to the boil with the Armagnac. Whisk in enough dissolved arrowroot to thicken the sauce lightly and taste it for seasoning. Remove the foil chimneys and pour some sauce in each dumpling.

Cassoulet
——— MEAT CASSEROLE ———

The cooking of cassoulet must be leisurely and, as with all such complex casseroles, the flavour improves on standing. Plump garlic sausages about 2 inches/5 cm in diameter for poaching to serve hot are popular throughout France; Polish kielbasa sausage is a good substitute.

Serves 8

2 lb/1 kg dried white beans
salt and pepper
10 oz/300 g garlic poaching sausage
7 oz/200 g pork rind (optional)
1 lb/500 g bacon or salt pork, cut in lardons (p. 184)
1½ lb/750 g lamb breast
3 lb/1.5 kg lamb shoulder, boned
¼ cup/60 g goose or duck fat or lard
10 oz/300 g baby onions
1½ lb/750 g pork loin, cut in 2 inch/5 cm cubes
10 oz/300 g saucisses de Toulouse
2 lb/1 kg tomatoes, peeled, seeded and coarsely chopped
(p. 186)
6 fl oz/¾ cup/175 ml white wine
2⅓ pints/1½ quarts/1.5 litres white veal stock (p. 186)
or water, more if needed
bouquet garni (p. 183)
3–4 cloves garlic, chopped
1 tbsp tomato purée/paste
4 pieces of duck or goose confit (p. 158)
⅔ cup/60 g dry breadcrumbs

To cook the dried beans: bring the beans to the boil with enough water to cover by 2 inches/5 cm. Cover the pan, remove from the heat, and allow the beans to stand and soften for an hour. Drain them, put them in a pan with enough water to cover generously and bring to the boil. Cover and simmer for 25 minutes, add salt and continue to cook for another 25–30 minutes or until nearly tender. Add more water during cooking if necessary so the beans are always covered.

Meanwhile poach the garlic sausage in a pan of water for 30 minutes; drain and slice it. Blanch (p. 182) the pork rind if using, rinse it under cold running water, drain thoroughly and mince/grind it. If the bacon is very salty, blanch it also.

Bayonne hams at the Bordeaux autumn fair.

Preheat the oven to No 5/375°F/190°C. Trim skin and excess fat from the lamb and cut it into cubes. Heat half of the goose fat in a large heavy casserole and lightly brown the bacon and baby onions; remove them and add the remaining fat. Heat it, brown the lamb cubes on all sides and remove them. Add the cubes of pork, brown them also and remove. Lightly brown the fresh sausages in the fat and remove them.

Put the chopped tomatoes in the large casserole with the minced/ground pork rind, white wine, stock or water, bouquet garni, garlic, tomato purée/paste and a little salt and pepper. Bring to the boil, skimming occasionally. Cover and bake in the oven for 50–60 minutes or until nearly tender, adding more stock or water if the pan becomes dry. Cut each piece of duck confit in two and add to the tomato mixture with the fresh sausages and garlic sausage. Cover and continue to bake for 30 minutes.

Drain the beans and put in large or medium baking dishes with all the meats and the onions. The dishes should be almost full, with the meats half-covered by the beans. Taste the meat cooking liquid for seasoning and discard the bouquet garni. Ladle enough of the cooking liquid into the dishes to moisten the cassoulet well without being soupy. Sprinkle it with breadcrumbs. It can be stored up to 2 days in the refrigerator. To finish: heat the oven to No 6/400°F/200°C. Bake the cassoulet for ½–1 hour, depending on the size of the dishes, or until a golden-brown crust has formed. Serve hot from the baking dishes.

Jarret d'Agneau en Gasconnade

— SHANK ENDS OF LAMB WITH ANCHOVY, GARLIC AND TOMATO —

Slow cooking is of the utmost importance in this recipe, a version of the 'gasconnade' of Chef André Daguin at Auch.

Serves 10–12
2 shank ends of lamb leg (about 3 lb/1.4 kg each)
salt and pepper
2 tbsp olive oil
4 onions, sliced
3 carrots, sliced
white part of one leek, sliced
1 turnip, sliced
3 tbsp flour
12 anchovy fillets, chopped
1 tbsp tomato purée/paste
1 bottle (3 cups/750 ml) full-bodied red wine such as Cahors
14 cloves garlic, peeled
3 tomatoes, peeled, seeded and chopped (p. 186)
bouquet garni (p. 183)
water, if needed

Preheat the oven to No 3/325°F/160°C. Sprinkle the lamb with salt and pepper. Heat the oil in a large heavy casserole and brown the lamb thoroughly on all sides. Take the meat out and discard all but 2 tablespoons of the fat. Add the onion, carrot, leek and turnip and cook them, stirring occasionally, until soft. Stir in the flour, anchovy and tomato purée/paste and cook 1 minute. Add the wine, bring to the boil and simmer for 10 minutes.

Stir in the garlic, tomatoes, bouquet garni, salt and pepper and replace the lamb shanks. If necessary, add water so they are completely covered. Add the lid and cook the shanks in the oven for 3–4 hours until very tender (test with a two-pronged fork). Stir and turn the lamb from time to time during cooking and add more water if it looks dry. At the end of cooking, discard the bouquet garni and season the sauce to taste. It should be dark and rich but if it is thin, boil to reduce and concentrate it.

The shanks can be stored up to 3 days in the refrigerator, or they may be frozen. Serve them in the casserole, with boiled, fresh noodles (p. 91).

Croquants

——— ALMOND COOKIES ———

These meringue-based cookies bake to be very firm, and are designed to be dipped in a glass of wine and soaked for a few seconds before eating. They should be thoroughly baked so the almonds develop a toasted flavour.

Makes 3 dozen
4 oz/⅔ cup/125 g blanched almonds
2 egg whites
8 oz/1¼ cups/250 g sugar
½ tsp vanilla
4 oz/1 cup/125 g flour
1 egg, beaten to mix with ½ tsp salt (for glaze)

Coarsely mince/grind the almonds in a food processor, or chop them with a knife. Whisk the egg whites until frothy and gradually beat in the sugar. Continue whisking until a thick meringue mixture is formed, 2–3 minutes. Note: it will be soft, not stiff. Add the vanilla. Using a wooden spoon, stir in the flour and almonds. Note: do not overwork it or the croquants will be tough. Refrigerate the dough for 30 minutes.

Butter and flour a baking sheet. On a well floured surface press down the dough to ⅜ inch/1 cm thickness using your hand. Cut into ¾ inch/2 cm × 3 inch/7.5 cm bars and set them on the prepared baking sheet, leaving room to spread slightly. Refrigerate until very firm, at least an hour.

Heat the oven to No 7/425°F/220°C. Brush the croquants with the glaze and bake them near the top of the oven until firm and brown, 8–12 minutes. Let them cool slightly, then transfer to a rack to cool completely. Leave them to dry in the open air for 12 hours before storing in an airtight container for up to 1 month.

Jarret d'Agneau en Gasconnade.

To macerate the fruit: bring the water to the boil, pour it over the tea and leave to infuse 5 minutes. Strain the tea over the prunes in a bowl, cover and leave to soak for 12 hours. Drain the prunes, pack in a jar and pour over enough Armagnac to cover. Cover tightly and leave to macerate for at least a week at room temperature.

For the ice cream: make the vanilla custard sauce, adding the cream with the milk. Strain it and chill. Drain the prunes. Purée the fruit in a food processor or blender, or work it through a sieve. There should be 8 fl oz/1 cup/250 ml of purée.

Stir the purée into the cold custard and chill until very cold. Freeze the mixture in an ice cream churn, then transfer to a bowl and put in the freezer. The ice cream can be stored for up to a month in the freezer. Let it soften in the refrigerator for 30 minutes before serving.

Boule de Neige
CHOCOLATE SNOWBALL

Chocolate arrived early from Mexico in this corner of France, brought from Spain through the gateway of Bayonne where it still remains a speciality. This snowball is completely coated with whipped cream so the dark filling, half mousse, half fudge, comes as a surprise. Bitter chocolate with cinnamon gives it a typically Gascon flavour, but dessert chocolate can be substituted if you prefer a sweeter effect.

Serves 8
8 oz/250 g bitter chocolate, chopped
6 fl oz/¾ cup/175 ml strong black coffee
8 oz/1 cup/250 g unsalted butter, cut into pieces
6½ oz/1 cup/200 g sugar
1 tsp ground cinnamon
4 eggs
crème Chantilly (p. 183) made with 16 fl oz/2 cups/500 ml
double/heavy cream, 2 tbsp sugar, and a
few drops/½ tsp vanilla
fresh mint sprigs or candied violets (for decoration)
*8 ramekins (4 fl oz/½ cup/125 ml each); pastry bag and
a small star tube*

Thoroughly butter the ramekins, line the base with grease-

Glace aux Pruneaux à l'Armagnac
PRUNE ICE CREAM WITH ARMAGNAC

Advance planning is needed for this alcoholic ice cream, as the prunes which flavour it must be macerated in Armagnac for at least a week. Reserve the Armagnac to drink after dinner!

Makes 1 quart/1¼ quarts/1.25 litres
16 fl oz/2 cups/500 ml water
2 tbsp dry black tea
6 oz/¾ cup/175 g stoned/pitted prunes
16 fl oz/2 cups/500 ml Armagnac, more if needed
vanilla custard sauce (p. 187) made with 16 fl oz/2 cups/
500 ml milk, 8 fl oz/1 cup/250 ml double/heavy cream,
1 vanilla bean, 7 egg yolks and 5 oz/¾ cup/150 g sugar
ice cream churn

proof/wax paper and butter the paper. Preheat the oven to No 4/350°F/175°C.

In a heavy pan, heat the chocolate gently with the coffee, stirring until melted. Cook, stirring until the mixture is thick but still falls easily from the spoon. Add the butter, sugar and cinnamon and heat, stirring until melted. Bring the mixture almost to the boil and remove from the heat. Whisk in the eggs, one by one. Note: the eggs will cook and thicken from the heat of the mixture.

Strain the mixture into a jug/pitcher, then pour it into the ramekins. Set the ramekins in a water bath (p. 187) and bring to the boil on top of the stove. Bake in the oven until a light crust forms on the chocolate, 15–18 minutes. Cover and refrigerate for at least 24 hours and up to a week, so that the flavour mellows.

To finish: not more than 2 hours before serving, run a knife around the ramekins and turn the snowballs on to individual plates, discarding the paper. Note: if the mixture sticks, scoop out and remould it on the plate. Make the crème Chantilly, and scoop it into the pastry bag. Completely cover the chocolate moulds with tiny rosettes of cream, then top the centre of the snowballs with a single large rosette. Decorate them with a mint sprig or a candied violet and chill until serving.

Petits Pignolas
——— PINENUT TARTLETS ———

Gascon desserts run the gamut of 'clafoutis', a batter pudding flavoured with unpitted cherries or prunes, and feuilleté Gasconne', made with paper-thin leaves of dough brushed

with goose fat and flavoured with sliced prunes or apples, sugar and Armagnac, to these pinenut tartlets from the Landes.

Makes 8 tartlets
pâte sucrée (p. 185) made with 6 oz/1½ cups/175 g flour, 4 oz/½ cup/125 g unsalted butter, 4 egg yolks, ½ tsp salt, 3¼ oz/½ cup/100 g sugar and a few drops/½ tsp vanilla
For the filling
4 oz/½ cup/125 g unsalted butter
3¼ oz/⅔ cup/100 g pinenuts
3½ oz/¾ cup/110 g whole blanched almonds, ground
4½ oz/⅔ cup/135 g sugar
3 eggs
1 oz/¼ cup/30 g potato flour/starch or cornflour/starch
½ tsp baking powder
pinch of salt
eight 3 inch/7.5 cm individual tartlet tins/pans

Make the pâte sucrée and chill until firm, about 30 minutes. Roll out the dough to a thickness of ⅛ inch/3 mm and line the tartlet tins/pans. Prick the bases and chill for 15–20 minutes. Heat the oven to No 5/190°C/375°F.

For the filling: heat 2 tablespoons of the butter in a frying pan, add the pine nuts and sauté, stirring over medium heat until lightly browned, 2–3 minutes. Leave them to cool. Melt the remaining butter in a small saucepan and leave to cool.

Mix the ground almonds and sugar in a bowl and add the eggs one by one, beating well after each addition. Continue beating until the mixture is very light and thick, 4–5 minutes. Sift the potato flour/starch or cornflour/starch with the baking powder and salt over the mixture; fold them in as lightly as possible. Just before they are completely mixed, carefully fold in the melted butter. Pour the mixture into the lined tins/pans, put them on a baking sheet and bake until the batter begins to set, about 10–12 minutes.

Working quickly, take the tins/pans from the oven and scatter the pinenuts over the tops in one even layer. Return the tins/pans to the oven and continue baking until the pastry is brown and the filling is firm, 10–15 minutes longer. Note: if the tartlets begin to brown too quickly, turn the oven temperature down to No 2/150°C/300°F. Unmould the tartlets and transfer to a rack to cool. They are best eaten the day of baking, but can be stored in an airtight container for several days.

Left: Le Vigan, a remote hill
town in the Cévennes.
Below: The walled town of
Aigues Mortes – an old centre
for the salt trade.

LANGUEDOC

*Montpellier to Nîmes, a circular tour of
eastern Languedoc encompassing all its diverse elements
from Mediterranean seafood to coarse-cut
charcuterie in the Cévennes*

Languedoc is a province of many faces, of sophisticated, ancient cities like Nîmes and Montpellier, of flashy beachside tourism and of migrant shepherds who with their tattered flocks have followed the same paths for a millenium. Much is a question of geography, for Languedoc is sandwiched between the Mediterranean and the Cevennes mountains. The terrain divides clearly into three parts: the mountains, the 'causses' or plateaux sloping southwest into the sun, and the coastal plain with its limestone foothills, known as 'garrigues' because of the distinctive Mediterranean scrub. Distances are quite large, particularly in the mountains where any step forward seems to involve a dozen to the side, so here I suggest looking only at the eastern part of the province.

As hub of the coastal plain, the graceful town of Montpel-

Above: Almost all roads in the Languedoc lowlands lead to vineyards.

Below: 'Tielles' are a local speciality, filled with mussels, squid and anchovy.

Opposite: For its main street, Sète has a canal, photogenically lined with fishing boats and restaurants.

early, cutting short the tourist season after a bare six months of warmth. In summer a searing sun is the rule, with inland temperatures rising high.

Today the covered market in the centre of the city is a microcosm of what you will see in the surrounding countryside. The baby vegetables and salad greens rival California for freshness and variety, and the mushrooms are truly wild, with cèpes measuring 6 inches/15 cm across. A couple of stalls are devoted to dried beans, lentils, chickpeas, rice and the seasonings that go with them – saffron, cloves and hot red peppers. The splendour of cassoulet, with its half-dozen different meats, comes from further north (p. 71); around here dried beans tend to be cooked more simply to serve with some tomato and a sausage or two.

The luxuriant, overflowing stalls of fresh fish are a reminder that Montpellier is less than 6 miles from the sea and even closer to huge 'bassins' or saltwater inlets used since Roman times to raise oysters and other shellfish. A good place to absorb the flavour of coastal Languedoc is Sète, a major fishing port, which deals in African tuna and Mediterranean fish as well as the teeming shoals raised in the Bassin de Thau. Taking the N112 instead of the autoroute from Montpellier, you'll pass through Frontignan, home of one of the famous 'vins doux naturels' with at least 15 per cent alcohol content. Made from the muscat grape, Frontignan is languorously sweet and makes an excellent sorbet.

Smollett remarked on the high price of Frontignan, adding: 'The wine of the country is strong and harsh, and never drank but when mixed with water.' The practice of

lier, served by airport, autoroute and fast train, is a good place to start an exploration. By local standards, Montpellier is young, dating only from the 10th century, when it developed as a centre of the salt trade. Almost all of France's salt still comes from near here, evaporated from great seawater pans on the coast behind the walled town of Aigues Mortes. First the brine is concentrated sufficiently for sand and other impurities to be filtered off, then it is run into pans where, as the water evaporates, salt crystallizes and falls to the bottom. This is the purest salt, 96 per cent sodium chloride, though the exact composition varies with the weather and time of year.

Montpellier is full of students, for it has been a centre of learning since medieval times (philosopher John Locke spent several years at the university). Life revolves around the cafés on an enormous oval space called 'l'oeuf' (the egg) and 'faire l'oeuf' means to go promenading and drinking there. Another visitor to Montpellier with a sharper nose for the table was Tobias Smollett. In December 1763, he remarked on the superiority of Montpellier markets 'well supplied with fish, poultry, butcher's meat and game at a reasonable rate'. Smollett hurried away to escape the cold northwest wind, the Tramontane, which blows more than 200 days in the year. Be warned that both the weather and the terrain in Languedoc run to extremes. In the mountains winter comes

blending continues, for local wines provide the base for such well known apéritifs as Dubonnet, Cazalis, St Raphael and Taillan. Colour ranges from ruby to honey depending on the original wine, and the apéritif flavour may be bitter with quinine or herbal with verbena. For the faint-hearted, there's even a non-alcoholic version called Palermo.

The main street of Sète features in every guide book for it is a canal, photogenically lined with fishing boats and restaurants. However, Sète is more than just a pretty picture – thanks to vigorous commercial activity, it escapes the tourist gloss that is spoiling so much of this coastline. Pick any one of the bistros lining the quay and you'll be guaranteed a platter of the freshest shellfish, its composition an interesting contrast to the offerings in Dieppe on the English Channel. In Sète I counted five varieties of oyster, three of snails, a sea urchin or two, plus half a dozen different bivalves including cockles, mussels, little 'pétoncles' (variegated scallops), plus soft and hardshell clams. Less attractive were the 'violets' relished by my neighbour – fist-sized molluscs containing soft yellow meat and tasting, it seemed to me, of nothing but iodine. However, another local speciality proved unexpectedly good. 'Tielles' are yellow double-crust pies with a fluted edge, filled with a piquant mix of mussels, squid and anchovy.

The classic fish soup of Languedoc is 'bourride', a white soup served with 'aïoli', garlic mayonnaise, in contrast to the more famous and colourful Provençal 'bouillabaisse' (p. 175), which comes with rusty 'rouille' sauce flavoured with hot red pepper. The fish needed for bourride and bouillabaisse is expensive, so locals more often opt for a simple 'soupe de poissons' made with baby fish sold by the kilo. A sharp eye ensures that a good proportion of the essential 'rascasse' or scorpion fish is included, as well as some bream, mullet, and conger eel. Flavouring varies from cook to cook; personally I like to use lots of everything – onion, tomato, garlic, saffron, herbs like thyme and bayleaf, and a hot pepper or two. Rouille sauce, toasted croûtes and grated cheese are standard accompaniments.

Sète is picturesque but noisy. For a quiet night, I'd suggest skirting the Bassin de Thau as far as Mèze. The Hôtel de la Côte Bleue at Bouzigues has a pool and a peaceful view of the oyster parks – wooden, fence-like structures which stretch half a mile into the Bassin. In the village you can find more details on the cultivation of oysters and mussels in the

Left: Petits pâtés de Pézenas.

Right: At La Brasucade in Mèze, the chef roasts spiny lobsters in an open hearth filled with vine-stock.

Musée de Conchyculture, or you can talk as I did to an expert like François Bondon, president of the local oyster-growers' association. Monsieur Bondon explained that the raising of shellfish remains an artisan, often family affair with the men working from small boats and the women on shore, cleaning and sorting the catch. Growth in the warm waters is rapid and production continues year-round – 'Ici on ne se "r" pas.' Given the concentration of shellfish in such a small space, pollution is always a danger. Only a week after I was there fishing was suspended for several weeks because of the bacteria count.

In a Mèze café we asked where we should eat. 'Can't go wrong at the Brasucade,' came the reply, and indeed they were right. In true Languedoc style, the chef was roasting outsize spiny lobsters in an open hearth fired with vinestocks. I opted for 'baudroie', the southern name for anglerfish/monkfish which are raised in the Bassin, while my husband dug into a huge bowl of mussels 'à la marinière'. The fish came with 'aïoli' but for a change I would suggest 'beurre de Montpellier', a herb and shallot butter softened with a few spoons of olive oil. Other local specialities include squid stuffed with spiced meat, and paella. While we were eating a guitar sounded, and the whole restaurant seemed to pause in the light of the candles and the smoke of the fire. The songs were new, but the spell was timeless – this is the

land of troubadours and romantic ballads dating from the Middle Ages. They were sung in 'langue d'oc', the historic language of the south where the familiar *oui* (yes) transformed itself into the crisper *oc*.

From Mèze the main road turns abruptly inland towards Pézenas. As the seat of the governor, Pézenas was known as the 'Versailles of Languedoc'. The town still has many fine 17th-century buildings, such as the Hôtel de l'Alfonce, where Molière produced his plays for the Prince de Conti. Pézenas has grown little since its heyday, retaining a sturdy country prosperity reflected in the open market which runs between houses of creamy gold stone. Here I fell into conversation with Pierre Martin, self-styled 'artisan grower' and member of the Association of Forgotten Fruits of the Cévennes. He lamented the disappearance of fruits too small or shy-bearing to be economic in a modern orchard, of ancient apples like the Rose of Gloucester and 'reinette royale', of quinces and butter pears – 'here, you must taste one.' An almost forgotten intensity of juice bursts in my mouth. The crates of pears are draped with tresses of garlic. 'White is the earliest,' explains Monsieur Martin, 'mild enough to eat a whole raw clove.' Violet comes mid-season, then rose is the late variety for winter storage. The flavour, it seems, is all a question of age, not of colour. 'This here has been dried in the ground, not like supermarket stuff. It will keep a year,' says Monsieur Martin. Somewhat sceptically, I took home a sample. My friend was quite right.

From garlic we turn naturally to onions. Pézenas calls itself the 'Capital of the Sweet Onion' and Monsieur Martin tells me how to cook them in their skins. Simply trim the

Pierre Martin, 'artisan grower' and member of the Association of Forgotten Fruits of the Cévennes, at Pézenas market.

Grazing land on the 'causses'.

root and remove any loose outer dry skin, but leave the peel. Bake the onion in a No 4/350°F/175°C oven for about 50 minutes until tender, then serve it hot and juicy in the skin like a baked potato. It is the prefect accompaniment to roast Languedoc lamb, fragrant from grazing the herbs of the 'garrigues'.

Monsieur Martin is unusual these days in growing a wide range of produce, ranging from apricots to zucchini. For labour he relies on 'helpful Moroccans', a reminder of how many immigrants arrived here after the French pulled out of North Africa. We could have talked for hours. The other stallholders have long since vanished for lunch when finally I tear myself away from an involved discussion about chestnuts bred for boiling versus those best roasted/grilled. (Boilers are larger and peel well, roasters have more taste.)

Laden with two infant pear trees, a plait of garlic, a brown bag of chestnuts and a pot of herbal honey so dark as to be almost black, I stagger along the street in search of 'petits pâtés de Pézenas', the much-touted town speciality. They turn out to be appealing little mushroom-shaped pies with a mincemeat filling credited to the native cook of Lord Clive of India, who visited Pézenas in 1766. Certainly they taste spicy, if a bit soggy. Better still was a walnut tart, a dense crunchy mixture of ground walnuts and sugar in the double crust which is typical of Languedoc.

Driving north from Pézenas along the valley of the Hérault – the river gives its name to the region – you might think vines were a weed. Never did I imagine tiring of their geometric patterns, but in Languedoc they seem interminable. No wonder nearly half of France's wine comes from here, not in great vintages but as rough 'vin ordinaire', priced according to its alcoholic strength. Fortunately quality is improving, with more and more growers upgrading to 'vin du pays', and even to V.D.Q.S. status (vin délimité de qualité supérieure). The better wines are grouped under the appellation Côteaux du Languedoc, often followed by village name, while the very best come from the highest land and include the reds of St Chinian, north of Béziers, and the dry white Clairet du Languedoc from north of Montpellier.

Finally, at Lodève, the road winds up a hillside and the horizon clears dramatically to an empty plain bordered with peaks. We have arrived on the famous 'causses', granite plateaux thinly clad with grass and fissured with steep ravines. Not for nothing did Robert Louis Stevenson make his tour of the Cévennes on a donkey. Even today, the tourist circuit is hard going as the road plunges down from

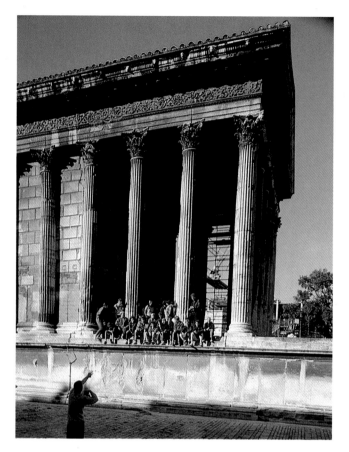

The Maison Carrée at Nîmes.

dogs are needed to round up strays. The milk goes to Roque-fort, some 30 miles away, to make the famous cheese. Madame Cazoul still cooks over an open fire, insisting that her sauté of lamb with turnips develops a particular savour if baked in a covered pot in the ashes. She prefers mutton of course, mature meat from an animal at least a year old which needs long slow cooking to be tender.

Wedged in a narrow river valley, Le Vigan is not a pre-possessing town, but the Mas Queyrol hotel, perched a thousand feet up the mountainside, is a good place for the night. Here you are poised to tackle the switchback circuit north to Mont Aigoual, the high point of the Cévennes which commands views east to Mont Blanc and west as far as the Pyrenées. Plan to take your time, for the road is slow and views spectacular, and make provision for a picnic of the excellent coarse-cut, zesty mountain sausages and ham that are offered in restaurants hereabouts as an alternative to the standard 'assiette de charcuterie'.

In Le Vigan I talked to Madame Fabre, whose 'saucissons secs' enjoy the seal of approval of the Fédération Nationale de la Charcuterie. When I looked curiously around the bare, shiny shelves of her little shop, she laughed: 'No, no, every-thing is stored at the back to sell fresh when we need it. We slaughter our own pigs and they must be the right size, not too fat, but nicely marbled within the lean meat. We use natural casings, no plastic, and the only seasoning is salt, pepper and "sel rose" [a preservative used instead of salt-petre].' Curing the sausages takes two to three months in a dry atmosphere at a constant temperature of around 55°F or 12°C: 'We are only just high enough here, at 750 feet.'

This altitude is too low for hams, which demand at least four months of drying, with the better ones matured for six months or more. Before that, the raw ham is rubbed with salt, then left to pickle for two weeks and then hung up to dry. (Brining and smoking, the two other methods of preserving, are not customary here.) The result is a dark, full-flavoured ham that needs to be thinly sliced because of its chewy texture. Not, perhaps, the most refined of meats, but very much in keeping with the rustic mountain style. When I enquired about other local specialities, Madame Fabre proffered a pan of 'caillettes', plump balls of sausa-gemeat wrapped in caul fat and baked in the oven. Her version is lightened with chestnuts, a common tree in the region. Called 'poor man's bread', until quite recently

the 'causses' through a zigzag of hairpin bends. You'll see crumbling stone barns and abandoned terraces of olive trees, for much of the population has foresaken the tough life of highland agriculture for the bright lights of the coast.

Not so Simone Jeysse, who runs a 'ferme auberge' near la Vacquerie at the edge of the sweeping Causse de Larzac. She caters 'en famille' meals for up to 40 in the summer season, raising chickens, making brawn/head cheese and serving wild rabbit and hare liberally laced with garlic. 'I like to roast whole peeled cloves with rabbit,' she explains, 'and to put a few as flavouring inside a pigeon or quail. Those who like garlic can eat it afterwards. In a stew,' she warns, 'be careful not to cook garlic too much or it will be bitter – it should go in after the onion.'

Her neighbour, Madame Cazoul, raises sheep in the old way with the help of one farmhand. Once she had a flock of 2000, but now it is down to 200 as 'there are no more shepherds'. Much of the causses are unfenced, so vigorous chestnuts took the place of bread in Languedoc and other regions where grain was scarce.

Heading east from Le Vigan, the Cévennes mountains give way to the 'garrigues', thin soil covered with aromatic plants of thyme, rosemary, oregano and juniper – picturesque but poor. Near St Hyppolyte, Marc and Françoise Chanial run a typically mixed farm raising sheep, fruit trees, olives and a few vines. When one crop fails, with luck another will compensate. 'Everything depends on the supply of water,' they say.

In early June, Marc often joins the annual transhumance of shepherds and their flocks following ancient packroads from the plain up to summer pastures in the mountains. (This practice is still so common in the area that there is a 'transhumance' phone number to call for dates and routes.) The 60-mile journey takes two or three days, and by journey's end thousands of sheep are united in a long rippling column, led by the rams with bells around their necks.

Françoise is an enthusiastic cook and once ran a restaurant. 'It did well,' she says, 'but there was never enough time.' 'Ah,' chimes in Marc, 'on a farm, the wife is a safety net, she must stand by for emergencies.' Yet Françoise still seems to find time to cure olives and make jam, to hunt wild rabbits, and to rush out after a shower of rain to gather emergent snails in the garrigues. Best of all are 'cagarolettes', tiny shells the size of winkles which cluster on the bushes. Their white meat is a delicacy but persistence is needed to extract a satisfying serving. Most locals settle for the larger 'petit gris' or common grey snail. Whatever the type, the snails must be starved for at least a week to clean them of toxic herbs, for the garrigues harbours poisonous rue and aconite, as well as the wild fennel, yellow mustard, anise, and more common cooking herbs which give such intensity of flavour.

Continuing along the D999 to Nîmes, the road branches northeast towards Uzès just beyond the pretty medieval village of Sauve. Long a key fortress in the Protestant wars, Uzès is so famous for its visual delights that you might expect a disappointment. However, for the moment the souvenir shops are camouflaged. The winding lanes around the arcaded Place aux Herbes are charming; here you will find wild asparagus at the Saturday market in spring, and truffles in the winter. At Le Buron, a side street cheese shop, I was counselled on roquefort, aged deep in mountain caves

to the west. The milk is treated with a bacillus found only in the caves of Roquefort-sur-Soulzon and the cheese is ancient, praised by Julius Caesar and Pliny. Now most production comes from the société coopérative, reliable but ordinary, and I was glad to have my long standing mistrust confirmed. 'Always buy cheese from a small producer if you can find it,' I was urged. 'Société roquefort is expensive and inferior. Or try some "bleu des Causses". It's made from cow's milk but with a similar bacillus to Roquefort.' On the counter are baskets of 'pélardons' and 'pérails', little round sheep cheeses at varying stages of dryness. The wheels of Cantal, a cow cheese from over the mountains in Auvergne, resemble a pock-marked Cheddar, tangy with age.

From Uzès it is but a short run to Nîmes, 'the Rome of France', known for its ruins, garden fountains and biannual 'brivada' when the populace downs tools as fighting bulls roam the streets. They come from the nearby Camargue, the marshy delta of the Rhône with its wild white horses and black cattle, the only area in France hot and wet enough for the cultivation of rice. It is said that denim (de Nîmes) was developed to clothe the tough 'guardians' or cowboys of the Camargue. 'Boeuf guardiane' is a beef stew with red wine, onions, garlic, tomatoes and olives. Nîmes is also known for the questionable treat of 'amourettes' or bull's testicles, more delicately dubbed as 'fries'.

The Maison Carrée, the Roman temple at the heart of the city is, with the arena, one of the beauties of Nîmes. The quaint Maison Villaret in a nearby back street was founded in 1775, and is still baking its almond 'croquants' – crisp cookies for dipping in wine (p. 72) – on the same premises. Not far away the Maison Raymond packages olive-based 'tapenade' spread and the famous Nîmes 'brandade' for dispatch worldwide. Brandade is a purée of salt cod, potato and olive oil – the nickname in 'langue d'oc' for the people of Nîmes is 'manjo merlusso', or cod-eaters. The flavour of brandade is addictive and it has become quite a cult.

Languedoc was never a region known for its grand cuisine, so keep an eye out for cafés and simple fare. Such restaurants as are listed in the guides all too often serve phoney 'nouvelle' versions of traditional dishes. Local treats are best summed up by a platter of raw shellfish, a steaming casserole of wild snails, a leg of lamb studded with garlic and roasted over a fire of vinestocks – the very essence of 'goût du terroir'.

RECIPES FROM LANGUEDOC

Soupe de Poissons Languedocienne

LANGUEDOC FISH SOUP

Scorpion fish and conger eel are key ingredients for an authentic 'soupe de poissons', while other possibilities include mullet, bass, bream, and members of the cod family such as hake and whiting. The greater the variety, the better the soup. After sieving, the consistency should be thick and rich but not pulpy. The leftover pounded bones and skin, says one cook, 'are the delight of chickens in the farmyard'.

Serves 6–8

3 lb/1.4 kg mixed fish with their heads, scaled and cleaned
1 lb/500 g scorpion fish, or more mixed fish
1 lb/500 g conger eel
salt and pepper
2 fl oz/¼ cup/60 ml olive oil
3 large onions, sliced
3 cloves garlic, crushed
1 lb/500 g tomatoes, peeled, seeded and chopped (p. 186)
3 tbsp cognac
large pinch of saffron, soaked in 3–4 tbsp boiling water
3¼ pints/2 quarts/2 litres water, more if needed
bouquet garni (p. 183)
2–3 tbsp tomato purée/paste
cayenne pepper
For serving
12 toasted croûtes (p. 183)
3¼ oz/ 1 cup/100 g grated Gruyère cheese
sauce rouille (see recipe below)

Wash and dry the fish and cut them in 1½ inch/4 cm slices, including the heads. Sprinkle them with salt and pepper. In a frying pan, heat half the olive oil and add a layer of fish. Sauté it until lightly browned, about 2 minutes, turn and brown the other side. Remove the fish pieces and sauté the rest in the same way. Heat the remaining oil in the frying pan and fry the onion until soft but not brown, about 5 minutes; remove it.

Pack the fish in a casserole in layers with the onion, garlic, tomato, salt and pepper, setting the slowest cooking fish such as monkfish and conger eel, and the largest pieces, at the bottom. Add the cognac to the frying pan and flame it (p. 184), stirring, to dissolve the pan juices. Pour it over the fish. Add the saffron and liquid, and just enough water to cover the fish. Add the bouquet garni, cover and simmer until the fish flakes very easily, about 1 hour. Meanwhile, prepare the sauce rouille (see below).

Remove the fish and vegetables from the casserole, discarding the bouquet garni, fish heads and as many bones as possible. If necessary, boil the cooking liquid to reduce it until well flavoured. Work the fish and vegetables through a food mill or coarse strainer. Alternatively, purée it in a food processor, taking great care to remove skin and bones beforehand. Whisk the fish purée back into the pot of fish liquid and bring to the boil. Whisk in enough tomato purée/paste to colour the soup a deep orange. Taste the soup for seasoning, adding cayenne pepper and salt to taste and, if you like, more saffron. The soup and rouille sauce can be refrigerated up to 2 days.

To finish: toast the croûtes. Bring the soup back to the boil; if it is very thick, add more water. Serve it very hot, with separate bowls of croûtes, sauce rouille, and grated cheese. Alternatively, spread the croûtes with rouille and add some to each bowl of soup.

SAUCE ROUILLE

½ dried or fresh red chilli pepper
4–6 cloves garlic
2 egg yolks
salt
4 fl oz/½ cup/125 ml olive oil
2–3 tsp tomato purée/paste (optional)

If using a dried pepper, soak it in cold water for 20 minutes or until soft enough to remove the seeds. For both fresh and dried pepper, discard stem, core and seeds, then cut it in pieces.

Work the pepper, garlic, egg yolks and a little salt in a food processor until smooth. With the blades running, pour in the olive oil in a thin stream, so the sauce thickens and becomes creamy. Note: if the oil is added too quickly, the mixture will separate. Add tomato purée/paste for colour if you like. Season the sauce to taste with salt and with cayenne pepper if needed; the flavour should be quite hot.

Soupe de Poissons Languedocienne.

Wooden fence structures in the oyster park at Mèze.

the omelette pan, add the eggs and stir briskly with a fork, pulling the cooked eggs from the sides to the centre of the pan. After 10 seconds, stir in the snail mixture and continue cooking for 5–10 seconds longer until the mixture is almost as thick as scrambled eggs. Leave the omelette on the heat until browned on the bottom and still soft on top if you like a soft omelette, or almost firm if you like it well done.

Fold the omelette, tipping the pan away from you and turning the edge with a fork. Half roll, half slide the omelette on to a warm serving dish so it lands folded in three. Serve at once.

Tielles de Sète

——— PIES WITH MUSSELS, SQUID AND ANCHOVY ———

As the dough for 'tielles' is robust, you'll find a spoonful of Montpellier butter (p. 87) (if the pies are hot) or 'aïoli', garlic mayonnaise (p. 84) (if cold) does not come amiss.

Makes 6 pies
pâte brisée (p. 184) made with 1 lb/4 cups/500 g flour,
8 oz/1 cup/250 g unsalted butter, or 1 part lard,
2 parts unsalted butter, 1 egg, 1½ tsp salt and
8–10 tbsp cold water
8 oz/250 g squid
2 lb/1 kg mussels, cleaned (p. 184)
4 anchovy fillets
2 cloves garlic, finely chopped
3 tbsp chopped mixed herbs – parsley, thyme, oregano
pepper
1 egg, beaten to mix with ½ tsp salt (for glaze)
six 4 inch/10 cm tartlet tins/pans: fluted pastry cutters
5 inch/12.5 cm and 4 inch/10 cm diameter

Make the pâte brisée dough and chill 30 minutes. Meanwhile clean the squid: pull the body from the head and, if the ink sac is unbroken, pierce it and catch the ink in a small bowl. Open the tentacles to reveal the 'beak' in the centre. Squeeze it outwards, cut off and discard it. Cut the tentacles from the head and intestines; discard the head and intestines also. Cut the tentacles into slices and the body into rings.

Put the cleaned mussels in a large saucepan, cover and cook over high heat, stirring once, until the mussels open, 4–5 minutes. Discard any mussels that do not open. Lift out the mussels and take the meat from the shells, discarding the

Omelette de la Garrigue

SNAIL, HAM AND WALNUT
——— OMELETTE ———

Snails, like caviar, are no use served in small quantities, so when the supply is depleted, Noelle Chanial cooks them in this garlic-flavoured omelette.

Serves 2
2 oz/½ cup/60 g canned snails, drained and rinsed
1½ oz/3 tbsp/45 g unsalted butter
1 oz/⅓ cup/30 g country ham, finely diced
1 clove garlic, chopped
salt and pepper
3 tbsp coarsely chopped walnuts
2 tbsp chopped parsley
5 eggs
9–10 inch/22–25 cm omelette pan

Cut each snail in 2–3 pieces. Melt half the butter in a frying pan, add the snails, ham, garlic, salt and pepper and cook them gently for 4–5 minutes. Take the pan from the heat and stir in the walnuts and parsley.

To cook the omelette: whisk the eggs with a pinch of salt and pepper until they are well mixed. If necessary, warm the snail mixture over a low heat. Heat the remaining butter in rubbery 'ring'. Pour the mussel liquid into a small saucepan, leaving sand and grit behind. Add the squid with enough water to cover. Simmer the squid until tender, 2–3 minutes.

For the stuffing: chop the mussels, squid and anchovy in a food processor or by hand with a knife. Stir in the squid ink (if the ink sac was unbroken), garlic, herbs and plenty of pepper. Taste, adding salt only if necessary. The stuffing should be highly flavoured.

Roll out the pastry dough to ⅛ inch/3 mm thickness and stamp out 8 rounds with each pastry cutter. Line the tartlet tins/pans with the larger rounds of dough, overlapping the edges over the tins/pans. Brush the edges with egg glaze. Spread the stuffing inside and top with the smaller rounds. Press the dough edges together then decorate them, folding the double layer with your finger and thumb alternately inwards and outwards so the edge of the pies is fluted. Cut a hole in the pies for steam to escape, brush them with egg glaze and chill 15 minutes. Preheat the oven to No 6/400°F/200°C.

Set the pies in the lower half of the heated oven and bake until crisp and brown underneath as well as on top, 25–30 minutes. They are best eaten the day of baking, but can be refrigerated 2 days and warmed just before serving.

Baudroie Rotie au Beurre de Montpellier

—— GRILLED/BROILED MONKFISH WITH PIQUANT HERB BUTTER ——

The herb butter on this fish is an old classic but a new-style chef would be justly proud of its lightness.

Serves 6
a 4½ lb/2 kg monkfish (or two 2 lb/1 kg monkfish)
2 tbsp olive oil
2–3 sprigs thyme
2–3 sprigs oregano or marjoram
salt and pepper
lettuce leaves (for garnish)
Montpellier butter (for serving – see recipe below)

Skin the monkfish, also cutting away the membrane under the skin. Cut horizontally along one side of the central bone towards the backbone to remove the fillet. Repeat on the other side to remove the second fillet. Brush the olive oil over the fish, add the herbs and sprinkle with salt and pepper. It may be prepared up to 2 hours ahead; cover and keep in the refrigerator. Meanwhile, prepare the Montpellier butter.

Preheat the grill/broiler. Put the monkfish fillets on a baking sheet lined with foil and baste again with the oil and herbs. Set the pan 3 inches/7.5 cm from the heat and grill-/broil the fillets until lightly browned, about 10 minutes for small fish or 15 minutes for a larger one, basting occasionally with oil and herbs. Turn them and grill/broil the other side until brown and the fish is no longer transparent in the centre when tested with a fork, 5–7 minutes.

Arrange the lettuce leaves on a serving platter and set the fish on top. Serve the Montpellier butter separately in a sauceboat.

MONTPELLIER BUTTER
a medium bunch (½ oz/15 g) watercress
a medium handful (½ oz/15 g) spinach leaves
a medium bunch (½ oz/15 g) parsley sprigs
a medium bunch (½ oz/15 g) fresh chervil
2 anchovy fillets, soaked in water or milk
1 small gherkin pickle
2 tsp capers, drained
½ clove garlic, peeled
2½ oz/⅓ cup/75 g butter, softened
3 tbsp olive oil
1 tsp Dijon mustard
a few drops lemon juice
salt and pepper

Discard the stems from the watercress and spinach and the large stalks from the parsley and chervil. Blanch (p. 182) the leaves, drain them, then squeeze them dry in a cloth.

Drain the anchovies and work them in a food processor with the pickle, capers and garlic until finely chopped. Add the butter gradually, continuing to purée until smooth. Add the herbs and purée until finely chopped. With the blades turning, slowly pour in the olive oil. Add the mustard and season with lemon juice, salt and pepper to taste.

If not using a food processor, finely chop the blanched herbs, anchovies, pickles, capers and garlic together with a knife. Cream the butter, beat in the herb mixture and mustard until smooth and then gradually beat in the oil. Season the sauce with lemon juice, salt and pepper to taste.

Brandade de Morue aux Olives Verts
——————— PURÉE OF SALT COD WITH GREEN OLIVES ———————

Brandade can be made by hand, but the food processor will greatly lighten the work. The purée should be served with fried garlic croûtons and a jet-black garnish of ripe olives, or occasionally of truffles. It is at its best piping hot, creamy white and fluffy, with the cod thoroughly blanched of its salt and highlighted by fruity olive oil.

Serves 6–8
1½ lb/750 g salt cod
1 lb/500 g potatoes, peeled
8 fl oz/1 cup/250 ml olive oil
8 fl oz/1 cup/250 ml milk
1½ oz/⅓ cup/45 g green olives, stoned/pitted
1 clove garlic (optional)
12 triangular fried croûtes (p. 183),
rubbed with a halved garlic clove
pinch of grated nutmeg
a few drops of lemon juice
white pepper
salt (optional)

Soak the cod in cold water for 1–2 days, changing the water several times. Drain it, put it in a large pan of cold water, cover and bring just to the boil. Poach over a low fire for 8–10 minutes or until barely tender, drain and cool it slightly. Flake the flesh with a fork, discarding all skin and bone.

Cook the potatoes by simmering them in lightly salted water until tender, 15–20 minutes. Drain them, return them to a low fire for a few seconds to dry, then cut them into small pieces.

Heat two-thirds of the oil in a saucepan until very hot. Scald the milk in another saucepan. Put the flaked cod in a food processor and with the blades turning, slowly pour in the hot oil. Add the olives and the garlic, if using, and purée thoroughly. Then add the remaining oil, little by little, alternating with the hot milk. Finally, add the potato pieces a few at a time to the cod mixture with the blades running; purée just until smooth.

If not using a food processor, heat two-thirds of the oil in a saucepan until very hot; scald the milk in another saucepan. Add the flaked cod to the oil and beat vigorously with a wooden spoon over a low fire, crushing and separating the fibres; to prevent the cod from browning move the pan on and off the fire as you beat. Finely chop the garlic and olives and stir them in. Beat in a tablespoon of the remaining oil alternately with a tablespoon of the milk. Work the potato through a fine sieve, or purée it with a potato masher. Beat it into the cod purée.

Fry the croûtes. Season the brandade to taste with grated nutmeg, lemon juice and pepper; salt may not be needed as the cod is salty. The finished purée should be white, smooth and stiff enough to hold its shape. If it is very stiff, beat in a little more milk. Pile the brandade in a shallow bowl, surround it with the croûtes, and serve at once.

Caillettes aux Marrons

——— PORK SAUSAGEMEAT WITH CHESTNUTS ———

Caillettes are good served hot or cold, with baked tomatoes Provençale (p. 178). If caul fat is not available, encircle each ball of meat with a strip of smoked bacon.

Serves 6

1 large piece of caul fat (about 4 oz/125 g)
8 oz/250 g chestnuts, peeled (p. 183)
1⅔ pints/1 quart/1 litre white veal stock (p. 186)
2 oz/¼ cup/60 g lard or oil
1 onion, chopped
2 cloves garlic, chopped
4 oz/125 g streaky bacon
8 oz/250 g lean pork
8 oz/250 g pork liver
3 tbsp chopped parsley
pinch of thyme
½ tsp each ground allspice and ground nutmeg
salt and pepper
3 bay leaves

Soak the caul fat in cold water for about 30 minutes to make it pliable. Heat the oven to No 5/375°F/190°C. Put the peeled chestnuts in a pan with the stock, cover and simmer them until tender, about half an hour. Drain them, allow to cool, then coarsely crumble them.

Heat half of the lard in a frying pan, add the onion and sauté until soft but not brown. Add the garlic and cook 1 minute. If the bacon is very salty, blanch it (p. 182). Mince/grind the bacon, pork and pork liver using the coarse blade of the grinder, or coarsely chop them in a food processor. Put the meats in a bowl and stir in the chestnuts, onion, garlic, parsley, thyme, allspice, nutmeg, salt and pepper. Sauté a small piece and taste for seasoning.

Drain the caul fat and spread it on a work surface. Shape the meat mixture into 6 balls, each about the size of a medium potato, and put them on the fat. Cut around each ball, leaving enough fat to fold over it. Wrap the balls and set a half bay leaf on each. Put them in a greased baking dish, packing them tightly. Melt the remaining lard and spoon it on top. Bake the caillettes, basting frequently, until crusty brown on top 40–50 minutes. The caillettes can be refrigerated up to 2 days and reheated.

Ragoût d'Agneau aux Navets

——— RAGOÛT OF LAMB WITH TURNIPS ———

Ragoût of lamb is a winter dish, at its best when lamb is mature and full of flavour. Root celery/celeriac or artichoke bottoms may be substituted for the turnips. Rice would be an appropriate accompaniment since it grows in the Camargue near Nîmes.

Serves 6

4 lb/1.8 kg boneless lamb shoulder or breast
2 tbsp oil
1½ lb/750 g onions, sliced
1 tbsp flour
6 fl oz/¾ cup/175 ml white wine
12 fl oz/1½ cups/375 ml brown stock (p. 186), more if needed
8–10 cloves garlic, halved
2 large tomatoes, peeled, seeded and chopped (p. 186)
bouquet garni (p. 183)
salt and pepper
1 lb/500 g turnips

Trim the excess fat from the meat and cut it into 2 inch/5 cm chunks. Heat the oil in a heavy casserole, add the meat and brown it well on all sides over fairly high heat. Remove the meat, add the onions and cook over a low fire, stirring often, until soft but not brown, about 10 minutes. Sprinkle the onions with the flour and continue to cook until brown, 2–3 minutes. Stir in the wine and stock, return the meat to the casserole and add the garlic, tomatoes, bouquet garni, salt and pepper. Bring to the boil, cover and simmer for 30 minutes on top of the stove or in a moderate oven (No 4/350°F/175°C).

While the meat is simmering, peel and trim the turnips. Cut medium turnips in quarters and smaller ones in half. Add them to the meat and simmer an hour longer or until the meat and turnips are tender. Stir occasionally and if the stew becomes dry, add more stock. Skim off any excess fat and discard the bouquet garni; taste for seasoning. Serve the ragoût directly from the casserole. It can be refrigerated up to 3 days, or frozen, and flavour improves on reheating.

Salade aux Haricots Blancs Languedocienne

————— WHITE BEAN SALAD —————

In summer this salad is good with cold roast lamb, or the spicy 'merguez' sausage made popular in Languedoc by the sizeable Arab population. (To conform to the Islamic code, merguez are usually made with lamb, not pork.)

Serves 6–8
For the beans
1 lb/500 g dried white beans
1 onion studded with 2 cloves
bouquet garni (p. 183)
1 clove garlic, cut in half
salt and pepper
For the salad
vinaigrette dressing (p. 187) made with 4 tbsp wine vinegar,
salt, pepper, 6 fl oz/¾ cup/175 ml olive oil and
1 clove garlic, finely chopped
3–4 sprigs fresh thyme, or 1 tsp dried thyme
3–4 sprigs fresh oregano, or 1 tsp dried oregano
2 medium tomatoes, peeled, seeded and chopped (p. 186)
1 shallot, finely chopped
1 small onion, cut in thin rings (for decoration)

Put the beans in a bowl, cover them generously with cold water and leave to soak 6–8 hours.

Drain the beans and transfer them to a large saucepan. Cover with water and add the onion studded with cloves, bouquet garni, garlic and pepper. Bring slowly to the boil and simmer until the beans are tender, 1–1½ hours. Add water when needed so the beans are always covered. Note: season the beans with salt only halfway through cooking or they will be tough. Drain the beans and discard the onion, bouquet garni and garlic.

Make the vinaigrette and whisk in the chopped garlic. Chop half the thyme and oregano, reserving the rest for decoration. In a large bowl stir together the drained beans, tomatoes, shallot, and chopped herbs. Pour over the vinaigrette, stir and taste the salad for seasoning. Allow the salad to marinate for at least 2 and up to 24 hours before serving, so that the flavours mellow.

Just before serving, decorate the top with onion rings and herb sprigs.

Aligot

————— POTATO AND CHEESE PURÉE —————

Aligot is a lighter version of cheese fondue and at least one restaurant I know makes its preparation a theatrical performance: a large copper pan of creamy mashed potato is heated over a burner, then little by little the grated cheese is beaten in by lifting the purée with a wooden spoon and letting it fall in great arcs back into the pan. The whole operation takes at least five minutes, leaving the waiter pink and perspiring, the diner round-eyed with suspense.

Aligot can be served with crusty bread as a first course, or as a main course with hot garlic sausages or baked ham. Like fondue, it easily cooks into strings if overheated, so the cheese must be beaten into the potatoes only at the last moment.

Serves 4
2 lb/1 kg potatoes, peeled
salt
2 oz/¼ cup/60 g butter
8 fl oz/1 cup/250 ml double/heavy cream or crème fraîche
(p. 183)
12 oz/4 cups/375 g grated cantal cheese
pepper

Cut the potatoes into 2–3 chunks, put them in a pan of cold salted water, cover and bring them to the boil. Simmer until the potatoes are tender when pierced with a knife, 15–20 minutes. Note: they should be quite soft.

Drain the potatoes and, while still hot, push them through a sieve or purée in a hand food mill. Note: if you use a food processor to purée the potatoes, they will become gummy and elastic. Put the purée in a heavy saucepan, add the butter and beat the potatoes with a wooden spoon over a low fire until light and fluffy, 2–3 minutes. Gradually beat in the cream, still working over a low heat. Little by little add the cheese and continue beating constantly with a wooden spoon until the aligot forms long ribbons when it falls from the spoon. Add pepper, taste for seasoning and serve very hot. The aligot is best if served immediately, but can be kept warm over a water bath (p. 187).

Pâtes Fraîches Cévenole

——— PASTA WITH HAM, PINENUTS AND BASIL ———

Try this pasta with grilled jumbo prawns. Pinenuts add an attractive crunch to the sauce and you can use homemade or ready-prepared fresh green pasta.

Serves 8
large bunch (2 oz/60 g) fresh basil
4 fl oz/½ cup/120 ml olive oil
4 lb/2 kg fresh tomatoes, peeled, seeded and chopped
(p. 186)
8 cloves garlic, chopped
8 oz/250 g smoked raw ham such as prosciutto, diced
4 oz/½ cup/125 g pinenuts, toasted
salt and pepper
For the pasta
12 oz/3 cups/375 g flour
6 eggs
1 lb/500 g spinach, cooked (p. 186) and finely chopped
2 tbsp oil
1 tsp salt

For the pasta: sift the flour on to a work surface and make a well in the centre. Beat the eggs, spinach, oil and salt together with a fork and pour into the well. Gradually draw in the flour, working the dough lightly between the fingers so it forms large crumbs, adding a little water if the crumbs are dry. Shape the dough into a ball and knead on a floured surface until very smooth and elastic, about 10 minutes. Cover with an upturned bowl and allow to rest for ½–1 hour.

Roll the dough out as thinly as possible. Sprinkle it with flour, roll loosely and cut into ¼ inch/6 mm strips as noodles. Spread them on a floured surface, tossing them until lightly coated. Leave them to dry for 1 hour, or up to 8 hours.

To finish: shred the basil, reserving 8 sprigs for garnish. Heat half the olive oil in a deep saucepan. Add the tomatoes and garlic and sauté, stirring, until slightly thickened, about 5 minutes. Add the ham and pinenuts and sauté until they are heated. Add the chopped basil and toss until mixed. Season with pepper and taste, adding salt only if needed as the ham is salty.

Bring a pan of salted water to the boil, add the noodles and cook until they are tender but still firm, about 2 minutes for fresh pasta and 5–10 minutes for prepared pasta. Drain them.

Heat the remaining olive oil in a pan, add the drained pasta and toss in the oil until hot, 1–2 minutes. Pile the pasta on individual plates, top with sauce and add a sprig of basil.

Tarte aux Noix

——— WALNUT TART ———

This walnut tart is a new twist on the little regional mincemeat pies found in Pézenas.

Serves 8–10
pâte sucrée (p. 185) made with 8 oz/2 cups/250 g flour,
5 oz/⅔ cup/150 g unsalted butter, 6 egg yolks, 1 tsp salt,
4 oz/10 tbsp/125 g sugar and a few drops/½ tsp vanilla
For the filling
7 oz/2 cups/200 g walnuts
5 oz/¾ cup/150 g light brown sugar
2 tbsp unsalted butter, melted
For the glaze
1 egg white, beaten until frothy
sugar (for sprinkling)
8 inch/20 cm tart tin/pan with removable base

Make the pâte sucrée and chill until firm, about 30 minutes. For the filling: finely chop the walnuts in a food processor. Add the sugar and continue working for 1 minute. Pour in the melted butter and continue to work the mixture until it forms coarse crumbs, 1–2 minutes longer. Without a food processor, work the nuts through the fine blade of a grinder with the sugar. Stir in the melted butter and work the mixture in a bowl with your hand until it forms crumbs.

Butter the tart tin/pan. Roll out about two-thirds of the pastry dough and line the tin/pan – the dough will be quite thick. Spread the filling on top. Roll out the remaining dough and cover the filling, pressing the dough edges together to seal them. Roll the rolling pin over the top of the tart tin to cut off the excess dough. Make 2–3 holes in the centre of the tart for steam to escape and chill it 30 minutes. Heat the oven to No 5/375°F/190°C.

Set the tart low down in the heated oven and bake it 15 minutes. Turn down the heat to No 4/350°F/175°C and continue baking until the tart is crisp and brown, 25–30 minutes. Brush the top with egg white and sprinkle generously with sugar. Continue baking to form a crisp white glaze, about 5 minutes longer.

Right: The Loire is the longest
river in France, rising in the
Massif Central.
Below: The abbey of
Fontevrault.

THE LOIRE

*Wandering the gardens of medieval abbeys and
grand châteaux between Tours and Angers, sampling the
apples and pears, champignons and charcuterie
in this gastronomic refuge from Paris*

The Loire is the longest river in France. It rises over 370
miles from the sea in the austere uplands of the Massif
Central and flows through narrow gorges and featureless
farming country, until near Orléans it takes a sharp turn west
and becomes the river we think of: majestic, languid, star-
studded with great châteaux. There is much to see along
these lower reaches. Distances are small, and vistas a tan-
talising invitation to linger in indolence, absorbing the
famous 'douceur de la Loire'.

At Angers, an easy three-hour trip by autoroute or train
from Paris, the stone walls of the 13th-century fortress loom
black and menacing. Invisible until you reach the moat are
flowered parterres which hark back to the 15th century and
King René of Sicily, Count of Provence and Anjou. Many

These distinctive black-topped fishing boats called 'toues' are a feature of the lower reaches of the Loire.

Ages, or more modest 'gentilhommières', essentially country houses built by gentlemen rather than nobility. The town of Château Gontier, with its lively Thursday market, is the leading market in Europe for veal.

Nearby Craons has long been famous for its breed of white-backed pigs, now crossed with Norman animals to produce a leaner beast. It was in a nondescript back street that I talked to the mother of Bertrand Vignais, artisan charcutier who prepares a score of terrines, sausages and meats in the little kitchen behind the shop. (The word 'charcuterie' originally meant cooked meat.) Because the pig is so versatile, edible from snout to tail, a charcutier is self-sufficient. Monsieur Vignais, for instance, buys only salt, pepper, sel rose (an age-old preservative which also colours pork a healthy pink), chilli pepper, and 'quatre épices', a mixture closely resembling allspice. He salts bacon and ham, he grinds and stuffs half a dozen varieties of fresh and dried sausages, he bakes liver pâté, country pâté, brawn/head cheese, and a meaty pâté en croûte which tastes rather like English pork pie. 'This is country charcuterie,' remarks his mother, 'it has the pure taste of pork, not adulterated as in the big towns.'

High point of the week at the Vignais charcuterie is the cooking of 'rillettes', a name given not just to the classic coarse-textured pork pâté, but to a vast cauldron of pig's ears, tails, feet and trimmings which are simmered on the stove with only a light seasoning of salt and pepper. As they cook, pieces are removed one by one, tails first, then ears (which remain crunchy) and finally after six or seven hours the feet, which should be falling from their bones (all 32 of them). Delicacies like these are bespoke a week in advance. The meat which remains is skimmed ('our customers look for less and less fat'), gently stirred and tasted for seasoning before being packed in pots as rillettes pâté. Good country rillettes are lean, slightly chunky, with no trace of stickiness from overstirring or too much fat; they keep at least a week and mellow in flavour.

The 60-mile run along the banks of the Loire from Angers to Blois must be the best-trodden tourist track in France. Yet it still holds surprises. Curious black-topped fishing boats called 'toues' net pike ('brochet'), pickerel ('sandre'), carp, eel and the occasional salmon. In the old days the boatmen were equally eyecatching, clad in blue blouses sashed in red. Troglodyte houses are hollowed deep in the soft stone cliffs

châteaux were begun at this time, and King René introduced many ornamental plants from his Mediterranean kingdom, starting a tradition of fine gardens in which he was followed by others who came to build the great châteaux of the Loire. A hundred years later famous species like 'reinette' apples and 'reine Claude' or greengage plums, named for the wife of François I, were developed in horticultural gardens at Angers. The tradition has continued; you can see magnificent trees in the Arboretum de la Maulévrie at Angers, and Anjou itself is home to thousands of greenhouses, and nearly 9000 acres of orchard. Not for nothing is the Loire Valley called the garden of France.

You can appraise the riches of the Loire in the central Halles market of Angers, a harsh modern structure which inside gives way reassuringly to the familiar, noisy stalls. Amid the multicoloured mounds of fruit and vegetables, be sure to pause at the charcuterie to inspect the mounds of pork 'rillettes' and the temptingly crisp 'rillons' (squares of roasted pork). Both are specialities of the Loire Valley, as are 'andouilles' – a connoisseur's item composed only of pig's intestines, cooked and smoked as a black-skinned sausage. Next door at the butcher's, the quality of pearly pink veal is equally high, for north of Angers is cattle country, a rich landscape graced by fine defensive châteaux of the Middle

bordering the river, their coziness appreciated for thousands of years. At Cunault, once a rich bishopric, the church vies with Vézelay for Romanesque purity, but in this region of grand monuments it is almost ignored. Be sure to take the D952 along the northern bank, where the road runs atop a protective 'levée' which affords a view of the deceptively placid waters and the old stone houses sheltering deep on the far side, seemingly unchanged over the centuries. From royal châteaux to simple cottages, the local building material is white tufa stone, quarried by tunnelling into the river banks. One restaurant is called 'Feet in the Water' – although the Loire is notorious for floods, a recent project for damming the waters has been rejected as damaging to the environment.

Soon you'll reach Les Rosiers and the Hôtel Jeanne de Laval (much-loved wife of King René). Slow your pace a decade or two in keeping with the flock wallpaper and well-aged furniture. Dinner evokes the surrounding countryside and begins with hors d'oeuvre of homemade rillettes, chicken pâté, baby asparagus vinaigrette, spicy mushrooms and courgettes 'à la grecque', crayfish swimming 'à la nage' in court bouillon, mixed vegetable salad, and a slice of melon. After that the main course classics of pike with 'beurre blanc' and pickerel with sorrel seem almost redundant. Craning from your bedroom window, on one side you can see the river, on the other the vegetable fields: flat, sandy, and punctuated by ranks of fruit trees. So sheltered is this region that produce ripens here as early as at Valence, 250 miles to the south in the Rhône valley.

One famous product of the area, however, is invisible. Despite being called 'champignons de Paris', three-quarters of the national output of mushrooms is grown in the Loire, using caves which were once stone quarries. (Mushroom caves once existed along the Seine near Paris, but were long ago overwhelmed by urban sprawl.) Growers cluster around Saumur, home of the Ecole Nationale de la Cavalerie, as even today horse dung is an essential constituent of mushroom compost. An 88lb/40 kg bag, a potent mixture of earth and dung, topped with crushed gravel, will produce 18 lb/8 kg of mushrooms. At St Hilaire and at Loches you can see them sprouting in mushroom 'museums', glowing creamy white in the moist semi-darkness of tunnels that extend by the mile into the cliffs. At one establishment the guide claimed there were 500 miles of such burrows.

Within 24 hours of popping up, a mushroom is ripe, the gills delicately pink and the cap detached from the stem. I'm fond of the dark, flat specimens sold in Britain, but in French eyes these are overripe – 'like umbrellas' teased a chef. When freshly picked, a cultivated mushroom is snow-white, almost crisp in texture, with no sogginess or tinge of brown. They make an excellent raw salad if thinly sliced and marinated for an hour or two with lemon juice, salt, pepper, and chopped garlic. Just before serving I like to add fresh tarragon (a favourite Loire herb) and a few spoons of thick cream, but that's a matter of taste. Cultivation of more exotic mushrooms like Japanese 'shiitake' has also begun along the Loire – these need a compost based on oak tree pulp to survive. There are also floppy white oyster musrooms which at triple the price have little more taste, it seems to me, than a 'champignon de Paris'.

Don't forget that this is wine country, home to some of the most popular middle-priced vintages in France. Balzac gave fine descriptions of Saumur and its inhabitants in his novel *Eugénie Grandet:* 'They all know the exact value of sun or rain at the right moment . . . each has his little farm and his patch of vineyard.' Champigny, just east of Saumur, gives its name to a ruby red wine with a raspberry flavour. From south of Angers, around Savennières and the Côteaux du Layon, comes 'rosé d'Anjou', noted for its slight sweetness and golden pink colour. At Chinon, cellars deep inside the cliffs house vats of earthy, tannin-laden red wines with a taste, so they say, of blackcurrant. Those from nearby Bourgueil and St Nicolas are lighter, more refined. Even good white wines are not lacking. The village of Vouvray near Tours produces inexpensive sparkling wines of that name. They are a bit sweet for my taste but lately local vintners have been turning out still wines with a crisp dry finish. All these wines find their way into the kitchen and feature in specialities like eel stew with Bourgueil, chitterling sausages ('andouillettes') with Vouvray, 'coq au vin de Chinon', and sautéed rabbit with Anjou white wine.

The abbey of Fontevrault, a short distance upriver from Saumur, was built two centuries before the châteaux boom, constructed according to the Benedictine rule. Much of the original structure still stands, including fine cloisters and an infirmary, now a cultural centre where you can stay in comfort with modern plumbing. The great octagonal kitchen has also survived; designed to feed 500, it has fireplaces in each

A Loire mushroom cave – three quarters of France's national output comes from this area.

Left: The medieval octagonal
kitchen at Fontevrault.
Right: Villandry, 'the ultimate
kitchen garden'.

Tours and Angers. Fishing simply requires a licence from the 'mairie', so no wonder the sport preoccupies amateurs. The day I was in Chinon the bank of the Indre was lined with hopeful anglers including an enterprising youth poised precariously on a punt in midstream. But fishing in today's waters is an unrewarding pastime. A few perch, tench, or tiny gudgeon (called 'petite friture' because they are best tossed in flour and deep-fried) are the most that can be expected. Commercial fishing has almost disappeared – the carp, pike and pickerel lying so innocently on ice in the market are likely to have come from eastern Europe. Loire salmon and shad ('alose'), once the pride of the region, have virtually vanished, though salmon trout is raised on farms in the area. Shad is famous for its innumerable bones, and one ancient recipe calls for baking it slowly on a bed of sorrel – the acidity is said to dissolve the bones.

Chinon itself is a town of great charm and antiquity, its ruined château overhanging the river. Tradition has it that King Richard the Lionheart died here. This is also the childhood home of Rabelais, where perhaps he first learned that 'the appetite grows by eating'. The town is dotted with modest hotels, one on the tree-shaded square, another on the river. Beyond Chinon and up to Blois stretch the great châteaux whose construction boggles the mind. On a first visit to the Loire, it is hard to miss Azay-le-Rideau, Chenonceau, Amboise, Chambord, and Blois itself, but pick your time as guided tours are usually mandatory and draw king-size crowds.

Lesser names can be equally rewarding. Take Villandry, with its great garden inspired by the Italian landscapers brought to France by King Charles VIII. The simple medieval garden at Fontevrault is a mere cabbage patch beside the swirling Renaissance fantasies of Villandry. Here 18 acres are laid out in a series of squares enclosed by knotted hedges of box, no two of them alike. Individual beds run into the hundreds, each small enough to till without putting a boot on the soil. There are nine squares of vegetable garden, six or more for ornament, while a third water garden is set high above the others to simplify irrigation.

It was in 1906 that Dr Joachim Carvallo, founder of the Vieilles Maisons Françaises preservation society, began the restoration of Villandry. Now his granddaughter by marriage, Marguerite, presides over six gardeners who each year cultivate upwards of 120,000 plants, prune over 1,000

angle and an array of conical chimneys for ventilation. To guard against fire, the kitchen roofs as well as its walls were built in stone, and once the building was freestanding though now it is linked to the main abbey by a vast refectory. In the palmy days of Fontevrault, when royal daughters were sent there to be educated, a dozen other such kitchens existed along the Loire. Only this specimen remains, an architectural triumph, half medieval high-tech, half gothic folly.

Part of the abbey plan included several types of garden, all essential to the life of the community. Today you can see a re-creation, divided according to medieval logic into plants for flavour (garlic, leek, aromatic herbs like thyme), for medicine (camomile and angelica), and for industry (hemp for rope, reseda for yellow dye, thistles or 'cardons' for carding wool). You can see the frail ears of early strains of wheat; flowers had their uses too, in pot pourri or for church decoration.

Half a dozen considerable rivers join the Loire between

pulling abandoned orchards back into production. Antoine feeds his trees with compost, not chemicals. 'The average grower sprays 25 times, more than twice a week during the season.' Antoine's crop is smaller, he freely admits, but so are his costs. His yield of pears is half that of conventional growers, and his apples scarcely a tenth, but Antoine can turn a profit with a sales price that is only double the average because he saves so much on chemicals. Customers are glad to avoid the mass-produced Golden and Granny Smith, which now account for 80 per cent of French production, and pay extra for full-flavoured fruit varieties.

Antoine cultivates more than a dozen varieties of apple and half a dozen pears, their names a roll call of honour for the cook. Poire Williams forms the basis of the finest pear liqueur; russet-skinned Beurré Hardy is historic, one of the first meltingly juicy 'butter' pears to be developed in the early 19th century; Bonne Louise is also a butter pear, best picked a week or two before maturity so the delicate flesh is not bruised; Bon Chrétien came from the gardens of Louis XI near Tours, where it was grown from a cutting by St Francis of Paola, the King's confessor; Conférence is an English pear and Passe Crassane a late-ripening keeper. Comice, developed in the Jardins du Comice in Angers, is the queen of them all, plump, pink-blushed with generous perfumed juice. In autumn they are given royal treatment, each one cocooned in soft paper with the stem dipped in red sealing wax to prevent evaporation. (Table grapes are equally well preserved by inserting the cut stalk in a sealed vial of water, then suspending the bunch from a rack.)

At the Domaine de la Giraudière 2 miles up the hill from Villandry, Roland de Montferrier combines tradition with modern technology in making goat cheese. He's been at it 10 years now, abandoning a business career in New York 'with no regrets'. To maintain the quality of milk, the goats are fed on a balanced diet including barley, oats, soy concentrate and fresh alfalfa grass. The cheese is aged in a climate-controlled dairy, using unpasteurized milk. Roland's half dozen cheeses – all moulded by hand – include little round 'crottin', conical 'pyramide', Valençay (a truncated pyramid coated in ashes), and a log called Ste Maure, a local speciality which has earned the national 'appellation contrôlée' guarantee of quality.

A feature of goat cheese is that it can be eaten at any stage of ripeness, from one day old to crumbly dry and piquant.

limes/lindens and 140 yews, and trim 32 miles of box hedge. Bedding plants are raised in greenhouses, while compost is made on the property following organic principles. Each year the layout of bedding plants is different, determined by the staff with Madame Carvallo as 'chef de culture'. Machines are of little use, given the tiny, irregular plots within the box hedges. 'We work as in the old days,' observed one of the gardeners, true to form as he leant on his hoe. To meander through beds of aromatic herbs, burgeoning leeks, celery, lettuces, the pumpkin family, and half a dozen kinds of cabbage is indeed a step into the past. Other historic French vegetable gardens have been restored – notably at Versailles – but none compares with Villandry. Hugh Johnson calls it 'the ultimate kitchen garden, for it is an attempt to create beauty with fruits and vegetables'.

The nostalgia of Villandry is echoed by young Antoine Moreau, a neighbouring market gardener who is laboriously

It's a matter of personal preference, and you can make a trial at La Giraudière with a tasting of cheese, rounded out by a salad dressed with walnut oil and a slice of fresh fruit tart. Often a toasted cheese croûte is added to the salad. 'A favourite of mine,' says our host. 'You need round crottin cheeses that are dry but not crumbly. Slice them in half horizontally, set them on a round of bread, and toast them in a very hot oven for about five minutes until they melt inside and the skin bursts. Simple!'

The production of goat's milk, and therefore of cheese, is seasonal, though it can be regulated with the help of hormones. Most smaller producers let nature take its course, so milk production ceases altogether for a month or two in winter until kids are born in the new year. She-goats, or 'nannies', are kept for milk so you see only a few he-goats ('billies'), needed for breeding. The remaining males end on the table and a dish of baby goat is a common delicacy along the Loire in late spring, appreciated in rural areas at least as much as baby lamb. Sometimes the meat is deliciously smoky from barbecuing outdoors. A serving should include a few ribs as well as slices from the loin and leg – perfect with tiny glazed turnips and carrots.

You can reach Tours from Villandry in less than half an hour. The city has been a centre of learning and of trade for over 1,000 years. In the old town, the Musée du Compagnonnage gives a vivid glimpse of commerce in the Middle Ages, displaying masterpieces created by appentice craftsmen as part of their graduation exercise. The Compagnons were trade guilds – the name denotes sharing of bread, from the Latin 'cum panis' – and they still continue as a self-help group for many crafts, including that of the charcutier and pâtissier. The wine museum nearby contains a bewildering assortment of quaint objects and is worth a glance. Note the magnificent pillared cellar of the Abbaye St Julien which dates from the 13th century.

After a century of decline, traditional open markets flourish once more in Tours. The flowers on display on Wednesdays and Saturdays, under the trees on the Boulevard Béranger, are a sight to see. An unexpected boost to local horticulture was provided by the four nuclear power stations along the Loire which came up with the bright idea of diverting their heated waters to greenhouses so that the final run-off into the Loire itself is back to normal temperature. When at the market, don't miss the covered

food hall beneath the flowers, which rivals any along the valley. What choice for a picnic!

As you buy, snatch a cup of coffee in the airy central café and glance at *La Nouvelle République*; nothing equals a local newspaper for colour. Here you'll find announcements of the seasonal fairs that flourish hereabouts. The tomato fair just outside Angers is timed for the third week in June, the garlic and basil fair in Tours for St Anne's Day (26 July), the melon fair in Amboise for early September, and the apple fair in Azay-le-Rideau for late October. Most lively of all is the medieval market held in Chinon on the first weekend in August, which attracts thousands to a costumed banquet in the château.

As any restaurant guide will tell you, Tours has its share of fine cooks, including up-and-coming Jean Bardet, who is installed in a grand mansion and prides himself on using local products. His rival is grand old man Charles Barrier, long-time culinary star of the city, who after a spell off-form has catapulted his kitchen back into prominence with country dishes like pig's foot stuffed with sweetbreads. Both chefs lend their own names to the restaurants they head. At about half the price, at les Truffeaux in the rue Lavoisier, you'll fare more simply but perfectly well on local dishes like

Goats at Roland de Montferrier's farm near Villandry – you can taste half a dozen different varieties of goat cheese here.

The Pecqueurs are among the few in France to raise wild boar.

navarin of lamb with baby spring vegetables and 'crémets', the fresh cream cheese dessert usually moulded in a heart shape. Little porcelain moulds, pierced to drain the whey, are a pretty gift to take home.

From Tours to Blois the road continues along the river, past imposing Amboise whose gardens once rivalled those of Villandry. A jog south brings you to Chenonceaux, its kitchens poised over the river, so handy for fishing or disposing of vegetable trimmings. You will notice a change in the countryside; fewer open fields and much more forest, scene of the hunts that attracted rulers such as Catherine de'Medici, her husband Henri II and his mistress Diane de Poitiers (her symbol was a hunter's bow and quiver). Leonardo da Vinci is buried in the small Chapelle de St Hubert, patron saint of hunters, at the foot of the Château of Amboise.

In the autumn, rich Parisians weekend here and in next-door Sologne, pursuing the slender stocks of wild partridge, pheasant and deer. Of the two common species of partridge, grey-legged are superior, ideal for roasting, while red-legged are coarser and more often braised. In any case, the age of a game bird should determine the method of cooking, for partridge or pheasant more than a year old can be very tough. To test, lift the bird by its lower beak, which will snap if the bird is young. Also the tip of the breastbone should be flexible, the feet without callouses, and the legs on the male without spurs.

Little wild game reaches the retail market. Laws governing hunting date from the Revolution, when many seigneurial rights were transferred from individuals to local communes. Nowadays hunters may consume their own bag, but sale of game is limited to licensed businesses. The resulting scarcity has encouraged more and more experiments with raising wild game, as I discovered when I visited Nadine Pecqueur and her husband. At Autrèche, just north of Tours, they raise wild boar; theirs is one of only a handful of such farms in France. The animals are fed on cereals and potatoes, running freely in great woodland pens, where they rootle like pigs and destroy the undergrowth. 'A couple of wild boar can ruin a field of potatoes in a single night!' exclaims Nadine. 'We have to change their pens regularly if the trees are to survive.' The age of a wild boar is indicated by the colour of its pelt, which is striped up to three months, rust coloured in adolescence, then darkens to black at a year old. A 'marcassin' is six to nine months old and should have the juicy tenderness of lean suckling pig. The classic two-day soak in red wine marinade is harsh treatment for such delicate meat, I think, but certainly needed for dark, mature wild boar from a 'sanglier' over a year old. As well as selling fresh game, the Pecqueurs make wild boar pâtés and rillettes – 100 per cent pure, they point out, unlike the supermarket equivalents which need only contain 20 per cent wild boar to qualify for the name. Game rillettes is an interesting idea to try at home. Simply substitute any game such as venison or pheasant for goose in the rillettes recipe on p. 157.

To enjoy the very best of game cooking, drive to the village of Bracieux, deep in hunting country just east of Blois. For more than a decade at Le Relais, Bernard Robin has been cooking dishes like noisettes of wild boar with devil sauce, and civet of hare 'à l'ancienne'. You can overnight modestly at the Hôtel Bonheure and be poised the following morning to view the elegance of Cheverny, with its kennels for 70 hounds, or the overbearing splendour of 365-chimneyed Chambord. Blois itself is the most royal of the Loire towns and was the favourite retreat of François I.

The longer you wander along the Loire, the more there is to discover. Somehow, Paris fades in the memory, though it is barely 100 minutes away on the autoroute. Is it the charm of the landscape, or the softness of the climate? Or is it the lazy reaches of the Loire itself, curling through sandbanks and dangling willow trees, which exerts such a powerful inertia? Medieval monks had a name for it: 'accidie', one of the seven deadly sins.

RECIPES FROM THE LOIRE

Tarte au Fromage de Chèvre et sa Salade de Chou Vert aux Noix

FRESH GOAT CHEESE QUICHE, CABBAGE AND WALNUT SALAD

The best Loire cooking is simple, but with a twist of originality. In this recipe shredded cabbage and crumbled soft goat cheese are baked in a custard filling, while more cabbage is tossed with walnuts in a walnut oil dressing to serve with the finished tart. Walnut groves have largely disappeared from the region, remarks goat cheesemaker Roland de Montferrier wistfully, but a taste for the nut remains.

Serves 6
pâte brisée (p. 184) made with 6½ oz/1⅔ cups/200 g flour,
3¼ oz/7 tbsp/100 g butter, 1 egg yolk, ½ tsp salt
and 3–5 tbsp cold water
1 small Savoy cabbage (about 1½ lb/750 g)
8 oz/250 g fresh goat cheese
For the white sauce
12 fl oz/1½ cups/375 ml milk
3 tbsp butter
3 tbsp flour
6 fl oz/¾ cup/175 ml crème fraîche (p. 183) or
double/heavy cream
salt and pepper
pinch of grated nutmeg
1 egg
2 egg yolks
For the cabbage salad
vinaigrette dressing (p. 187) made with
2 fl oz/¼ cup/60 ml red wine vinegar, salt and pepper,
1 tsp Dijon mustard, 2 fl oz/¼ cup/60 ml walnut oil and
2 fl oz/¼ cup/60 ml salad oil
3–4 tbsp coarsely chopped walnuts
10 inch/25 cm tart tin/pan

Make the pâte brisée and chill it for 30 minutes. Roll out the dough and line the tart tin/pan. Blind bake the shell (p. 182).

Trim the outer leaves from the cabbage and finely shred it, discarding the core. Boil a large pan of salted water, add the cabbage and bring just back to the boil. Drain, rinse with cold water and drain thoroughly.

For the white sauce: scald the milk. Melt the butter in a heavy saucepan, whisk in the flour and cook until foaming,

about 1 minute. Remove the pan from the heat and strain in the hot milk, whisking constantly. Bring the sauce back to the boil, whisking constantly, until it thickens. Note: it will be very thick. Add the crème fraîche, season to taste with salt, pepper and nutmeg and simmer for 2 minutes. Let the sauce cool to lukewarm.

Heat the oven to No 5/375°F/190°F. Spread about a third of the cabbage in the pie shell. Crumble the goat cheese on top. Stir the egg and egg yolks into the sauce and season again to taste. Pour the mixture into the pie shell.

Bake the quiche in the heated oven until brown and firm, 40–45 minutes. A skewer inserted in the centre should come out clean. Let the quiche cool, then unmould it and serve at room temperature. It is best eaten the day of baking.

For the salad: make the vinaigrette. About 30 minutes before serving, toss the remaining cabbage with the walnuts and dressing and serve with the quiche.

Omelette Gargamelle
—— OMELETTE WITH MUSHROOMS, CHEESE AND PARSLEY ——

At the restaurant Gargantua in Chinon, installed in an elegant Renaissance town house, you can feast on puffy 'omelette Gargamelle' filled with mushrooms, cheese and parsley, topped with a cheese sauce. Gargamelle was one of the carousing characters in the 16th-century *Chronicles of Gargantua* by Rabelais, who spent his childhood in the town.

Serves 2
3 tbsp butter
1 shallot, chopped
4 oz/125 g mushrooms, finely chopped
salt and pepper
5 eggs
2 tbsp chopped parsley
2 oz/¼ cup/60 g soft cream cheese
1 tbsp grated Gruyère cheese (for sprinkling)
For the cream sauce
8 fl oz/1 cup/250 ml milk
1 tbsp butter
1 tbsp flour
2 fl oz/¼ cup/60 ml crème fraîche (p. 183)
or heavy/double cream
salt and white pepper
a pinch of nutmeg
8 inch/20 cm omelette pan; 2 small oval baking dishes

Melt a tablespoon of the butter in a frying pan, add the chopped shallot and cook until soft. Add the mushrooms, salt and pepper. Cook over high heat, stirring occasionally, until their liquid evaporates, 5–10 minutes. Taste the purée for seasoning.

Whisk the eggs with the mushroom purée, salt and pepper until frothy. Stir in the chopped parsley. Heat a further tablespoon of butter in the omelette pan until foaming and add half the eggs. Cook, stirring constantly with a fork, until lightly set and brown on the bottom. Spread half the cream cheese in the centre, leave it to warm for 30 seconds and then fold the omelette, tipping it into an oval baking dish. Repeat with the second omelette.

For the cream sauce: scald the milk. Melt the butter in a heavy saucepan, whisk in the flour and cook until foaming, about 1 minute. Remove the pan from the heat and strain in the hot milk, whisking constantly. Bring the sauce back to the boil, whisking constantly, until it thickens. Add the crème fraîche, season to taste with salt, pepper and nutmeg and simmer for 2 minutes. The sauce will be quite thin. Pour it over the omelettes and sprinkle with the grated cheese. They can be prepared up to 4 hours ahead.

To finish: heat the oven to No 6/400°F/200°C. Bake the omelettes in the heated oven until the cheese is melted and the sauce is bubbling, about 5 minutes. Serve at once.

Feuilletés aux Asperges
—ASPARAGUS WITH TARRAGON BUTTER SAUCE IN PUFF PASTRY —

The soft sandy soil of the Loire valley is ideal for asparagus. In spring, if you see a carefully tilled field that is apparently empty, you can be sure that prized stems of white asparagus lurk underground. As soon as they poke through, they are snipped with a special tool 8 inches/20 cm below the surface so they remain bleached. Here, the asparagus is set in a puff pastry case and topped with the lightest of herb sauces made only of butter whisked with chopped tarragon and a squeeze of lemon juice. If asparagus is out of season, green beans are an excellent alternative.

Serves 8
pâte feuilletée (p. 185) made with 8 oz/2 cups/250 g flour,
8 oz/1 cup/250 g butter, 1 tsp salt, 1 tsp lemon juice, and
4 fl oz/½ cup/125 ml water
1 egg mixed with ½ tsp salt (for glaze)
1½ lb/750 g asparagus
6 oz/¾ cup/180 g chilled, unsalted butter, cut in pieces
4 tbsp chopped tarragon
squeeze of lemon juice
salt and pepper

Make the pâte feuilletée dough and chill thoroughly. Roll the dough to a sheet ⅛ inch/3 mm thick. Cut eight 4 inch/10 cm diamonds and brush them with the egg glaze. With the tip of a knife, mark a line inside each diamond to make a lid, cutting halfway through the dough. Trace an asparagus spear on each feuilleté. Scallop the edges of each diamond with a knife to help rising and transfer them to a baking sheet. Chill until firm, about 30 minutes.

Heat the oven to No 7/425°F/220°C. Bake the feuilletés in the heated oven 8–12 minutes. Lower the heat to No 5/375°F/190°C and continue baking until puffed and golden, 12–15 minutes. Transfer to a rack, cut the lids from the feuilletés and scoop out any uncooked dough. The feuilletés can be stored 2 days in an airtight container, or frozen.

Peel the lower part of the asparagus stems with a vegetable peeler and trim to equal lengths. Tie them with string in 8 equal bundles. Cook the asparagus in a large pan of boiling salted water until tender but still slightly firm, 7–10 minutes. Drain it, rinse with cold water and drain again thoroughly.

Heat the oven to No 1/275°F/140°C. Warm the feuilletés on a baking sheet in the oven. If necessary, warm the asparagus in a steamer over boiling water. Cut the asparagus spears in 3 inch/7.5 cm lengths, discarding the strings. Dice the asparagus trimmings and spread them in the feuilleté cases. Top with asparagus spears, draping them over one edge of the pastry. Half cover the feuilletés with a pastry lid to keep warm.

Make the tarragon butter sauce: put a teaspoonful of water with 2–3 pieces of butter in a small heavy pan. Heat gently, whisking constantly, until the butter softens creamily. Add the remaining butter a few pieces at a time, moving the pan on and off the heat so the sauce softens without melting to oil. Note: do not heat it above blood temperature. Whisk in the chopped tarragon and lemon juice and season to taste with salt and pepper. Serve the sauce in a bowl with the warm feuilletés.

Terrine de Legumes à la Mousseline de Veau

—————— VEGETABLE TERRINE WITH VEAL MOUSSELINE ——————

A novelty 20 years ago when 'nouvelle cuisine' was launched, vegetable terrine has become a classic. This recipe has more body than most, a mosaic of sliced carrots, turnips, green beans and chopped spinach, all held together with a veal mousseline. The terrine is good served hot with tarragon butter sauce (see above) or Montpellier butter (p. 87), or cold with garlic and chilli pepper mayonnaise ('rouille', p. 84).

Serves 10
1 lb/500 g fresh spinach
1½ oz/3 tbsp/45 g unsalted butter
salt and pepper
pinch of grated nutmeg
8 oz/250 g carrots, sliced
8 oz/250 g turnips, sliced
8 oz/250 g green beans, trimmed
For the veal mousseline
1½ lb/750 g lean veal
1 egg
1½ oz/3 tbsp/45 g unsalted butter, softened
6 fl oz/¾ cup/175 ml crème fraîche (p. 183) or double/
heavy cream
salt and white pepper
pinch of grated nutmeg
rectangular terrine mould (1 quart/1 litre capacity)

Remove the stems from the spinach and wash thoroughly. Blanch in a pan of boiling salted water for 1 minute. Drain, rinse with cold water and drain again thoroughly, patting it dry with a towel and keeping as many leaves whole as possible. Thoroughly butter the terrine mould and line the bottom and sides with the whole spinach leaves, overlapping the edge of the mould. Chop the remaining leaves. Sauté the chopped spinach in most of the remaining butter until the moisture has evaporated, 2–3 minutes. Season with salt, pepper and nutmeg.

Put the sliced carrots in a pan of cold, salted water, bring to the boil and simmer until tender, 7–10 minutes. Drain thoroughly. Put the turnips in a pan of cold, salted water, bring to the boil and cook until tender, 5–7 minutes. Drain thoroughly. Cook the green beans in a large pan of boiling salted water until just tender, 5–7 minutes. Drain, rinse them in cold water and drain again thoroughly. Sprinkle all the vegetables with salt and pepper. The vegetables can be prepared up to 24 hours ahead and refrigerated.

For the veal mousseline: work the veal in a food processor to a smooth paste. Work in the egg and the softened butter. Set the mixture in a metal bowl over a bowl of ice. Beat until well chilled, then gradually beat in the cream. Season with salt, pepper and nutmeg. Sauté a small piece of mousseline and taste for seasoning.

Heat the oven to No 4/350°F/175°C. Spread a sixth of the mousseline over the spinach leaves. Arrange the carrot slices on top and cover with more mousseline. Continue adding layers of turnip, mousseline, green beans and spinach, ending with a layer of mousseline. Fold the overlapping spinach leaves on top of the mould. Cover with buttered parchment paper and the lid.

Put the terrine in a water bath and bring to the boil on the stove. Bake in the heated oven until the veal mousseline is set and a skewer inserted in the terrine for 30 seconds comes out hot to the touch, 55–60 minutes. Let stand in a warm place for 10 minutes. If serving hot, turn out the terrine and slice it; if serving cold, let it cool completely in the mould.

Ballotine de Brochet Rabelaisienne

BALLOTINE OF PIKE AND SALMON TROUT WITH PRUNES, RED BUTTER SAUCE

Even though fish is scarce in the Loire itself, a tradition of fish recipes continues in the region. One of the most interesting recipes I found was this pâté of pink salmon trout mousse sandwiched between fillets of pike and studded with prunes (Plums are so common that a local expression 'pour des prunes' means 'for nothing'.) Red butter sauce is also typical of this region, with its excellent red wines from Chinon and Bourgueil; white butter sauce comes from downriver at the mouth of the Loire and the vineyards of Muscadet. Any firm white fish can be substituted for the pike.

Serves 12
24 prunes
1 bottle (750 ml) Chinon or other fruity red wine
2 pike fillets (1¼–1½ lb/600–750 g), skinned
For the sauce
8 oz/1 cup/250 g chilled unsalted butter, cut into pieces
2 onions, sliced
2 stalks celery, sliced
2 carrots, sliced
bouquet garni (p. 183)
4 cloves garlic
1 lb/500 g fish bones
4 shallots, chopped
2½ fl oz/⅓ cup/75 ml red wine vinegar
1 tsp tomato purée/paste
2 tbsp double/heavy cream
For the mousseline
1 lb/500 g salmon fillet
1 egg
1½ oz/⅓ cup/45 g butter, softened
salt and pepper
pinch of nutmeg
5 fl oz/⅔ cup/150 ml double/heavy cream

Soak the prunes in half the red wine overnight. Strain, reserving the wine and cut the prunes in 2–3 pieces.

For the mousseline: mince/grind the salmon fillet in a food processor. Blend in the egg then blend in the softened butter. Season to taste with salt, pepper and nutmeg. Set the mixture in a metal bowl over a bowl of ice. Beat until well chilled, then gradually beat in the cream. Note: do not over-beat or the cream will separate. Sauté a small piece of the mousseline and taste for seasoning.

Cut a horizontal slice off the thickest part of the pike fillets and lay it beside the tail end to form a rectangle. Lay one of the rectangles on a large piece of buttered parchment paper and spread half the mousseline on top in a band 3 inches/7.5 cm wide. Cover with the chopped prunes, add the remaining mousseline and top with the second fish fillet. Fold any overlaps of the fish fillets along the sides of the mousseline to make a neat cylinder. Wrap in the parchment paper, then in foil, tying the ends tightly. Poach in a large pan of salted water until a skewer inserted in the centre is hot to the touch when withdrawn after 30 seconds, 30–40 minutes. Let stand 10 minutes then remove the foil. Tighten the parchment and leave the ballotine to cool. It can be cooked up to a day ahead and refrigerated.

For the sauce, make fish stock: melt 2 oz/¼ cup/60 g of the butter in a large pot. Add the onions, celery, carrots, bouquet garni and garlic and cook over low heat, stirring occasionally until soft but not brown, about 20 minutes. Add the fish bones, the remaining wine and water to cover and simmer 20 minutes. Strain the stock, discarding bones and vegetables, and boil until reduced to a glaze (p. 184). In a heavy saucepan boil the reserved liquid from the prunes with the shallots, red wine vinegar and tomato purée until reduced to a glaze. Combine with the fish glaze, stir in the cream and cook for 1 minute. The glaze can be made 2–3 hours ahead.

To finish: if necessary, reheat the ballotine by rewrapping the parchment paper package in foil and heating it in boiling salted water for about 10 minutes. To finish the sauce, heat the saucepan of glaze; add the remaining butter, a few pieces at a time, whisking constantly and moving the pan on and off the heat so the sauce softens without melting to oil. Strain it and taste for seasoning.

To serve: unwrap the ballotine and cut it in ½ inch/1.25 cm slices with a sharp knife. Coat individual plates with sauce, set a slice of ballotine on top and serve.

Fishing on the Indre.

Fricandeau de Veau à l'Oseille

FRICANDEAU OF VEAL WITH SORREL

Sorrel is a favourite ingredient along the Loire. Its lemony bite combines well with rich fish like shad, with venison, and with this braised veal. A mixture of spinach and watercress leaves can be used instead of sorrel. Fricandeau is a firm cut from the rump which holds up well to long cooking.

Serves 8
2½–3 lb/1.25 kg rump of veal
8 oz/250 g pork or bacon fat, cut in lardons (p. 184)
4–5 slices fat bacon
2 carrots, thinly sliced
2 onions, sliced
6 fl oz/¾ cup/175 ml white wine
16 fl oz/2 cups/500 ml brown stock (p. 186), more if needed
bouquet garni (p. 183)
salt and pepper
For the sorrel purée
1½ lb/750 g sorrel
1 oz/2 tbsp/15 g unsalted butter
4 fl oz/½ cup/125 ml double/heavy cream
string

Heat the oven to No 3/325°F/160°C. To lard the veal roast pierce the meat with the point of a very sharp knife and insert lardons into each cut. Tie the roast in a neat cylinder with string. Lay the bacon slices in the bottom of a casserole just big enough to contain the veal. Add the carrots and onions, set the veal on top, pour over the wine and simmer until reduced by half. Add enough stock to just cover the meat, the bouquet garni, salt and pepper. Cover the pan and bring to the boil. Cook the veal in the heated oven until very tender, 1½–2 hours. It can be cooked up to 48 hours ahead and refrigerated.

For the sorrel purée: wash the sorrel thoroughly and pick over it, discarding the stems. Pack it in a large pan, add a little salt, cover and cook over high heat until the sorrel is wilted, 3–5 minutes, stirring once or twice. Drain it. Melt the butter in a pan, add the sorrel and cream and cook, stirring, until the sorrel thickens to a purée which just falls easily from the spoon, about 5 minutes. The purée can be prepared up to 6 hours ahead and kept covered.

To finish: heat the oven to No 6/400°F/200°C. Reheat the meat on top of the stove, if necessary. Transfer it to a carving board, discard the strings and keep warm. Boil the cooking liquid until reduced to about 1 cup. Carve the veal in ¾ inch/2 cm slices, set them in a shallow baking dish and spoon over the cooking liquid. Cook the veal in the heated oven, basting often, so that the liquid evaporates and the meat becomes coated with a shiny glaze.

Reheat the sorrel purée, if necessary. Pile the purée down the centre of a serving dish and arrange the veal slices overlapping on top. Spoon over any remaining cooking liquid and serve.

Marcassin au Genièvre et Champignons Sauvages

WILD BOAR WITH JUNIPER BERRIES AND
WILD MUSHROOMS

Golden 'chanterelles' and their cousin 'trompettes de mort', so-called because of their black colour, are relatively common in the forests of the Loire, but for this recipe any edible mushrooms may be used. If wild boar proves difficult to find, you may substitute noisettes of pork – after being marinated for a day or two you'll be surprised how closely they resemble the real thing.

Serves 4
4 wild boar noisettes, cut 1½ inches/4 cm thick
4 oz/125 g wild mushrooms, cleaned (p. 187) and sliced
4 fried croûtes (p. 183), in rounds slightly larger
than the noisettes
bunch of watercress (for garnish)
For the marinade
2 tbsp oil
1 onion, sliced
1 carrot, sliced
2 shallots, sliced
1 stalk celery, sliced
16 fl oz/2 cups/500 ml red wine
1 tsp peppercorns
2 tsp juniper berries, crushed
bouquet garni (p. 183)
1 tbsp vinegar

For the sauce
2 oz/¼ cup/60 g butter
1 oz/¼ cup/30 g flour
1 tsp juniper berries, crushed
16 fl oz/2 cups/500 ml brown stock (p. 186)
1 tbsp oil
salt and pepper
3 tbsp crème fraîche (p. 183)
1 tsp redcurrant jelly

For the marinade: heat the oil in a saucepan, add the onion, carrot, shallots and celery, and cook slowly until soft but not brown. Add the wine, peppercorns, juniper berries, and bouquet garni, bring to the boil, and simmer until the vegetables are tender, about 30 minutes. Leave until cold and add the vinegar.

Put the wild boar noisettes in a deep dish just large enough to hold them and pour the cold marinade over them. Cover and leave in the refrigerator 1–2 days. The longer the meat is marinated, the stronger the gamey flavour.

Lift the meat out and pat dry with paper towels; reserve the marinade. For the sauce: in a saucepan melt half the butter. Whisk in the flour and cook slowly, stirring constantly until golden brown. Stir in the marinade, the juniper berries and all but ½ cup of the stock. Bring to the boil, stirring, and simmer over low heat for 1 hour, stirring occasionally. The sauce can be prepared up to 8 hours ahead and kept with the noisettes in the refrigerator.

To finish: put the wild mushrooms in a small saucepan with the remaining stock. Simmer until the mushrooms are tender and the stock has evaporated, 5–7 minutes. Heat the

oil in a sauté pan. Season the noisettes with salt and pepper and sauté over medium heat until rare, about 4 minutes on each side. Fry the croûtes.

Set the steaks on the croûtes and discard the fat in the pan. Pour in the crème fraîche and bring to the boil, stirring to dissolve the pan juices. Strain the sauce into the pan and bring to the boil again. Stir in the mushrooms and redcurrant jelly and taste for seasoning – pepperiness is characteristic of the sauce. Cut the remaining butter into small pieces and add it to the sauce off the heat, shaking the pan so the butter is incorporated. Arrange the steaks on individual warm plates, spoon a little sauce on top and garnish each with watercress. Serve the remaining sauce separately.

Sauce Beurre Blanc
——————— WHITE BUTTER SAUCE ———————

White butter sauce originated near the mouth of the Loire and uses the best of local ingredients: white Muscadet wine, shallots, and unsalted butter from Charentes. This is the classic recipe, but Parisian chefs ring innumerable changes on the sauce by adding herbs or spices and using red wine instead of white. White butter sauce is the perfect accompaniment to poached fish such as salmon, pike, or sea bass.

Makes 8 fl oz/1 cup/250 ml sauce
3 tbsp white wine vinegar
3 tbsp Muscadet or other dry white wine
2 shallots, finely chopped
1 tbsp crème fraîche or double/heavy cream
8 oz/1 cup/250 g very cold unsalted butter, cut in cubes
salt and white pepper

In a small heavy pan, boil the vinegar, wine and shallots to a glaze (p. 184). Add the cream and re-boil to a glaze.

Whisk in the cold butter a few pieces at a time, moving the pan on and off the heat so that the butter emulsifies and the sauce thickens creamily. Note: if it gets too hot, the butter will melt to oil and separate.

Work the sauce through a sieve, or leave in the shallots, as you prefer. Season to taste. It can be kept warm for a few minutes on a rack over a pan of warm water, but should be served as soon as possible.

Crémets

————— MOULDED FRESH CHEESE —————

Crémets or 'coeur à la crème' is a fresh cheese often moulded in a heart shape. The most delicate is based on crème fraîche, but soft cream cheese mixed with double/heavy sweet cream is an acceptable substitute. It is a summer dessert, at its best with fresh red berries, sugar and cream.

Serves 6
16 fl oz/2 cups/500 ml crème fraîche (p. 183) or
12 fl oz/1½ cups/375 ml double/heavy cream and
4 oz/125 g cream cheese
4 egg whites
For serving
fresh raspberries or strawberries
sugar or vanilla sugar
crème fraîche or crème Chantilly (p. 183)
coeur à la crème mould (1 quart/1 litre) capacity or
several small moulds; muslin/cheesecloth

Line the mould with muslin/cheesecloth. In a large bowl whip the crème fraîche until it holds soft peaks. Alternatively, beat the double cream with the cream cheese. In another bowl, whip the egg whites until stiff. Stir about a quarter of the egg whites into the crème fraîche then fold the mixture into the remaining egg whites. Spoon the mixture into the mould and cover with plastic wrap. Set it on a dish and leave to drain in the refrigerator for at least 8, or up to 36 hours.

An hour or two before serving, turn the crémets out on to a serving dish. Arrange the raspberries or strawberries around the crémets. Serve it with separate bowls of sugar or vanilla sugar and the remaining crème fraîche or crème Chantilly.

Tarte aux Poires et Chocolat

————— CHOCOLATE PEAR TART —————

Blois used to be the home of Poulain, one of France's largest chocolate manufacturers, and open fruit tarts are a Loire speciality, so to find chocolate combined with pears in an open tart is a logical, delectable conclusion. Extra crispness is added to the crust by coating the tart tin/pan with butter and sugar.

Serves 8
pâte brisée (p. 184) made with 6 oz/1½ cups/175 g flour,
1 egg yolk, 3 tbsp sugar, ¾ tsp salt, 3¼ oz/7 tbsp/100 g
unsalted butter
4 oz/125 g semisweet chocolate, chopped quite finely
3 ripe dessert pears (about 1 lb/500 g)
2–3 tbsp sugar (for sprinkling)
For the custard
1 egg
1 egg yolk
4 fl oz/½ cup/125 ml single/light cream
½ tsp vanilla, or 1 tsp kirsch
10–11 inch/25–28 cm tart tin/pan

Butter the tart tin generously, then sprinkle with sugar. Make the pâte brisée and chill it for 30 minutes. Roll out the dough to ⅛ inch/3 mm thick and line the tart tin/pan.

For the custard: beat the egg, egg yolk, cream and vanilla until thoroughly mixed.

Heat the oven to No 6/400°F/200°C. Sprinkle the bottom of the tart with the chopped chocolate. Peel and thinly slice the pears crosswise; flatten the slices lightly. Arrange them in a flower petal design on the chocolate so that the slices overlap. Spoon over the custard so the surface of the pears is coated. Note: the custard should be just visible between the pear slices. Sprinkle the pears with sugar.

Bake the tart well down near the base of the oven so the bottom cooks, 10 minutes. Reduce the heat to No 4/350°F/175°C and bake until the crust is brown and the custard is set, 15–20 minutes longer. If the pears are not caramelized, brown them under a hot grill/broiler for 2–3 minutes.

Tarte aux Poires et Chocolat.

Right: Sunset in the Pays de
Dombes.
Below: Traditional Bresse
farmhouse near St Trivier.

THE LYONNAIS

*Traditional cooking by the famous 'mères' and
star chefs of Lyon, at the heart of a region rich in the
finest of French gastronomy*

Lyon took the lead in French gastronomy long before Paris.
The culinary authority of Lyon was already established in
the early 16th century, when Rabelais remarked on the excellence of Lyonnais specialities in his satires *Pantagruel* and
Gargantua. He praises 'soupes lionnaises', 'boutargues' (mullet caviar, which is again very much in vogue), and a host of
meat ragoûts and hotpots. History counts: the cooking of
this elegant city and its surrounding province of the Lyonnais
radiates the confidence of a distinguished past.

Even more than Paris, Lyon is spoiled in the provenance
of its ingredients, so generously supplied by the surrounding
countryside. Beef from Charolles, chickens from Bresse,
crayfish, wild mushrooms and Comté cheese from the
foothills of the Alps, walnuts and potatoes from the

Peaceful fishing country in the Dombes.

Dauphiné, game from Forez, and baby vegetables from the Rhône valley is but a start. As for wine, with Beaujolais and the Côte Mâconnaise on the doorstep, it is no wonder three rivers are said to flow through Lyon – the Rhône, the Saône and the Beaujolais. Don't miss a 'pot' of the latter, a scant two cup measure unique to the region.

A 20-minute drive to the north-east takes you to the curious Pays de Dombes, a triangular area bounded on three sides by autoroutes, and with Bourg-en-Bresse at its north-ern end. The land is riddled with lakes, big ones, little ones, ringed with reeds, dotted with swans, and ruffled by the constant breeze. Surprisingly, the water still teems with fish thanks to a century or more of careful conservation. At the fish cooperative near Pérouges, Fabius Gadouillet is part of a team servicing more than 20,000 acres of water. 'It's all

natural you know,' he says, pointing to the sky, 'the water comes from there!' Once a year the fish in each lake are netted, first in fine mesh so the stock can be assessed. Most are then set free to grow, while only the larger fish are separated with coarser nets for the market. If breeding stock is lacking, it is made up from another lake. Plump, dark-fleshed carp, much of it exported to Germany, form more than half of the catch, with the rest a mixture of perch, pike, eel and a few rather tasteless tench. After spending all his days among fish, I asked Fabius if he often eats it: 'Never!' he admitted.

A pleasant morning awaits as you meander through the Dombes. Pretty châteaux and quiet villages punctuate the woods and fields of maize. This is fine hunting as well as fishing country; 'faire le maïs' means to tramp through the maize stubble to put up pheasant, partridge, and hare. Typical towns are St Paul de Varax, with its 14th-century brick-ornamented château, part-medieval Chalamont, and Chatillon sur Chalaronne with its timbered old houses. At Villars is a much-advertised bird sanctuary, where a pavilion sells local products such as smoked carp and wild duck breast. If you are near Bouligneux, you might drop in for lunch at the Auberge des Chasseurs, or the more contemporary Le Thou across the street. Both specialize in freshwater fish, frogs' legs, and dishes like grilled quail with tart cherries and pheasant with red and green grapes.

At the end of the day, there are at least two attractive places to stay. Commercial reconstructions of the past are not my style, but the medieval village of Pérouges at the southeast corner of the Dombes is an exception. The tall houses with their carved façades have been restored with sensitivity and a night spent at the Ostellerie du Vieux Pérouges, furnished in period style, is comfortable as well as evocative. Lean out of your window as the sun goes down and you can picture the marauding Saracens ranging the wooded valley below the stone walls.

As a more urban alternative, head for a hotel in the prosperous city of Bourg-en-Bresse. On the N83 you'll pass the giant dairy, resembling nothing so much as a petro-chemical plant, which mass-produces Bresse Bleu cheese. (Its look-alike, Bleu de Bresse, has a milder flavour). Bourg itself is unremarkable, though you might want to take home a souvenir 'oeuf Bressane' eggshell filled with chocolate praline ganache from Au Prieuré de Brou on the avenue Alsace Lorraine. Destination for the evening is the Auberge Bressane in Brou, on the edge of Bresse itself. The Auberge is an institution, albeit a modernized one, still serving the same dishes of frogs' legs with herbs and garlic, and magnificent Bresse chicken with tarragon in a cream sauce, as 25 years ago. You can buy pink and white plates embellished with a chicken from nearby Meillonnas, where potters flourished in the 18th century. The Auberge is easy to find, for it faces one of the great monuments of France, the fretted, flamboyant gothic church of Brou. Tour the church early in the morning before the crowds arrive to best appreciate the austere faces and intricate carving on the tombs of Philibert of Savoy and the two Marguerites, his mother and his wife.

Bourg-en-Bresse is barely inside the province of Bresse. Driving north along the D975 towards Chalons, the lakes of the Dombes are gone. Here the terrain is undulating, the soil thin with apparently little promise for the gastronome. But look more closely, for the fields are dotted with small white chickens, their feet blue and their crests a patriotic red. This is the home of the aristocrat of all chickens, the 'poulet de Bresse', raised in the open air and fed an exclusive diet of dried or skim milk and maize.

The chickens of Bresse, and those of Louhans just to the north, are part of the selective 'appellation contrôlée' system for ingredients which are produced under carefully regulated conditions in order to guarantee their quality. Roquefort and Brie cheeses, walnuts from Grenoble, olives from Nyons, and butter from Poitou and Charentes are among the privileged products to be marketed with a coveted red label, and a high price to match it. Bresse chickens, for instance, cost three times as much as a supermarket bird.

To earn the red label of excellence, Bresse chickens must be divided into groups of 500, with 12 square yards of ground per bird. Their number is declining – not surprisingly, for production of Bresse chickens seems astonishingly primitive. The birds are left to roam cornfield and pasture at will and are only brought into the barn to fatten for the last 10 days. In the fields a constant agitated pecking is in progress. 'Chickens must be free to pick up insects – grasshoppers are full of protein,' Armand Mazuy tells me. For 50 years he has raised birds near the little town of St Trivier de Courtes. A Bresse bird takes 16 weeks to grow, as compared with 6½ for a supermarket chicken. 'There's the secret,' he says, 'time, breed, and feeding.' For those used to bloated commercial birds, the rangy Bresse chicken seems puny, the meat dark and chewy – but what taste! To do it justice, in Bresse a chicken is commonly poached to serve in a rich cream sauce, perhaps flavoured with mushrooms or herbs; outsize rolls come with it to sop up the juice.

The Mazuy family farm is typical of Bresse, constructed of timber and brick with wooden balconies and a low roof. Two miles east of St Trivier, at La Ferme de la Fôret, you can visit such a farm dating from the 16th century, complete with kitchen. The magnificent carved furniture, often in pear and other gnarled fruit woods, remains a Bressane speciality. The farmhouse is crowned with one of the 'cheminées sarrasines' peculiar to the region – elaborate chimneys designed to draw smoke from an open hearth. From St Trivier our route heads west towards the Saône and Pont-de-Vaux, a

Carp, perch, pike and eel are the main catch of this region.

La Ferme de la Fôret, a 16th-century farm near St Trivier. The Saracen chimney, typical of farmhouses of the region, was designed to draw smoke from an open hearth.

Opposite: Drying corn – eventual chicken feed – is a characteristic sight against the timber and stone of a farmhouse.

season for outdoor gathering is very short, basically from mid-April to end-May. As soon as they arrive from the east – for once Customs delays are welcome as a week's fast in a truck is exactly what's needed for cleansing – the snails are blanched, removed from their shells, and frozen. Eighty per cent of the snails are consumed before and just after Christmas but they are processed year-round. This involves discarding the black intestine, blanching, sorting by size, cooking in court bouillon, then packing plain or in their shells in herb butter. No wonder cooks avoid all the bother and pay a hefty price for prepared snails. The most expensive snail is the 'petit gris' or common snail which is about half the size of the white-shelled 'escargot de Bourgogne' and is usually shipped to France from Spain or Syria.

Monsieur Migeon is an enthusiast, and on parting insisted I must visit his friend who is one of the five or six French dealers in frogs. So in a Mâcon back street I heard about (and inspected) the sacks of live frogs that arrive in summer from Turkey by truck and in winter from Egypt by air. I learned that Parisians consume only the legs, but that the Lyonnais like the backs as well. Apparently a few frogs are still caught locally in the Dombes, with the dazzle of an electric torch and a red handkerchief. To foster the home-caught illusion, some local restaurateurs serve only frogs of the smallest size.

In the Lyonnais I came across frogs' legs cooked with herbs in cream, sautéed with anchovy and walnuts, even simmered with snails as a soup. But I still think you can't beat them sautéed with garlic in butter. Allow half a pound or five medium legs per person, toss them lightly in seasoned flour and fry briskly in a couple of tablespoons of unsalted butter (it burns less easily). When the legs are brown on one side, they should be turned and sprinkled with very finely chopped garlic, less or more to your taste. Then continue frying until both sides are golden brown, sprinkle with chopped parsley and serve very hot on some fresh green pasta.

If you cross the Saône near Pont-de-Vaux and meander westwards through sheltered valleys, you will soon reach the abbey town of Cluny. Here again the landscape changes dramatically, for we follow part of the 'route des vins Mâconnais' through Viré, with Lugny just to the north. If wine is your passion, allow for a leisurely detour around here to sample a vintage or two. Cluny is dominated by the Benedictine foundation dating from the 10th century and was rapidly recognized as 'the light of the world' in the words of

town notable for two thoroughly good restaurants. (Rivalry is healthy – note how often one good cook leads to another.) At Le Raisin you can snap up your chicken with morel mushrooms; at the Hôtel de Commerce an eggcup of chicken pâté was offered 'to help you wait', for in Bresse a chicken in cream sauce is always cooked to order.

It was just south of Pont-de-Vaux that I tracked down Burgundian snails, not in the fields but in a processing plant. As I talked to young Patrick Migeon the manager, many illusions were dispelled. Commercially speaking, the famous 'escargots de Bourgogne' are no longer gathered, nor even raised, in Burgundy. They come by the million from Poland, Hungary and Yugoslavia, 10 tonnes to a truck. (At 5 grams a snail, you can work it out for yourself.) Monsieur Migeon insists the snails are wild, but somehow I doubt it as the one pope. Its history is a kaleidoscope of power play and decadence. 'Wherever bloweth the wind, Cluny collects its dues,' went the saying. At its height around 1150, 10,000 French monks were under the rule of the abbot, who by papal decree was independent of the French King. In fact it was the shameless opulence of Cluny which prompted the Cistercians to found their own order, with its strict austerity. By the 17th century the great days of Cluny were over but the vast fruit and vegetable gardens were still said to rival those of Versailles. Alas they have long since disappeared, as has most of the abbey, once the most imposing of all Christian foundations.

The market town of Charolles further west may lack the centuries-old lustre of Cluny, but it generates plenty of excitement during the November sales of some of the world's most expensive cattle. A prime bull will fetch 100,000 francs or more. Now one and a half million strong, pure-bred Charollais are raised in 26 countries (including Brazil and India) and are tracked in a herdbook, just like racehorses. The breed is valued by butchers for its high yield of lean meat and by farmers for its docile nature – no bullfights here! In France, the very best grassfed Charollais, raised on the spot, earn 'appellation contrôlée' status like the chickens of Bresse.

From Charolles we head back to the wine, south through la Clayette, via les Echarmeaux and the D37 to Beaujolais. A turn left in Beaujeu plunges you at once into remote, Italianate countryside carpeted with vines. 'End of the World' reads one sign pointing down a singularly precipitous dirt road. The vineyards seem endless – officially they cover 32,000 hectares or over 100 square miles. No wonder so much Beaujolais arrives on the table! Famous names appear – Morgon, Chiroubles, and finally Fleurie, where a shop on the central square sells trappings for the small winemaker and corkscrews for the mere consumer. In Fleurie you may dine on foie gras with the leading vintners at the classy Auberge du Cep, or on 'andouillettes' sausages with their workers at the bistro opposite.

Better still head for the railway station and the inn of Les Maritonnes, where a little renovation and an astonishing number of flowers have transformed an unpromising location. To call Les Maritonnes old-fashioned would be inaccurate, for it is timeless. The terrine of game, the quenelles, the frogs' legs 'fines herbes', the floating island flavoured with

Above and right: Spring and winter in the Dombes.

pralines, are as up-to-date as they were 50 years ago. The 'poulet au Beaujolais' was the best chicken braised in red wine that I have ever tasted, and the wine list was exemplary.

The maturity of a bird for braising is important and it was Monsieur Mazuy in Bresse who explained to me French terminology. A 'poulet' is young but plump, weighing from 2½–5½ lb (anything smaller lacks taste he reckons, not worth the eating). A 'poularde' does not necessarily weigh more but is full-grown with more flavour, while a 'poule' is a boiling fowl, an old bird of up to 6½ lb which has laid eggs. Prized in country districts is a cock of 9 lb or more, but as they are only to be found in an old-fashioned farmyard they are rare indeed. When marinated for several days their dark fresh resembles that of a game bird.

After Fleurie, Lyon beckons from the heart of the Lyonnais. Make for the open-air market on the Quai St Antoine, where each morning chefs jostle stout women with string bags for the best that local farmers can offer. You need a sharp eye, for a good many tired greens and fruits from the cold store are mixed with the fresh raw milk cheese and baby leeks picked that morning. It was here I spotted four different kinds of green beans on a single stall, artichoke hearts already trimmed for simmering, quince and medlar, those antiquated fruits which are now a rarity, and an odd root looking like overgrown kohlrabi, which I was told was root cabbage. When I took it home in triumph, the La Varenne chefs laughed. 'My mother used to grow that,' said one. 'Better blanch it well, it's powerful stuff!'

My market initiation was conducted many years ago by Mère Léa, one of the famous women cooks of Lyon whose restaurant, La Voûte, was just across the road. (Léa has retired but the restaurant is still there.) Armed with handcart and bullhorn, she was adept at extracting the best prices by playing one merchant against another. Magnified by the bullhorn, a chiding word had miraculous effect. The Lyonnais history of women cooks goes back at least a century and I asked Lyonnais businessman Albert Convert whether any 'mères' remain. 'You'll find the tradition carried on at Mère Brazier,' he said. 'She died in 1977, but her daughter-in-law and grand-daughters carry on the same menu of artichoke heart stuffed with foie gras, quenelle au gratin, and chicken "en demi-deuil" (half-mourning, with black slices of truffle inserted under the skin). It hasn't changed at all.'

The Charollais cattle market at St Christophe en Brionnais.

pepper. My encounter that evening with 'cochonailles lyonnaises' was never to be forgotten, an immense cauldron of pig's head, loin, ribs, feet and ears simmered with sausages and vegetables, and served with a potato and onion salad.

Throughout the Lyonnais you will be offered soft fresh cheese, to eat with herbs and chopped garlic or a sprinkling of sugar (a taste mentioned by Rabelais). With a wink and a risqué remark, our cheerful waitress recommended the homemade 'fromage fort', a powerful mixture of fresh and dry cheeses, leeks, garlic and herbs. In Lyon fromage fort is known somewhat lugubriously as silk-weavers' brains or 'cervelle de Canut', after the famous Lyonnais weavers. (You can see intricate samples of their work over the centuries at the museum in the 18th-century Hôtel de Villeroy.) Classic onion soup, thick with bread and rich with cheese, is often called 'soupe des Canuts', for the Lyonnais love onions – potatoes fried with onions are termed 'lyonnaise'. In Lyon the potato is known as the 'truffle of the poor' – Stendhal claimed that in Lyon he found 20 ways of cooking potato as compared with only 10 in Paris.

Much of Lyon life centres around the imposing 18th-century Place Bellecour. Just off the western side you can see the appropriately named rue du Plat and the sleek windows of Chorliet, one of the finest charcutiers in the city. A sophisticated charcutier sells much more than just pork, and the window at Chorliet was decked with little cocktail hors d'oeuvre, fresh salads, salmon in aspic. Particularly famous is the 'rosette de Lyon', a dried salami-type sausage of raw pork stuffed into 50 cm/20 inches of pig's gut and offered in several seasonings and coarsenesses of texture. Half a dozen terrines tempt, not to mention head cheese, parsleyed ham in aspic, braised tripe and sauerkraut. The key to success is still to use every bit of the pig – tongues go in a terrine studded with pistachios, crunchy ears are set in jelly made from the bones. It's a messy job and I was amused to be told by the cashier (distinguished by the size of her diamonds) that Chorliet's products are made 'en laboratoire'!

Professional kitchen equipment shops tend to hide in back streets, so don't miss La Régionale right next door to Chorliet. Their range of heavy copper pans with rivetted handles, black metal bread pans, round, flat and rectangular, fish poachers and pastry cutters, is impressive. Best of all is their candy equipment, for Lyon has been a centre for chocolate since the mid-18th century, when Italian pastrycooks

The Converts have no time for trendy young chefs: 'worse than divas of grand opera,' snorted Albert. Instead they took us to their favourite backstreet bistro in the rue Guynemer. 'Don't expect much,' they warned, as we pushed open the steamy glass door to reveal an ancient zinc counter and walls so brown with age they had acquired their own patina. Restaurants like these are called 'bouchons', once frequented by workers who were known as 'mâchons' or good chewers.

The menu here was also a classic of inverted chic: garlic sausage with red wine sauce, tripe with tomato 'à la mode', calf's head with sauce gribiche (a piquant mayonnaise, p. 56), liver with onions, grilled pig's feet. This emphasis on innards is typical of Lyon, where a dish called 'sapper's apron', consisting of a slice of tripe, breaded and fried, is actually enjoyed. 'Tablier de sapeur' dates from the time of Napoleon III, when the military governor of Lyon, a lover of tripe, belonged to the corps of engineers and covered his uniform with the customary leather apron. Another oddity is 'couennes' made with shavings of pigskin tied in packets and poached in stock before being fried in lard with parsley and introduced chocolate to Lyon as a novelty from the New World. Exploring the streets surrounding the Place Bellecour, you'll find half a dozen fine chocolate shops each with its speciality, be it the bitter dessert chocolate at Weiss on the rue Childebert or the modernistic gold-leaved creations of Richart, back on the rue du Plat. Maurice Bernachon, son-in-law of Paul Bocuse, is another Lyonnais pâtissier and amid the chocolate-coloured marble of 42 cours Franklin-Roosevelt you can goggle at his astonishing 'gâteau président' with its ski-bonnet pompom of shaved chocolate. In the next-door tearoom there's a chance to sample one of his dozen chocolate cakes. Don't forget to walk around the corner to the back window and peer at white-coated chefs as they deftly coat rack after rack of chocolates.

No one should leave Lyon without a stroll around Le Vieux Lyon on the western bank of the Saône. The noise and fumes of the city die away amid the steep streets of fine Renaissance houses, their pinkish-yellow stone giving an impression of warmth on the dullest day. Students crowd the streets and artisans abound in the ancient 'traboules' or shortcuts linking the labyrinth of buildings perched on the precipitous hillside. Up the hill is Fourvière, where a still remains from Roman times as a reminder of millenia of good eating and drinking. In keeping with the atmosphere, I'd suggest you try one of the many bustling bistros where you won't go far wrong with a 'salade Lyonnaise' of hot bacon dressing with a lightly poached egg.

Bistro dining in Lyon is only one aspect of good food in the Lyonnais. The region shelters three or four out of the 20 or so restaurants given top rating in the Guide Michelin. 'L'Empéreur' Paul Bocuse is installed in Collonges au Mont d'Or, practically a suburb of Lyon. Mionnay acquired world renown under Alain Chapel, unfortunately no longer with us. Further north is Georges Blanc at Vonnas, with other members of the Blanc family at Thoissey. If you venture to the west, you will be in the territory of the Troisgros, père et fils, at Roanne. Like many stars of their generation, Paul Bocuse and Pierre Troisgros were trained in the 1950s by Fernand Point at Le Pyramide in Vienne, just down the Rhône from Lyon.

Fernand Point's simple, light style earned him recognition as the father of modern cooking. In his own words: 'The good cook has a duty to bequeath his culinary wisdom to future generations with all the fruit of his personal experi-

A winter vineyard in the Maconnais.

ence.' This tradition lies at the heart of fine cooking in France. Young cooks start out as apprentices in the kitchens of the great, much as the Renaissance artists studied in the great studios. A promising 'cuisinier' will work a year or two in a handful of top kitchens before starting out on his own.

Not for nothing does the word 'chef' mean leader; these men are in the forefront of French cuisine. They have a talent, a sureness of touch at the stove which is rare. Dishes such as Bocuse's 'soupe aux truffes' or Blanc's 'poularde de Bresse aux gousses d'ail et foie gras' are not for every day. Rather they are a glimpse of what can be done with the finest ingredients in the most sensitive hands, quite impossible to reproduce at home. Can anyone seriously resist the chance to try at least one temple of gastronomy, or possibly more?

RECIPES FROM
THE LYONNAIS

Salade Lyonnaise

────── HOT BACON AND EGG SALAD ──────

Chewy greens such as escarole or dandelion are best with a bacon dressing as the hot fat wilts the greens and makes them tender. The Lyonnais like to add a soft boiled egg, but sliced chicken livers or a few mushrooms are other possibilities.

Serves 4
4 eggs
a medium-size head of curly endive or escarole
(about 12 oz/375 g)
8 oz/250 g streaky bacon, cut in lardons (p. 184)
2 tbsp oil
3 fl oz/6 tbsp/90 ml wine vinegar
salt and pepper

To soft boil the eggs: put them in cold water, bring to the boil and simmer them 5–6 minutes. Transfer them to a bowl of cold water and leave to cool. Tap them gently all over to crack the shells, then peel them carefully under running water. Note: the yolks should be soft in the centre. Thoroughly wash the salad greens, drain and dry them. Put them in a salad bowl. If the bacon is salty, blanch (p. 182) and drain it. The eggs, salad and bacon can be prepared up to two hours ahead.

To finish: heat the oil and fry the bacon until lightly browned but still tender. Discard the excess fat, or add more oil to make about 3 fl oz/6 tbsp/90 ml. Heat the bacon and fat thoroughly, pour them over the greens and toss well. The heat will wilt the leaves slightly. Add the vinegar to the hot pan, standing back from the fumes, and cook until it has reduced by half. Pour it over the salad and toss again. Taste for seasoning and add salt and pepper if needed.

To serve: pile the salad on 4 individual plates and set an egg on top. Serve at once.

Pâté de Foie de Volaille à l'Ancienne

────── TRADITIONAL CHICKEN LIVER PÂTÉ ──────

An eggcup makes a pretty container for chicken liver pâté, just the right size for a single portion. Serve the pâté with toast or wholewheat bread.

Serves 8
8 oz/250 g chicken livers
salt and pepper
6 oz/¾ cup/175 g butter
2 shallots, finely chopped
1 clove garlic, crushed
1 tbsp brandy
2 fl oz/¼ cup/60 ml mayonnaise
1 medium tomato, peeled, seeded and chopped (p. 186)
8 egg cups or ramekins of 2½ fl oz/⅓ cup/75 ml capacity

Trim any membrane from the chicken livers and sprinkle them with salt and pepper. In a frying pan heat 2 tablespoons of the butter and fry the livers until thoroughly cooked and crusty brown on the outside, stirring often, 5–7 minutes. Add the shallots and garlic and continue cooking over low heat for 1 minute. Take from the heat, let cool to tepid and work the mixture in a food processor or blender so that it is puréed but there are still bits of the crusty liver to add texture. Cream the remaining butter and beat in the chicken liver purée with the brandy. Season the mixture to taste and spoon into the egg cups or ramekins, smoothing the top. Cover and chill. The pâté can be kept up to 2 days in the refrigerator.

To finish: thin the mayonnaise with a tablespoon or two of warm water so it pours easily. Season the chopped tomato with salt and pepper and pile it on the pâté. Coat the top with thin mayonnaise and serve at room temperature.

Escargots sur un Champ Rouge et Vert

———— SNAILS ON A FIELD OF TOMATO AND PARSLEY ————

The finest snails, say connoisseurs, are fattened on a diet of lettuce and herbs such as thyme. The snails for this recipe may be canned or frozen and their shells are not needed as the snails are set on a bed of tomato coulis and parsley purée.

Serves 4
2 oz/¼ cup/60 g butter
24 large or 36 small cooked snails
1–2 cloves garlic, finely chopped
1 shallot, finely chopped
salt and pepper
For the tomato coulis
1 tbsp butter
2 lb/1 kg tomatoes, peeled, seeded and chopped (p. 186)
bouquet garni (p. 183)
For the parsley purée
2 bunches of parsley (about 4 oz/125 g)
4 fl oz/½ cup/125 ml double/heavy cream

To make the tomato coulis: melt the butter in a saucepan and add the tomatoes, bouquet garni, salt and pepper. Simmer, uncovered, until the tomatoes are very soft and thick, 15–20 minutes. Discard the bouquet garni and taste for seasoning.

To make the parsley purée: discard the parsley stems. Blanch (p. 182) the sprigs, drain, rinse them with cold water and drain thoroughly. Purée the parsley in a food processor or blender with the cream and season to taste with salt and pepper. Tomato coulis and parsley purée can be stored up to 24 hours in the refrigerator.

To finish: warm the tomato coulis and parsley purée over low heat, adding a little water to the purée if necessary so it spreads easily. Heat the butter in a frying pan and sauté the snails for 2 minutes. Add the garlic, shallot, salt and pepper and continue cooking for 1–2 minutes until the snails are very hot. Spoon the tomato coulis on one side of 4 warm individual plates, then add the parsley on the other. Pile the snails in the centre and serve at once.

The open air market on the Quai St Antoine in Lyon.

Quenelles Sauce Nantua
—————— FISH DUMPLINGS WITH CRAYFISH SAUCE ——————

The Lyonnais way of dealing with pike, full-flavoured but bony, has become a classic. The flesh is filleted and skinned, then puréed to make 'quenelles Nantua' fish dumplings which are served in a crayfish sauce. (The town of Nantua, tucked in a dank, narrow valley to the east of the Pays de Dombes, is famous for its crayfish.) Any full-flavoured fish such as whiting, flounder, catfish, or even salmon can be substituted for the pike, with shrimps instead of crayfish; on no account should the fish be frozen or the quenelles will separate.

Serves 6–8 as a main dish
2 lb/1 kg pike fillets, with bones and head
pâte à choux (p. 185) made with 4 fl oz/½ cup/125 ml water,
½ tsp salt, ¾ oz/3 tbsp/20 g unsalted butter,
2 oz/½ cup/60 g flour and 2 eggs
6–7 egg whites
16 fl oz/2 cups/500 ml crème fraîche (p. 183)
or double/heavy cream
salt and pepper
pinch grated nutmeg
Nantua sauce (see recipe below)
gratin dish

For the quenelles: discard the skin from the fillets and reserve the head and bones to make fish stock for the Nantua sauce. Make the choux pastry and rub the surface with butter to prevent skin forming. Finely chop the fish fillets, pass them twice through the fine plate of a mincer/grinder or purée them in a food processor. For the best texture, also work the fish through a fine sieve. Refrigerate the fish purée in a bowl for about 30 minutes or until well chilled. Set the bowl of fish purée in a pan of ice and water. Lightly beat 6 of the egg whites and gradually work them into the fish purée, beating vigorously with a wooden spoon. Beat in the choux pastry, a little at a time; then gradually beat in the cream followed by salt, pepper and nutmeg to taste. If the quenelle mixture is soft, salt will stiffen it slightly. The beating can also be done in a food processor if the mixture is then refrigerated at least 30 minutes.

To poach the quenelles: heat a large shallow pan of salted water until simmering. Using two large serving spoons dip-ped in the water, shape an oval of quenelle mixture and drop it into the pan; if it starts to break up, add another lightly beaten egg white to the mixture and beat for another few minutes over ice. Shape the remaining mixture into 12–16 ovals and drop them into the simmering water. Poach them for 15–20 minutes, depending on size, or until firm. Lift them out with a slotted spoon and drain on paper towels.

Arrange the quenelles in a buttered gratin dish, scatter the crayfish tails (from Nantua sauce) in the dish and coat with the sauce. They can be kept covered in the refrigerator up to 2 days. To finish: heat the oven to No 6/400°F/200°C. Bake the quenelles until they are puffed and brown and the sauce bubbles, 15–20 minutes.

NANTUA SAUCE
6 oz/¾ cup/175 g butter
1 onion, finely chopped
1 carrot, finely chopped
2 lb/1 kg crayfish
2 tbsp brandy
4 fl oz/½ cup/125 ml white wine
1⅔ pints/1 quart/1 litre fish stock (p. 186)
made with the pike heads and bones
bouquet garni (p. 183)
salt and pepper
1½ oz/⅓ cup/45 g flour
16 fl oz/2 cups/500 ml crème fraîche (p. 183)
or double/heavy cream
1 teaspoon tomato purée/paste (optional)
pinch cayenne pepper

Melt a quarter of the butter in a large shallow pan and sauté the onion and carrot until soft. Add the crayfish and sauté, tossing over high heat until they turn red, about 2 minutes. Add the brandy and flame (p. 184). Add the white wine, fish stock, bouquet garni, salt and pepper and simmer for 8–10 minutes until the crayfish turn bright red.

Remove the crayfish from the cooking liquid and shell them, discarding the intestinal vein. Reserve the crayfish tails for garnishing the quenelles. Work the shells in a food processor with a little liquid from the pan until coarsely chopped, or work them a little at a time in a blender. Return them to the pan and simmer 10 minutes longer. Strain the mixture, pressing hard on the shells and vegetables to extract all the liquid.

Melt all but 3 tablespoons of the remaining butter in a saucepan, whisk in the flour and cook until foaming but not browned. Whisk in the shellfish liquid and bring the sauce to boil, whisking constantly until it thickens. Simmer for 10–15 minutes or until the sauce just coats a spoon. Add the crème fraîche or double/heavy cream and bring just back to the boil. If the sauce is pale, stir in a little tomato purée/paste, add a pinch of cayenne pepper and taste it for seasoning.

Poulet au Beaujolais

———— CHICKEN WITH BEAUJOLAIS WINE AND ONIONS ————

The light fruitiness of Beaujolais is clearly echoed in the sauce for this chicken. If you use red wine with different character, you'll have a different dish.

Serves 4–6
a 5 lb/2.3 kg roasting chicken or fowl, cut in 8 pieces
(p. 183)
2 tbsp oil
2 tbsp butter
4 fl oz/½ cup/125 ml chicken stock (p. 186), more if needed
1 clove garlic, crushed
2 shallots, finely chopped
salt and pepper
24–30 baby onions, peeled
kneaded butter (p. 184) made with 3 tbsp butter and
3 tbsp flour
8–12 fried croûtes (p. 183)
1 tbsp chopped parsley (for sprinkling)
For the marinade
1 bottle (3 cups/750 ml) Beaujolais wine
1 onion, sliced
1 carrot, sliced
1 stick celery, sliced
bouquet garni (p. 183)
1 clove garlic, sliced
6 peppercorns
2 tbsp olive oil

For the marinade: in a saucepan combine the wine, onion, carrot, celery, bouquet garni, garlic and peppercorns, bring to the boil and simmer for 5 minutes; let cool completely. Pour the marinade over the chicken, top with the oil, cover

A chicken trader at the Bourg-en-Bresse market.

and leave at room temperature for 12 hours or in the refrigerator for 24 hours, turning the pieces occasionally.

Drain the chicken pieces and pat dry with paper towels. Strain and reserve the marinade and vegetables. In a sauté pan or shallow casserole heat half the oil and half the butter. Add the chicken pieces, skin side down, and sauté over medium heat until brown, allowing at least 5 minutes. Turn, brown the other side, and remove them from the pan.

Add the reserved vegetables and bouquet garni from the marinade and cook until slightly soft, stirring occasionally for 5–7 minutes. Stir in the marinade, bring to the boil and simmer for 5 minutes. Add the stock, garlic, shallots, salt and pepper and replace the pieces of chicken. Cover and simmer on top of the stove or in a moderate oven (No 4/350°F/175°C) until the chicken is tender, 30–45 minutes for a roasting chicken, 1–1½ hours for a fowl. If the pan gets dry during cooking, add more stock. Heat the remaining oil and butter in a frying pan, add the baby onions, salt and pepper, and sauté until the onions are tender, 15–20 minutes. Shake the pan occasionally so the onions brown evenly.

Remove the chicken pieces from the liquid and strain it. Discard the vegetables and the bouquet garni. Taste and, if necessary, boil the liquid until concentrated. Whisk in enough kneaded butter so that the sauce lightly coats a spoon. Taste it for seasoning, stir in the sautéed onions and replace the chicken. The chicken can be prepared up to 3 days ahead and kept in the sauce in the refrigerator, or it can be frozen.

To finish: if necessary, reheat the chicken and sauce on top of the stove. Fry the croûtes. Serve the chicken in the casserole or on individual plates, sprinkled with parsley and with the croûtes on the side.

Faisan en Cocotte Vigneronne
—— PHEASANT EN COCOTTE WITH RED AND GREEN GRAPES ——

Grapes and pheasant share the same season, so why not the same pot?

Serves 4
8 tear-shaped fried croûtes (p. 183)
2 pheasants weighing about 1½ lb/750 g each, with giblets
salt and pepper
2 thin slices of pork fat, or 4 slices streaky bacon
2 oz/¼ cup/60 g butter
1 tsp marc or brandy
1 bunch watercress
For the sauce
6 oz/175 g seedless green grapes
6 oz/175 g seedless red grapes
8 fl oz/1 cup/250 ml Chardonnay or full bodied white wine
1½ fl oz/3 tbsp/45 ml marc or brandy
8 fl oz/1 cup/250 ml white veal or chicken stock (p. 186)
2 tsp arrowroot dissolved (p. 182) in 2 tbsp water
salt and pepper
trussing needle and string

Preheat the oven to No 6/400°F/200°C. Fry the croûtes. Sprinkle the birds inside with salt and pepper and truss them. Cover the breasts with the fat or bacon and tie it on with kitchen string. Heat 1½ oz/3 tbsp/45 g butter in a flame-proof casserole and brown the pheasants thoroughly on all sides, for about 8–10 minutes. Add the giblets, including the liver, and cover the casserole. Cook in the oven for 25–30 minutes until the juices from the centre run pink rather than red. If you prefer the birds well done, or if they are tough, continue cooking until the juice runs clear and they are tender when pierced with a skewer.

After 10 minutes, remove the pheasant liver from the casserole, let it cool, and crush it with the remaining butter using a fork. Season it with the teaspoon of marc or brandy, salt and pepper and spread it on the croûtes. For the sauce, put the grapes in a pan with the wine and simmer them for 3–5 minutes until they are lightly cooked but not soft.

When the pheasants are cooked, pour off any excess fat, add the 1½ fl oz/3 tbsp/45 ml marc or brandy to the pan and flame (p. 184) it. Remove the pheasants from the pot, discard the fat or bacon and remove the trussing strings. With poultry shears or a heavy knife cut along each side of the backbone and remove it. Trim the leg bones to neaten them and cut the birds in half along the breastbone. Keep them warm.

Add the wine from cooking the grapes to the pot and boil it for about 2 minutes, stirring to dissolve the pan juices. Add the stock, bring it to the boil and strain the sauce. Reduce, if necessary, to concentrate the flavour. If the pheasant is well done, it can be stored for up to 2 days in the refrigerator with the sauce, keeping the garnish separate. If you like the bird rare, however, it should be cooked at the last minute and served immediately.

To finish: if necessary reheat the pheasants in the sauce on top of the stove, adding more stock if necessary to keep them moist. Arrange the pheasant pieces on a serving dish so they overlap and keep them warm. Mix the arrowroot paste if it has separated and whisk enough into the boiling sauce so it lightly coats a spoon. Add the grapes to the sauce, bring it just to the boil and spoon the sauce over the pheasant. Garnish the dish with croûtes and watercress.

Faisan en Cocotte Vigneronne.

Landscape near Cluny.

Steak aux Cinq Poivres
— STEAK WITH FIVE PEPPERS —

A large thick-cut steak such as sirloin in the US, or rump in the UK is good for this dish; in France individual entrecôtes would be used. A version of the traditional 'steak au poivre', the recipe calls for five different types of pepper. A commercial mix of peppercorns can be substituted for the four black, white, pink and green peppercorns as it is the fifth, spicy Szechuan pepper, which adds such character to this recipe. Add more or less to your taste and, to develop its aroma, toast the pepper before using.

Serves 2–3
1 tbsp Szechuan pepper
1 tbsp black peppercorns
1 tbsp white peppercorns
1 tbsp dried pink peppercorns
1 tbsp dried green peppercorns
1½ lb/750 g steak, cut 1 inch/2.5 cm thick
salt
1 tbsp oil
2–3 tbsp brandy
8 fl oz/1 cup/250 ml double/heavy cream

Toast the Szechuan pepper in a small dry pan over low heat, tossing and stirring the pepper, until it smells aromatic, 3–5 minutes. Mix it with the other peppercorns, put them in a double thickness of plastic bags and crush them finely with a rolling pin. Spread the pepper in a shallow dish, add the steak and coat it on both sides with pepper, pressing in the crushed grains. Cover and leave for up to 6 hours in the refrigerator to absorb the flavour.

If you like strong flavour, leave the peppercorns; for milder taste, scrape most of them from the meat. Sprinkle the steak on both sides with a little salt. Heat the oil in a heavy pan, add the steak and cook over medium heat until very brown, 3–4 minutes. Turn and brown the other side, allowing 3–4 minutes longer for rare steak, or 5 minutes for medium done meat. Rare meat will feel spongy when pressed with your fingertip and the meat will be resilient when medium done.

Add brandy to the pan and flame (p. 184) the steak. Transfer it to a carving board and keep warm. Add cream to the pan and boil it, stirring to dissolve the pan juices. Taste the sauce for seasoning. Carve a large steak in thick diagonal slices and arrange them overlapping on warm plates; leave individual steaks whole. Spoon the sauce over the steak and serve at once.

Gratin de Racines d'Hiver
— GRATIN OF WINTER ROOT VEGETABLES —

When mixed with potato in this gratin, the strong flavour of roots like kohlrabi is tamed. The same trick works well with turnips, root celery and Jerusalem artichokes.

Serves 6–8
2 pints/1¼ quarts/1.25 litres milk
salt and pepper
1 lb/500 g root vegetables
1 lb/500 g potatoes
1 clove of garlic, peeled
grated nutmeg
12 fl oz/1½ cups/375 ml crème fraîche (p. 183)
or double/heavy cream
3 oz/90 g grated Gruyère cheese

Divide the milk between two pans, adding salt and pepper. Peel the roots, slice them thinly and add them at once to one milk pan to prevent their discolouring. Bring them to the boil and simmer until they are almost tender, 15–20 minutes depending upon the vegetable.

Meanwhile, peel the potatoes, slice them thinly and add them quickly to the other pan of milk. Bring it to the boil and simmer also until they are almost tender, 15–20 minutes. Drain both vegetables, reserving 12 fl oz/1½ cups/375 ml of the milk and keeping the rest for another purpose such as soup.

Rub a shallow baking dish with the garlic and then butter it. Spread half the vegetables in the baking dish and season them with salt and pepper. Add the remaining vegetables and season again. Stir the reserved milk with the nutmeg into the cream and pour it over the vegetables. Spinkle with the grated cheese. The gratin can be prepared up to 12 hours ahead and kept in the refrigerator.

To finish: heat the oven to No 4/350°F/175°C. Bake the gratin for 25–30 minutes until it is very hot and the top has browned.

Lyonnais goats carry wooden restraints around their necks to hinder their escape through gaps in field hedges.

cool completely and measure the liquid, adding more water if necessary to make 4 fl oz/½ cup/125 ml.

Beat the cheese until very smooth. Whisk in the vegetable liquid, cream, marc or brandy, oil and vinegar. Stir in the garlic and chives with salt and plenty of pepper to taste. Spoon the mixture into a small bowl or crock. The flavour mellows if it is kept at least 3 days and up to 2 weeks.

Galette Vieux Pérouges
── LEMON SUGAR BREAD ──

The traditional wood-fired bread ovens of Pérouges turn out this galette by the dozen. Delicious with berries, it resembles a sugar-topped pizza; granulated or light brown sugar may be used.

Serves 6–8
4 fl oz/½ cup/125 ml milk
½ oz/15 g compressed yeast, or ¼ oz/7 g dry yeast
1 lb/4 cups/500 g flour
1 tsp salt
1½ oz/3 tbsp/45 g sugar
3 eggs
4 oz/½ cup/125 g butter, creamed
For the topping
2½ oz/⅓ cup/75 g butter, softened
grated zest of 2 lemons
3¼ oz/½ cup/100 g granulated or brown sugar

Scald the milk in a small pan and let cool until tepid. Crumble or sprinkle the yeast on top and leave until dissolved, about 5 minutes. Sift the flour on to a work surface with the salt and sugar and make a large well in the centre. Add the eggs and yeast mixture and work lightly with your hand until mixed. Using a pastry scraper or spatula, gradually draw in the flour, working the mixture until it forms large crumbs. Press it into a ball; the dough should be soft and slightly sticky; if necessary add more flour.

Flour the work surface and knead the dough until it is smooth and elastic, at least 5 minutes. Work in the creamed butter and continue kneading until the dough is smooth again, 2–3 minutes. Shape the dough into a ball, transfer it to an oiled bowl and flip it so the top is oiled also. Cover with a damp cloth and leave to rise in a warm place until doubled in bulk, 1–1½ hours.

Fromage Fort
── PIQUANT CHEESE SAUCE ──

'Fromage fort' is sometimes called 'claqueret' from the verb 'claquer', to slap, an action which keeps wives and cheese in order, say the Lyonnais men. Serve fromage fort with hot boiled or steamed potatoes or as a spread for bread or toast. Alternatively it can be thinned with cream and served as a dressing for potato or cucumber salad.

Serves 6–8
1 large or 2–3 small leeks, washed, trimmed and sliced
1 sprig thyme
1 tbsp tarragon leaves
1 lb/500 g fresh goat or cows' cream cheese
2½ fl oz/⅓ cup/75 ml double/heavy cream or crème fraîche, (p. 183)
2 tbsp marc or brandy
1 tbsp oil
1 tbsp wine vinegar
3 cloves garlic, finely chopped
3 tbsp chopped chives
salt and pepper
boiled or steamed potatoes, fresh bread or toast (for serving)

Put the leeks in a saucepan with the thyme and tarragon and add water to barely cover them. Bring to the boil and simmer for 20 minutes. Drain the liquid through a fine sieve, pressing hard on the vegetables to extract all the juices. Let it

The time-honoured Galette Vieux
Pérouges.

Gâteau au Chocolat de Fernand Point

———— FERNAND POINT'S CHOCOLATE CAKE ————

Among the more feasible of Lyon's chocolate treats is this gâteau of the legendary Fernand Point, father of modern cooking, whose career in the kitchen flourished just south of Lyon in Vienne. The speckled appearance of the cake is due to the use of grated rather than melted chocolate. It is delicious served with a coffee vanilla custard sauce (p. 187).

Serves 6–8

4 oz/125 g dessert/semisweet chocolate
4 oz/1 cup/125 g flour
4 oz/½ cup/125 g unsalted butter
4 eggs, separated
5 oz/¾ cup/150 g sugar
powdered cocoa or icing/confectioners' sugar
(for sprinkling)

9 inch/22 cm straight-sided cake tin/pan or springform cake tin/pan

Preheat the oven to No 4/350°F/175°C. Butter the cake tin/pan, line the base with a round of greaseproof/wax paper and butter the paper. Sprinkle the tin/pan with flour, discarding the excess. Work the chocolate in a food processor, finely chop it with a knife, or coarsely grate it. Note: the texture should be slightly granular. Sift the flour.

Warm the butter over a pan of hot water until it is soft enough to pour. Note: do not heat too much or it will melt to oil. Let it cool slightly. Beat the egg yolks with the sugar until thick and the mixture leaves a ribbon trail when the whisk is lifted, about 5 minutes. In a separate bowl, stiffly whip the egg whites.

Beat the butter into the egg yolk mixture, followed by the chocolate and then the flour, using an electric mixer if you like. With a spatula, fold in the egg whites in three batches. Pour the batter into the prepared tin/pan and bake in the heated oven 35–45 minutes until the cake shrinks slightly from the sides of the pan and the top springs back when lightly pressed with a fingertip.

Run a knife around the edge of the cake and turn it out on a rack to cool. It is best eaten the day of baking, but can be stored 2–3 days in an airtight container. For serving, sprinkle it generously with powdered cocoa or icing/confectioners' sugar.

Butter a baking sheet. Turn the dough on to a lightly floured work surface and knead lightly to knock out the air. Roll it to the largest possible round that will fit the baking sheet, preferably 20 inches/50 cm across. Transfer the dough round to the buttered baking sheet and with your knuckles, flatten the centre slightly to form a 1 inch/2.5 cm border around the edge to contain the butter and sugar topping. Dot the top with butter. Mix the lemon zest with the sugar and sprinkle it on the dough. Leave the galette in a warm place to rise until light, 15–20 minutes. Heat the oven to No 8/450°F/230°C.

Bake the galette in the heated oven until browned and the sugar has formed a crisp glaze on top, 15–20 minutes. Transfer it to a rack to cool. It is best served while still warm, but can be baked a few hours ahead and warmed for serving.

NORMANDY

Across orchards and grazing lands to Dieppe, along the chalk cliffs and into the Seine Valley, in quest of all that is essentially Norman, from Camembert to Calvados

Home ground in Normandy for me is the Pays de Caux, the land of chalk, a fertile windswept plain furrowed by a dozen narrow river valleys which shelter the famous apple orchards and black and white cows. In one of these valleys near Dieppe we had a weekend villa, where we carried our churn each morning to be filled with rich, unpasteurized milk at the farm, then crossed the road to buy croissants warm from the oven and moist with good Norman butter. On the seafront we watched open boats come in with the tide to land flapping-fresh fish – hake, plaice, John Dory, Dover sole and the occasional turbot. The stocky build of the locals took me back to my childhood in the Yorkshire dales. The grey, damp weather, propitious for crops and the development of rheumatism, held no surprises. After all, Normans and

130

swelling under her dress, that her succulence was exceed-ingly tempting. Her face was a red apple . . .' She sums up much of Norman cooking – the pork, the butter, the charcuterie, the apples, with the emphasis on generosity and solid worth. The Normans live on the income from their income, the saying goes.

The 17th-century dining room at the Hôtel du Cygne is equally evocative of the old Normandy, a museum piece with racks of plates from floor to ceiling, a pendulum clock 9 feet high, and the classic shallow Norman stone fireplace still equipped with a pot hook and spit mechanism. Famous visitors to the inn include Louis XIII and Madame de Pompadour but such glories are now in eclipse, drowned by the roar of heavy trucks as they grind through Tôtes on their way to the coast. To escape the fumes, take a quick jog eastward to the river valleys of the Scie, Varenne or Arques. All offer a foretaste of the riches of Normandy, with ample farmhouses and manors dating back 800 years and more.

This is cider country, where in the autumn you'll see sack after sack of apples by the roadside, awaiting the travelling press, which passes once a year. After years of decline, farmhouse cider is now common in local groceries, most of it sparkling and with a low alcohol content of 6 per cent or less. (Cloudiness is a good sign, indicating that the cider is unfiltered and with body.) Most is blended, but one enter-prising producer, Claude Havard, uses specific apple types to make varietal ciders in the manner of wine. Cider, it seems, was popularized in Normandy by the Moors from Spain in the 12th century. They brewed a similar drink from dates called 'sicera', hence cider. During the season from September to November, Monsieur Havard offers tours of his presses at the Duché de Longueville at Anneville, just south of Dieppe.

No permit is required to press cider at home, but the distillation of Calvados (apple brandy), is another matter. Like cider, the name for Calvados is said to come from overseas and the wreck of the galleon 'El Salvador', part of the Spanish Armada in 1588. Two hundred years later the name Calvados was given to the apple-growing area south of the Seine near Caen, source of the best Calvados. First the cider is left in the cask for up to two years, then the juice is distilled twice, like Cognac. However, there are no great brand names, as with Cognac, so mellow, vintage Calvados is harder to find, a matter of enquiry and then sampling the

Dalesmen are closely linked, both descended from the tough, sturdy Vikings who in the ninth century pillaged the coasts of Britain and sailed their longboats up the Seine.

Distances are small in the Pays de Caux, ideal for a leisurely long weekend whether you chug over on the ferry from Newhaven to Dieppe (3¾ hours) or make the 1½ hour drive from Paris to Rouen by autoroute, then strike north on the arrow-straight N27 to Dieppe. On the way from Rouen to Dieppe you pass through Tôtes, where Flaubert's Emma Bovary whiled away the time with her dull doctor husband. ('Tôt' comes from the Danish 'toft' or settlement, and appears in many local placenames.) It was here at the Hôtel du Cygne that Guy de Maupassant wrote the short story *Boule de Suif* ('ball of lard'); the eponymous heroine was 'short and round, fat as butter, her podgy fingers with their nipped–in knuckles looking exactly like strings of chitterling sausages; she was none the less so fresh with her ripe breasts

bottle. The 'petit Calva' taken in cafés on a winter morning is fiery stuff, a thump in the chest as it goes down.

A quick tot of Calvados may also be taken in the middle of a meal to clear the palate. 'Between each dish we tossed down a "trou Normand",' says Guy de Maupassant, 'with a glass of "eau de vie", which was a fire in the body and a joy to the soul.' Other regions follow the same custom with their own 'eau de vie', so you'll find a 'trou Gascon' of Armagnac, and a 'trou Bourguignon' of marc, for instance. In restaurants, a mild version of a 'trou' may be served mid-meal in the form of a sorbet flavoured with the relevant 'eau de vie'. Another variant of Calvados turns up in Pommeau, an aperitif of one third Calvados and two thirds apple juice, closely resembling Burgundian ratafia.

In cooking, Calvados is excellent for flaming meats like pork chop and kidneys, it balances the richness of tripe in 'tripes à la mode de Caen', and its vigour marries naturally with the overwhelmingly rich 'crème fraîche' of Normandy, a combination known as 'vallée d'Auge' after the river valley in Calvados where the finest Calvados is made. Crème fraîche tastes like cream before the days of pasteurization – of course, the French do pasteurize their cream, but they have the sense to add back lactic enzymes so as to restore the nutty flavour of natural fermentation. Crème fraîche keeps better than cream, thickening and acquiring a slightly cheesy taste, but remaining quite useable after two or three weeks. In most other countries you now find only sweet cream, or crème fleurette as it is called in France.

Normandy is also source of some of the world's best butter. In the rest of France, bread is eaten dry with a meal, but here and in Brittany butter appears routinely beside bread on the table just as it did in Yorkshire when I was a child. Butter is the key ingredient in brioche – in our village of Bourg Dun, pensioners were presented with a brioche loaf each Christmas by the commune – and in crumbling 'sablé' cookies. 'Exclusivement au beurre' declare the best Norman pastry shops with pride. In France, this is an endorsement of quality; in many other countries, obsessed with cholesterol, it would amount to a 'stay-away' sign. But the French live longer than most of us, say the statistics!

In Dieppe all roads lead to the seafront with its casino and half dozen old-style hotels with 'English bar'. Like the town itself, they offer a timeless, slightly shabby welcome. On the pedestrian main street you can sit outside the Tribunaux café,

as did Oscar Wilde when he fled England after his release from prison in 1895. A narrow street leads to the high gothic Eglise St Jacques, much painted early this century by English School artists who found inspiration in the muted greys of France's northern coast. On Saturdays the church is surrounded by an outdoor market, notable for farm-raised poultry, cider, and in winter, for fresh scallops sold in their shells by the dozen.

Dieppe is the nearest port to Paris. For centuries before the railways a system of express coaches called the 'chasse marée' (tide-chaser) rushed the fish to market next morning in Paris. The street where they were sold is still called the Faubourg Poissonnière, though today's catch now ends up in Rungis wholesale market. Best bet for dining in Dieppe is to visit one of the fish restaurants under the 18th-century arcades lining the port. Here you'll find the freshest of seafood, at its best plainly poached, grilled or served meunière. Pride of place goes to spectacular 'plateaux de fruits de mer' of bewhiskered langoustines, prawns, little pink and grey shrimp, a crab or two, oysters, clams and mussels on the half shell, whelks and winkles, all resting on a bed of seaweed. It's a half hour of cracking and shelling to do justice to the feast with its accompaniment of fresh mayonnaise, shallot vinegar and lemon wedges.

On a cold day you might opt for a cauldron of Dieppe's famous little mussels, cooked 'à la marinière' with white wine, shallot and chopped parsley. These are 'moules de bouchot', grown on poles washed clean by the tide to taste extra salty and crisp. If you've still space for a main course, Dover sole must surely be your choice, whether grilled on the bone, or sautéed in butter with a few shrimps and mushrooms 'à la Joinville'. If mussels are included as well, the correct name becomes 'Dieppoise'. Most complex of all is 'sole Normande' in a white wine and cream sauce with a garnish of shrimps, mussels and mushrooms. You might also encounter a fish stew called 'marmite Dieppoise', flavoured with curry and dating back to medieval times when Dieppe merchants made fortunes in the trade of ivory, spice and armaments. The Château de Dieppe overlooking the sea houses a fine collection of locally carved ivories.

It was on the proceeds of trade that Jehan d'Ango built his Renaissance manor a few miles west along the cliffs. The house is a copybook of architectural styles in the local materials of black flint, brick and stone. In the centre of the

courtyard stands an imposing pigeonhouse, sure sign of prosperity and a common feature on old Norman farms. Historically, pigeons produced a number of benefits – not only eggs and meat but also manure for the fields – but because the birds are greedy, gobbling grain indiscriminately from neighbours' fields, ownership of a pigeonhouse was strictly controlled, being limited to established landowners until the revolution. By the time these exclusive rights were abolished in 1789, there were already some 40,000 pigeon-houses throughout France. After visiting the Manoir d'Ango, it's worth continuing to the Parc des Moutiers, classically landscaped in English style with a house by Edwin Lutyens, and then adventuring on to the beach head to visit the cliff-side church where Braque is buried.

As you drive westwards along the coast, the road switch-backs along chalk cliffs and sheltered valleys, each with its seaside settlement. A few, like Fécamp where Benedictine liqueur is made, are sizeable ports, but most have no anchorage and amount to little more than a string of bathing huts along the front, much as Boudin painted them 100 years ago. Pretty but precarious: 'Our only unmortgaged piece of real estate,' remarked my husband wryly after discovering that the hut conveyed to us in great pomp and ceremony only three months earlier had been washed away in an autumn storm.

Away from the main roads, many villages in the Pays de Caux are quite untouched by time. Most farms keep a family pig, fed on scraps and whey left from butter and cheese-making. I once attended a pig killing, a ritual held in the orchard and presided over by the local charcutier. The more easily to dismember it, the animal was suspended from an apple tree, next to an immense cauldron of boiling water needed first for scalding and cleaning the pig's hide, then for blanching the 'boudin noir' blood sausages, a Norman speciality which is at its best with sautéed apples. In the kitchen, the preparation of head cheese, country terrine, and 'andouillettes' (sausages made with the chitterlings) is soon under way. It might seem nothing had changed for centuries, but I noted a capacious freezer in the pantry: much fresh pork is now frozen rather than salted as bacon or 'petit salé', the poor man's ham. Petit salé is made with inexpensive bits such as the shoulder and sparerib, which are pickled in brine, then simmered in soup or braised with lentils, kidney beans or cabbage.

My authority on Norman charcuterie is Françoise Samson, the countrywoman who looked after my parents-in-law for nearly 20 years. It was she who taught me that the secret of crispy roast chicken is constant basting with lots of butter. Her sole meunière, downfall of many a professional, is exemplary, and her coquilles St Jacques – a perfume of scallops, mushrooms, and plenty of crème fraîche – is a delight. Françoise is that rarity, the born cook. When I asked how she learned, she looked confused. 'No one taught me. I never measure, but I taste and adjust. And I cook very, very thoroughly so everything toasts and browns. I'm a maniac for that.'

I talked to Françoise's neighbours Sylviane and Jean-Pierre Levasseur, who run a typical Cauchois farm, growing grain and sugar beet, fattening calves and steers, as well as sending milk to the cooperative. Like most farm wives, Sylviane raises chickens. In her grandparents' time, the favourite family dish for weddings and special occasions was 'poule au blanc' made from a tasty mature hen, in a sauce with plenty of cream. Her grandmother also made cheese in the style of Neufchâtel, which lies to the southeast of Dieppe. Neufchâtel, white like Camembert and slightly more piquant, is unusual in being sold in several shapes: a brick, a small square, a log called 'bondon', and an instantly recognizable heart-shaped 'coeur'.

Other Norman cheeses are few but famous – square, bold-flavoured Pont l'Evêque, its reddish crust latticed from drying on straw matting; punchy little Livarot, yellow, crusty and rich; round white-skinned Camembert, the melting interior gently yielding when pressed with a fingertip (at least when it can be found unpasteurized and in peak condition). Camembert has been around for three centuries or longer but was not commercialized until the railways made its rapid transportation possible in the familiar boxes of

shaved poplar wood. Scarcely cheese at all is 'petit Suisse', a walnut-sized nugget of fresh cheese which is a standard child's dessert when sprinkled with sugar. Petit Suisse has no connection with Switzerland but comes from the same area as Neufchâtel.

The Seine valley which forms the southern border of the Pays de Caux is very different from the chilly northern coast. No wonder the Vikings settled here with such alacrity, building castles like that of Les Andelys and churches including the Benedictine abbey of St Wandrille. Along the river bank from the hamlet of Villequier east to Bouille winds a road of singular charm. At Caudebec a Saturday market has been held since at least the 1400s in the shadow of the flamboyant Eglise Notre Dame. The chapels are dedicated to artisan guilds, with one window donated by Jean Thorel, baker. The emblems of his trade – rake, peel, and loaves of bread – are endearingly depicted in the bottom frieze, while the space above is devoted to the Holy Spirit whose heavenly flames recall the searing heat of a bread oven.

At Caudebec a modern suspension bridge soars over the Seine with its busy, ocean-going traffic (Rouen is the fourth port in France). You can take coffee on the sidewalk overlooking the river where a tidal bore called the 'mascaret' used to sweep up the river twice daily at certain seasons, drenching the unwary. At Villequier just downstream, Victor Hugo's daughter was swept to her death in 1843. My favourite restaurant spot is east at Duclair, where the Hôtel de la Poste serves traditional Rouennais duck prepared by the great grandson of the founder. Even on a rainy day the dining room is cheerful, with its backdrop of turn-of-the-century frescoes and a view of the many river ferries, their sides emblazoned with the lions of Normandy.

Rouennais duck is raised by a single producer across the river from Duclair. They are a special crossbreed, half wild, half domestic, and what makes them 'rouennais' is the method of killing – they must be strangled without bleeding so the flesh remains dark and full of taste. (When dispatched conventionally, the small plump bird is called 'sauvageaux', ideal for contemporary recipes which use only breast meat or 'magret'.) A 'canard rouennais' must be roasted for only 18 minutes until rare. At the table the breast is carved in classic needle-shaped slices called 'aiguillettes', while a concentrated sauce is created with the liver, a reduction of shallots, red Bordeaux wine, and the duck's blood extracted by

Normandy is famous for its orchard fruits and for its rich fruit tarts.

crushing the bones. All of this is mounted with butter and sharpened with just a squeeze of lemon juice. Or so insists Chef Guéret of the Hôtel de Dieppe in Rouen, president of Les Canardiers, a worldwide association of cooks devoted to serving only genuine 'canard Rouennais'.

Between Caudebec and Duclair, the river loops wide to enclose the graceful ruined abbey of Jumièges, founded in the 7th century by St Ouen, bishop of Rouen. The road meanders along the 'route des fruits', lined with timbered houses massed with pear and apple trees. Blossom time, usually in late April, is the moment to come here, as to so much of Normandy. To avoid the industrial sprawl of Rouen, at Duclair take the river ferry and road south to Bouille, a popular but still peaceful stop for a luncheon outing. With its northern exposure, Bouille is less of a sun-trap than towns further down the river, but its range of restaurants is superior.

In contrast to the time-capsule of the Norman countryside, Rouen plays very much the role of great city. The shops are international, set among black and white houses undergoing major, sometimes strident, restoration. The cathedral is a landmark, its fretted 'butter tower' financed in the 16th century by dispensations which allowed the faithful to consume milk and butter during the Lenten fast. To leave Normandy with Rouen as a last impression would be a pity. Better continue on small roads which hug the Seine as far as Les Andelys, with its fortress overhanging the river as an enduring reminder of Norman dominance. The town square is placid, with a restaurant or two beside the Seine. Further on towards Paris lies Monet's house at Giverny, high spot for garden lovers but remarkable too for its buttercup-yellow dining room and the kitchen tiled in iris blue. The same brilliant colours animate the porcelain sold for the benefit of the Monet Foundation. Don't expect sophistication: the glory of the house is its garden, a fitting backward look at Normandy, the orchard and dairy of France.

Pâté de Foie de Porc Campagnarde
—————— PORK LIVER PÂTÉ ——————

This rich pork liver pâté should be served with gherkin pickles, black olives and plenty of crusty brown or wholewheat bread.

Serves 12–15
8 oz/250 g sliced barding fat (p. 182)
1 lb/500 g pork liver
1 tbsp butter
1 onion, chopped
1 lb/500 g pork (half fat, half lean), minced/ground
8 oz/250 g veal, minced/ground
2 cloves garlic, finely chopped
½ tsp ground allspice
pinch ground cloves
pinch ground nutmeg
2 medium eggs, beaten to mix
3 tbsp Calvados, or Cognac
salt and pepper
2½ oz/½ cup/75 g shelled hazelnuts (optional)
bay leaf
sprig of thyme
terrine (2⅓ pint/1½ quart/1.5 litre capacity)

Line the terrine or casserole with barding fat, reserving a slice for the top. Heat the oven to No 4/350°F/175°C.

Discard the ducts from the liver and mince/grind it in a food processor or meat grinder. Melt the butter in a small pan and sauté the onion until soft but not brown. Mix it with the pork, veal, pork liver, garlic, allspice, cloves, nutmeg, eggs, Calvados, and plenty of salt and pepper. Beat with a wooden spoon until the mixture pulls from the sides of the bowl, 2–3 minutes. Sauté a small piece and taste – it should be quite strongly seasoned. Beat in the hazelnuts, if using.

Pack the mixture into the lined terrine and trim the barding fat level with the top. Cut the barding fat in strips and arrange on top of the mixture in a lattice. Set the bay leaf and sprig of thyme on top of the fat. Do not cover the terrine. Set the terrine in a water bath (p. 187), bring it to the boil on top of the stove and transfer to the heated oven. Cook until a skewer inserted in the centre of the terrine for 30 seconds is hot to the touch when withdrawn, 1¼–1½ hours.

Let the terrine cool until tepid, and then press it with a board or plate with a 2 lb/1 kg weight on top until cold. Keep the terrine in the refrigerator for at least 3 days and up to a week to allow the flavour to mellow before serving.

To serve, unmould the terrine, cut it in slices and arrange them overlapping on a platter. Alternatively, serve the terrine in the mould.

Marmite Dieppoise
—————— FISH STEW WITH VEGETABLES AND CREAM ——————

'Marmite Dieppoise' is a good deal more serious than the usual fisherman's stew of his leftover catch. A good marmite includes mussels, shrimps, scallops, and a scampi or two. In the old days, you might have found Dover sole and turbot among the white fish, but nowadays it is more likely to be lemon sole or whiting. The use of spice in the Dieppoise fish stew dates from medieval times when Dieppe was an important trading port.

Serves 10–12 as an appetizer, 8 as a main course
fillets of 4 lemon sole, flounder or whiting weighing about 1 lb/500 g each
8 cod steaks, weighing 1½ lb/750 g
1⅔ pint/1 quart/1 litre fish stock (p. 186)
2½ oz/⅓ cup/75 g butter
2 leeks, trimmed, split and chopped
2 large onions, chopped
1 tsp curry powder, or to taste
pinch of paprika
2 tomatoes, peeled, seeded and chopped (p. 186)
4 medium carrots, peeled and cut in sticks
4 stalks celery, cut in sticks
8 fl oz/1 cup/250 ml white wine
salt and pepper
8 scallops
3¼ pints/2 quarts/2 litres mussels, cleaned (p. 184)
8 fl oz/1 cup/250 ml crème fraîche (p. 183)
or double/heavy cream
pinch of cayenne pepper
8 oz/250 g cooked peeled shrimps

Cut each fillet in half crosswise. Cut each cod steak in 4 pieces, removing the bone. Use the heads, tails and bones of the fish to make a simple stock: wash them, put them in a

large pan and add enough water to cover, bring to the boil and simmer for 20 minutes. Strain; then add enough water to make 1⅔ pints/1 quart/1 litre liquid. Wash the pieces of fish and pat them dry.

Heat 2 tablespoons of the butter in a saucepan. Add the chopped leeks and onions and cook over low heat, stirring occasionally, until soft but not brown. Stir in the curry powder and paprika and cook for 1 minute. Add the tomatoes, carrots, celery, wine and fish stock with a little salt and pepper and simmer until the vegetables are almost tender, about 15 minutes.

Meanwhile layer the fish in a large saucepan, first the cod, then the scallops, sole, flounder or whiting, and mussels, sprinkling each layer with salt and pepper. Pour over the vegetable broth, bring to the boil and simmer until the fish just flakes easily and the mussels open, 3–5 minutes. Discard any mussels that do not open when heated.

Transfer the fish and mussels to serving bowls. Add cream and cayenne to the broth, bring to the boil and taste – it should be slightly piquant with cayenne. Add the shrimps and spoon them with the vegetables and broth over the fish. Serve at once.

Sole Sautée Joinville

———— SAUTÉED SOLE WITH SHRIMPS AND MUSHROOMS ————

Dover sole is the preferred fish for sautéing, but any white fish fillets can be substituted.

Serves 8 as an appetizer and 4 as a main course
8 sole fillets, about 1½ lb/750 g
2 oz/½ cup/60 g flour seasoned with ½ teaspoon salt and
pinch of white pepper
5 oz/⅔ cup/150 g butter
4 oz/125 g cooked, peeled, baby shrimps
8 oz/250 g mushrooms, thinly sliced
juice of 1 lemon
2 tbsp chopped parsley

Wash the sole fillets and dry them on paper towels. Dip them in seasoned flour, patting them to coat evenly.

In a heavy frying pan or skillet, heat half the butter until foaming, add the fillets, skinned (smooth) side down. (If all the fillets won't fit, fry them in two batches.) Fry over brisk heat until golden brown, 1–2 minutes, depending on the thickness of the fish; turn over and brown the other side.

Note: the fish will flake in pieces if overcooked. Transfer the fillets to a serving dish and keep warm.

Wipe out the pan and heat the remaining butter until foaming. Add the shrimps and heat, stirring for 30 seconds, remove them. Add the mushrooms and sauté until all the cooking liquid has evaporated, 5–7 minutes.

Stir the shrimps into the mushrooms with the lemon juice, salt and pepper, and taste. Spoon the mixture over the fish, sprinkle with parsley and serve at once.

Coquilles Saint-Jacques au Safran
SCALLOPS WITH SAFFRON

The combination of saffron with scallops recalls Dieppe's history as a spice port. Rice pilaf is a good foil for the rich sauce.

Serves 4–6
2 tbsp butter
6 oz/175 g mushrooms, thinly sliced
juice of ½ lemon
salt and pepper
2 lb/1 kg shelled sea scallops
large pinch of saffron threads, soaked in 2–3 tbsp boiling water
For the sauce
1 shallot, finely chopped
2 tbsp dry vermouth
2 tbsp white wine
½ pint/1¼ cups/300 ml crème fraîche (p. 183) or double/heavy cream
small pinch saffron threads, optional
3 oz/6 tbsp/90 g cold butter

Melt half the butter in a medium pan and add the mushrooms, lemon juice, salt and pepper and press a piece of buttered foil on top. Cover with the lid and cook gently until the mushrooms are tender, 4–5 minutes.

Melt the remaining butter in a frying pan, add the scallops and pour over the saffron and liquid. Cover and cook very gently until the scallops whiten, 3–5 minutes. Note: do not overcook them or they will be tough. Transfer them to a plate with a draining spoon.

For the sauce: add any cooking juices from the mushrooms to the scallop liquid with the shallot, vermouth and wine. Boil until reduced to a glaze (p. 184). Whisk in the cream, and boil until reduced by about a third, 5–7 minutes. Taste, adding more saffron if necessary. Scallops and sauce can be cooked up to 2 hours ahead.

To finish: reheat the sauce if necessary. Take the pan from the heat and whisk in the cold butter, working on and off the heat so that it softens without melting to oil. When all the butter is added, bring the sauce just to the boil. Add the scallops and mushrooms, heat gently for 1–2 minutes and spoon the mixture on to individual warm plates.

Poule au Blanc au Salsifis
POACHED CHICKEN WITH SALSIFY AND CREAM

Salsify adds flavour to this dish without disturbing its white purity; root artichokes or quartered baby turnips may be substituted. If you use a chicken rather than a boiling fowl, reduce the cooking time to 1 hour. Rice is the traditional accompaniment, cooked if you like in some stock from the chicken.

Serves 4
4 lb/1.8 kg boiling fowl
1 onion, studded with 2 cloves
2 carrots, quartered
2 cloves garlic
bouquet garni (p. 183), including a celery stalk and a stem of tarragon
½ pint/1¼ cups/300 ml white wine
3¼ pints/2 quarts/2 litres chicken stock (p. 186) or water, more if needed
salt and pepper
2 lb/1 kg salsify
For the sauce
2½ oz/⅓ cup/75 g butter
1½ oz/⅓ cup/45 g flour
1¼ pints/3 cups/750 ml stock (from cooking the chicken)
12 fl oz/1½ cups/375 ml crème fraîche (p. 183) or double/heavy cream
trussing needle and string

In Dieppe fresh scallops are sold in their shells by the dozen.

Truss the fowl and put it in a small pot so it fits quite tightly with the onion, carrots, garlic and bouquet garni. Pour in the white wine and enough chicken stock or water just to cover, add a little salt and pepper and bring to the boil. Cover and simmer over low heat, skimming occasionally until the thigh of the bird is tender when pierced with a two-pronged fork, 1¼–1¾ hours.

About a half hour before the end of cooking, peel the salsify and cut it in 2 inch/5 cm lengths. Put it in a saucepan and add enough stock from the chicken to cover it generously. (Add more stock or water to the chicken if needed.) Cover the salsify and simmer until tender, 15–20 minutes. Drain it and add the stock back to the chicken. The chicken can be cooked up to a day ahead and refrigerated in the stock.

If necessary, reheat the bird, remove it, cover it loosely with foil and keep warm. Skim any fat from the stock, boil until it is reduced to 1¼ pints/3 cups/750 ml, then strain it. For the sauce: melt the butter in a saucepan, stir in the flour and cook until foaming. Whisk in the reduced stock and bring the sauce to the boil, whisking constantly until it thickens. Simmer it for 2 minutes, then add the cream and taste for seasoning. Continue simmering the sauce until it lightly coats a spoon and the flavour is concentrated and mellow, 10–15 minutes.

Meanwhile carve the chicken in 6–8 pieces (p. 183), arrange it on a serving dish, cover it tightly with foil and warm it in a low oven. Add salsify to the sauce and heat gently for 2 minutes. Coat the chicken with the sauce, spooning the salsify down one side of the serving dish. Serve immediately.

Ragoût de Porc aux Lentilles

— STEWED PORK WITH LENTILS —

This is Françoise's recipe marrying lentils with fresh pork rather than the more common 'petit salé'. Spicy sausages add piquancy, while apple sauce and crisp fried potatoes would be the Norman choice as accompaniment.

Serves 8

2 lb/1 kg boneless pork breast, cut in 1 inch/2.5 cm cubes
salt and pepper
2 tbsp lard or oil
12 oz/375 g spicy fresh sausages such as chipolata
2 onions, chopped
6 cloves garlic, chopped
bouquet garni (p. 183)
big bunch of thyme
16 fl oz/2 cups/500 ml water, more if needed
10 oz/1½ cups/300 g lentils

Preheat the oven to No 3/300°F/150°C. Sprinkle the pork generously with salt and pepper. In a flameproof casserole heat the lard and fry the pork over high heat, a few pieces at a time, until browned on all sides, and set them aside. Then brown the sausages and set them aside. Add the onions to the pan and fry gently until brown, stirring occasionally. Add the pork with the garlic, bouquet garni, thyme, salt and pepper and enough water to cover. Cover tightly and cook in the heated oven for 30 minutes.

Meanwhile, pick over the lentils, discarding any stones, and wash them thoroughly. Stir them into the pork with water to cover by ½ inch/1.25 cm. Cover and continue cooking, stirring occasionally, until both pork and lentils are tender, 40–50 minutes. Stir the lentils from time to time, and add more water if they are dry. At the end of cooking they should be moist but not soupy.

Ten minutes before the end of cooking, immerse the sausages in the lentils so they heat thoroughly. Before serving, discard the thyme and bouquet garni and taste the lentils for seasoning. The dish can be refrigerated up to 2 days and reheated.

Brioche au Neufchâtel
—————— CHEESE BRIOCHE ——————

Camembert, Brie or any other soft cheese may be substituted for Neufchâtel in this cheese brioche. Indeed it is said that the name 'brioche' comes from the use of Brie cheese rather than butter in the original recipe.

Makes 2 medium loaves
½ oz/15 g compressed yeast, or ¼ oz/7 g dry yeast
2 fl oz/¼ cup/60 ml lukewarm water
1 lb/4 cups/500 g unbleached flour, more if needed
1 tsp salt
1 tbsp sugar
6 eggs, beaten to mix
6 oz/175 g cheese (after the rind is removed)
6 oz/12 tbsp/175 g butter, softened
1 egg, beaten to mix with ½ teaspoon salt (for glaze)
two medium loaf tins/pans (8½×4½×2½ inches/30×11×6 cm)

Sprinkle or crumble the yeast over the water and let it stand for 5 minutes or until dissolved. Sift the flour on to a work surface and make a large well in the centre. Sprinkle salt and sugar on to the flour. Add the yeast mixture with the beaten eggs to the well. With your hand, gradually work in the flour to form a smooth dough; it should be quite sticky. Knead the dough on the work surface, lifting it up and throwing it down until it is very elastic and resembles chamois leather, about 5 minutes. Work in more flour if necessary so that at the end of kneading, the dough is sticky but holds together in one piece.

Transfer the dough to an oiled bowl, turn it over so the top is oiled and cover the bowl with a damp cloth. Leave it in a warm place for an hour or until doubled in bulk. Butter the loaf tins/pans, line them with greaseproof/wax paper and butter the paper. Cut the cheese into cubes; if necessary leave at room temperature to soften.

Knead the dough lightly to knock out air. Work in the softened cheese and butter, squeezing with your fist until it is completely incorporated. Divide the dough in half and shape it into two loaves. Set the loaves in the prepared tins/pans, cover with a cloth and let them rise in a warm place for ½–1 hour, or until the tins/pans are almost full. Heat the oven to No 6/400°F/200°C.

Brush the loaves with egg glaze and score the tops with a sharp knife. Bake in the heated oven for 45–55 minutes or until the loaves start to shrink away from the sides of the pan and sound hollow when tapped on the bottom. Unmould and cool them on a rack. Cheese brioche is best eaten the day of baking; but day-old brioche also toasts well.

Gâteau aux Poires
—————— PEAR CAKE ——————

Françoise's recipe for pear cake is typical of her simple approach. The sliced pears are cooked in butter and sugar, then baked in a shallow layer of cake batter; apples or peaches do equally well. Crème fraîche, of course, is the mandatory accompaniment.

Serves 8
2 lb/1 kg medium pears
3 oz/6 tbsp/90 g unsalted butter
8 oz/1¾ cups/250 g icing/confectioner's sugar
juice of ½ lemon
8 oz/2 cups/250 g flour
1½ tbsp baking powder
4 egg yolks
4 fl oz/½ cup/125 ml milk
few drops/½ tsp vanilla
11 inch/28 cm porcelain or metal quiche mould

Preheat the oven to No 4/350°F/175°C. Butter the mould. Peel, core, quarter, and cut the pears in ½ inch/1.25 cm wedges. Melt half the butter. Add the pears and sprinkle with one third of the sugar and the lemon juice. Sauté briskly, turning the pears occasionally, until they are just tender, 7–12 minutes, depending on their ripeness. Lift out and drain them, reserving the juice.

Sift the flour and baking powder together on to a work surface. Make a well in the centre and add the remaining butter, remaining sugar, egg yolks, milk and vanilla. Mix the ingredients with your fingertips until the sugar is dissolved. Pour the mixture into the prepared mould and arrange the pears overlapping in concentric circles on top. Bake the cake in the heated oven until brown and starting to shrink at the edges, 30–40 minutes.

Meanwhile boil the reserved pear juice until reduced and syrupy. Shortly before the cake is done, brush the top with the juice and continue cooking until glazed and shiny, about 5 minutes. Let it cool a few minutes in the mould, then transfer to a rack to cool. The cake is best eaten the day of baking, but can be kept a day or two in an airtight container.

Sorbet Normande
APPLE SORBET WITH CALVADOS

The tarter the apples, the better the sorbet, and to extract their full flavour, in this recipe the apple cores and skins are simmered in syrup. Sugar should be added to taste: just a little if the sorbet is served in the middle of the meal, more if it is served as dessert.

Makes 3¼ pints/2 quarts/2 litres sorbet to serve 8–10
2 large Granny Smith apples, cut in ½ inch/1.25 cm dice
2⅓ pints/1½ quarts/1.5 litres water
8 oz/1¼ cups/250 g sugar, or to taste
stick of cinnamon
4 fl oz/½ cup/125 ml lemon juice
5 fl oz/⅔ cup/150 ml Calvados
ice cream churn

In a saucepan heat the apples, water, sugar and cinnamon stick, stirring occasionally until the sugar is dissolved. Cover and simmer for 10–15 minutes until the apples are softened

to a pulp. Work the mixture through a sieve, reserving the cinnamon stick to use again. Stir in the lemon juice and Calvados and taste the mixture, adding more sugar if needed.

Chill the mixture, then freeze in the ice cream churn. Transfer the sorbet to a chilled container, cover and store in a freezer. Sorbet is best eaten within 24 hours. If storing longer, let it soften in the refrigerator 1–2 hours before serving.

Pommes au Pommeau
APPLES IN LIQUEUR

For these baked apples in syrup, be sure to use a variety that holds its shape during cooking, such as Delicious or the Norman 'Calville'. As Pommeau is only available in Normandy, you can use one part Calvados to two parts apple juice for this recipe.

Serves 4
3¼ oz/½ cup/100 g sugar, more if needed
1⅔ pints/1 quart/1 litre water
8 fl oz/1 cup/250 ml Pommeau
8 cloves
stick of cinnamon
strip of lemon peel
juice of ½ lemon
4 large or 6 medium apples, peeled, cored and halved

Preheat the oven to No 2/300°F/150°C. Put the sugar, water, Pommeau, cloves, cinnamon, lemon peel and juice into a casserole or heatproof dish and stir to dissolve the sugar. Bring nearly to the boil. Add the apples, with a heatproof plate on top to weigh them down, and cover tightly. Poach in the oven for 30–45 minutes until the apples are very tender but still hold their shape. Cooking time varies very much with their ripeness.

Let the apples cool in the syrup then transfer them to a serving dish. In a saucepan boil the syrup until reduced and slightly thick, 30–45 minutes. Taste it, adding more sugar if needed, and strain it over the apples. They can be kept 2–3 days in the refrigerator, but should be served at room temperature. They are delicious, Norman-style, with crème Chantilly (p. 183) or crème fraîche (p. 183).

Le Bugue on the Vézère river.

PERIGORD

Driving east from Bordeaux and deep into the Dordogne, to the black, white and green earth of a region made paradise by truffles, walnut oil and foie gras

Stony, infertile, riddled with ravines and river valleys, Périgord is not at first glance the most desirable part of France. But look more closely; it was in the sheltered caves of Périgord that prehistoric man was inspired to draw the great frescoes. It was over this territory that the English and French warred for 300 years, leaving ruined castles and fortified towns as witness to their struggle. And most importantly, Périgord produces black gold, the mysterious truffle which to this day has not been cultivated with any success. When combined with the famous geese, results are celestial. 'The earth of Périgord is paved with truffles and transformed into paradise by foie gras,' exclaimed a local bard.

Geographers refer to eastern Périgord as Noir, black from the thickness of its forests, and to northern Périgord as

The bridge at Brantôme over the Dronne river in Périgord.

cellar of beautifully displayed cheeses, as well as row upon row of good wines to drink with your meal. Just to confuse you, many St Emilion growths are labelled 'grand cru classé', a much-coveted designation in neighbouring Médoc. In St Emilion it may not mean much at all.

Following the Dordogne river to the east you enter Périgord proper at Ste-Foy-la-Grande, a local centre for vineyard and orchard produce. Ste-Foy is a bastide – one of the many planned towns which still survive from the 13th and 14th centuries when both the French and English built feverishly in an attempt to secure disputed territory. Settlers were exempt from military service and granted rights of succession. Like many bastides, Ste-Foy is built on a grid plan and has ramparts beside the river as well as streets dotted with gems of medieval and Renaissance architecture. The Grand Hotel in the rue de la République offers country comfort and simple cuisine. However we were lucky enough to be the guests of Madame Laroche in nearby Mussidan.

We were greeted in a pretty, creeper-covered 'gentilhommière', a little manor house. Madame offered us tea and her own deliciously moist almond cake. Later, basking in the evening sun, we sipped a glass of chilled golden-rich Montbazillac wine and tasted Madame's foie gras. To a visitor, country France is reassuringly rooted in tradition, but not so for the inhabitants. 'It's a constant struggle,' laments Madame, 'life changes so fast.' We heard of the difficulty of finding tenants for the little farmhouse, tenants who could rear geese in the old way and help prepare confits, pâtés and rillettes. The immigrant Portuguese community is too busy working in the strawberry fields, while the French population of the village has been steadily declining.

Blanc, white from its limestone rocks and dusty soil. To this one might add a 'Périgord Vert', for there are lush green fields along the river valleys, particularly on the Dordogne and the Isle. On the confines of Périgord rises St Emilion, an enchanted town with its buildings of silvery stone amidst rustling vines. They were first planted in the time of the Roman governor and poet Ausonius; the vineyard at Château Ausone still ranks as one of the top in Bordeaux.

After a tedious exit from nearby Bordeaux, St Emilion provides an instant immersion in rural France. Vinous odours rise from cool cellars hewn out of the soft rock, as they have done for centuries. Through an open door you may glimpse a cooper shaving staves or heating a barrel over an open fire to make it watertight. Busy trucks laden with protective wooden boxes, packed with bottles nestling neck to bottom, are still used for exporting quality wines from these parts. Bordeaux has a tradition of shipping wine long distances by sea, with careful packing required.

St Emilion is famous for macaroons, at their best Chez Germaine, a modest restaurant on the Place Créneaux, which also sells macaroons to take away. For more substantial refreshment, make your way to the enterprising Boutique Fromagère on the rue de la Grande Fontaine. Half shop, half restaurant, the boutique offers a help-yourself

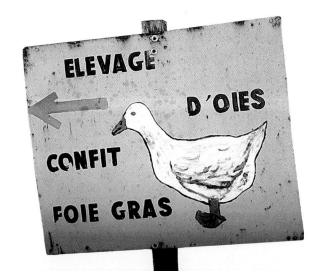

A fattened goose is a valuable prize even after the foie gras has been removed. The carcass is delicious roasted whole, yielding crisp golden skin and quantities of white fat for frying the world's best potatoes. (So sought-after is goose fat that you can buy it in tins/cans.) The meat from a fattened goose makes the finest of 'rillettes', a coarse, rich pâté baked in a closed pot until the meat is falling from the bone. Goose feathers go into pillows and the feet are dissolved for glue. Locals particularly appreciate the neck skin, which forms a lusciously rich sausage when stuffed with goose trimmings, pork and bits of liver. 'With a neck of goose, a loaf of bread and a bottle of wine, you can invite your neighbour to a feast,' they say.

However, fattened goose is so costly that the meat is usually removed in pieces, the breast to be sold fresh or smoked as 'magret' and the leg to be made into 'confit'. How long it has taken the culinary mainstream to discover this ancient method of preserving meat! Confit has existed for centuries, yet only in the last 30 years has it spread from southwestern France to kitchens as far afield as London, New York, and Tokyo. The principle is simple: the meat is salted – up to 3 days if it is to be used as a flavouring, 1–2 days for eating alone – then tightly covered and baked with a minimum of seasoning until meltingly tender.

The long slow cooking destroys bacteria, so that when packed in a crock and sealed with fat, confit can be kept for months in a cool place. One month is a minimum for the flavour to mellow. Fatty meats such as duck, goose and pork do best in confit, but in southwestern France you'll also find oddities like duck gizzard and pig's tail or tongue preserved

A vineyard in Fronsac, above the Dordogne river.

149

this way. Nutty and rich as the finest ham, confit is also a handy flavouring, adding indispensable patina to new-style salads of cabbage or green beans as well as traditional dishes like 'cassoulet' (p. 71). 'It's as integral a part of current cooking as foie gras,' remarked one chef to me.

Bergerac, only a few miles from Mussidan, is famous for its Wednesday and Saturday market in the streets around the church. Big fairs are held at Martinmas (11 November) and in mid-April. Each season brings its temptations – in spring the first little onions and shallots (the local preference), sorrel and asparagus; in early summer strawberries and mild garlic; in autumn, hazelnuts, chestnuts, and roots like salsify and celery to marry with wild partridge and boar during their all-too-short season; at Christmas, the finest poultry, foie gras and truffles. In the back streets of most market towns you may find an old-style bistro – a drinking house serving food cooked by the patron, while his wife tends the bar. Customers are regulars, collecting their rolled napkin from its pigeonhole on the wall, and sitting at paper-covered tables to a fixed menu of dishes like 'mique', a boiled dumpling of wheat and cornmeal served with cabbage, or 'enchaud Périgourdin', pot-roast pork liberally flavoured with garlic and herbs. A common custom is to 'faire chabrol', by adding a dash of red wine to the dregs of soup and drinking it out of the bowl.

The route east from Bergerac along the Dordogne is a traveller's delight. Placid and lush for the first few miles, after Lalinde the river becomes wilder and more picturesque, with wooded islets, stony beaches and long curves, sometimes overhung with rocky cliffs crowned with a romantic castle. Trémolat, with its twisting streets and massive fortress of a church entwined in two great bends, was the setting for Claude Chabrol's film 'Le Boucher'. You will eat well at Le Vieux Logis on such dishes as 'daube' of chicken with artichokes and foie gras.

Here a detour is tempting, following the more intimate valley of the Vézère via le Bugue to Les Eyzies. The limestone cliffs are riddled with caves dating from prehistoric times, for the countryside is hospitable, the water plentiful and the climate mild. It was 60 or 70 years ago that restaurants in this area were discovered by Curnonsky, whose pioneer series of guidebooks helped make travel and food writing an entertaining and respected career in France. He describes a visit to one of the caves at Les Eyzies where

Opposite: Near Sorges, in truffle country.

The walnut mill at Ste Nathalène where oil is made by traditional methods.

the pretty ankles of the barefooted guide were so distracting that his substantial frame became wedged in a narrow rocky passage. Like any serious gastronome of the day, Curnonsky was rotund. In Les Eyzies, I myself feasted on a menu of truffles with scrambled eggs, baked trout with herbs, and mouth-watering walnut tart at the Cro-Magnon restaurant. Just down the road, the recently acclaimed Le Centénaire was offering ravioli filled with snails and smoked goose and risotto with foie gras. What a happy dilemma!

A bit further off the tourist track to the southeast of Les Eyzies is the hill-top village of Marquay, where Madame Dalbavil, the charming owner of the Hôtel des Bories, preserves her own duck and goose confits as well as taking charge of the day-to-day fare. Far from routine was the 'tourin', a clear garlic and tomato soup that formed the classic opening to a delicious meal. 'Have you made soup?' is a

local way of asking whether you have eaten lunch. Vegetable-based 'tourins' are many and varied. As well as Madame's quick tomato-based version, a 'tourin' may be white, flavoured with onion and enriched with cream, or green and sharp with sorrel. In winter, root vegetables give body. Key to them all is goose fat, with a few slivers of confit if you wish to intensify the flavour.

Back on the main road, Sarlat is a distinguished town, headquarters for the English during the Hundred Years' War. The tall carved stone façades, many of them medieval and Renaissance, attest to centuries of prosperity and form an operatic backdrop to the famous Saturday market. The last time I was there it poured with rain, driving the stall-holders under a huddle of tarpaulins and dripping umbrellas. I prefer to remember a faraway sunlit autumn day when fattened livers, ochre, pink and beige, were laid out by the dozen on bare trestle tables, flanked by bushel baskets of craggy fresh truffles, brown with earth. (Only years later, on a visit to the luxury stores around the Madeleine in Paris, did I realise how much wealth was inherent in this casual display.) At almost any time of year Sarlat is a great place for wild mushrooms – with luck you might find rarities like wrinkled black morels, second only to truffles in intensity of taste, or frail 'mousserons' (fairy ring mushrooms) which are too delicate to ship far from where they grow.

Sarlat is capital of the Périgord Noir, which is dense with trees, notably the walnut. The Dordogne department ranks as the largest producer in France, together with the Isère, east of the Rhône valley. With their high oil content and earthy taste, walnuts are almost as versatile as the almond. They feature in desserts from walnut cake to walnut ice cream and walnut tart (p. 91). They make good soup, add crunch to salads and are excellent with pork and duck. The French like to eat their walnuts juicy and scarcely ripe, when they are still covered with their green husk (beware of the juice, which stains your hands an indelible brown). Périgourdin cooks also pickle walnuts in mouth-puckering sour grape juice, or verjuice. This ancient flavouring, the forerunner of lemon juice, is still used in Périgord for sprinkling on salads or on sautéed foie gras and fish.

Walnut oil is almost as important in cooking as the nut itself. Once it was so cheap in these parts that it was used as lamp oil. Today, if you find a cheap bottle, read the label carefully as the chances are it is diluted. Most walnut oil is factory-pressed, but just east of Sarlat, at Ste Nathalène, a traditional water mill is still in commission. A glorious perfume of crushed walnuts pervades the 16th-century stone buildings. The process is simple enough: the kernels are ground to a paste between stone wheels, then heated over a

Trompettes de Mort, one of Périgord's commoner wild mushroom varieties.

wood fire to extract any remaining oil before being pressed with two wooden blocks between layers of jute. Cloudy at first, the oil is left to stand for three days before being decanted and strained. Walnut oil has long been favoured for vinaigrette dressing, particularly with sherry or balsamic vinegar, and is now in vogue for sautéing vegetables and fish. 'It's delicious with prawns and shellfish,' beams the mill owner, Jean Pierre Bordier.

Continuing south from Ste Nathalène, the road winds down to Carlux and the Dordogne river, source of lamprey as well as salmon, pike and eel. Carp is sometimes stuffed luxuriously with foie gras, while gudgeon, baby roach and barbel are tossed in flour to deep-fry as 'friture Périgourdine'. High above the bridge near Carlux towers the Château de Rouffilhac, while westwards along the D703, the romantic castle of Montfort is just one of several mighty

A 'gariotte' or traditional storage hut.

diverted so the magnificent cathedral of Saint-Front and the winding streets around the place du Coderc can be better appreciated. In culinary parlance, 'périgueux' denotes truffles and in traditional restaurants you may still find 'sauce périgueux', a Madeira sauce flavoured with truffles and truffle juice, served with your tournedos steak. Northeast of Périgueux is prime truffle country; drive out on the little D8 road to Sorges and you arrive on the limestone plateau or 'causse' of the Périgord Blanc.

At the Maison de la Truffe in Sorge a video will fill you in on the biology of 'tuber melanosporum' though any hopes of finding a truffle for yourself near its favourite habitat of oak, blackthorn, juniper, spindle or dogwood trees is in fact forlorn. A trained dog or pig is indispensable for any serious detective work, though some treasure hunters claim they simply follow the silvery wings of the truffle fly and dig wherever it hovers. During the season from November to early April you are quite likely to encounter a truffle hunter with his stout pig (sows are most astute) and pointed stick at the ready to restrain the 'hound' from guzzling its quarry. A truffle may range in size from a hazelnut to a child's fist. Traditional decoy is a handful of maize, but on one expedition, our host rewarded his sow with a handful of Smarties each time she rooted a truffle from the ground!

Efforts to cultivate truffles continue both in France and the USA but with scant success. Meanwhile the crop diminishes and prices rise with almost every season. 'Dinde truffée', a Christmas turkey dating from the days when truffles were bought by the kilo rather than the gram, is now a millionaire's treat. A more affordable alternative is to make do with a warm salad of potatoes dressed with white wine and walnut oil, topped with slices of truffle. Slivers of truffle may be inserted into a 'magret' breast of duck – a natural marriage of richness and intensity of taste – or less expensive truffle peelings may be added to a sauce. Canned or frozen truffles lack the amazing heavy pungency of fresh and are a waste of money in my view, useful only for adding a dense black contrast to aspic decorations. But a fresh truffle, once tasted, is never forgotten. If you leave one in a basket of eggs, the aroma will penetrate the shells and flavour the egg within. With the autoroute, airport and high speed trains of Bordeaux only an hour away from Périgueux, what better souvenir could you take home than a single nugget of Périgord's black gold?

fortresses guarding the river. Until the late 19th century great flat-bottomed boats were used to transport wood and cheese from the Auvergne to the Atlantic. The water highway was safer than the road, though it is hard to believe this now, looking at the tricky bends and turbulent water. Montfort is a microcosm of local history, having been taken by storm four times, initially by Simon de Montfort in 1241. Its impressive pile is an endearing muddle of 15th-, 16th- and 19th-century buildings.

The circuit of Les Eyzies, Sarlat and Montfort completed, you arrive back at le Bugue and bid goodbye to the river to head north to Périgueux. The road is unremarkable, a pleasant meander through woods and fields marking the transition between Périgord Noir and the more spartan terrain of Périgord Blanc to the north. With luck you will spot a timbered pigeonhouse, or perhaps a 'gariotte' – an odd little conical storage hut built entirely from flat stones without any mortar. Look too for roadside potteries selling glazed earthenware garden pots, and for beekeepers selling dark, smoky honey flavoured with chestnut flowers. This is a tobaccogrowing area, and in early autumn you'll see the big-leaved plants growing as tall as a teenager. Their cultivation is described in the museum of tobacco at Bergerac.

Périgueux itself has undergone a face-lift, its chaotic traffic

RECIPES FROM PERIGORD

Le Tourin
— TOMATO AND GARLIC SOUP —

Some 'tourin' soups need long simmering, but this summer recipe is quick to make with a delightfully fresh flavour. For body, you may like to add a few slivers of confit or, for a lighter soup, the bread croûtes may be replaced by vermicelli, simmered a few minutes in the broth.

Serves 4
3 tbsp goose fat
2 onions, chopped
6 cloves garlic, thinly sliced
salt and pepper
½ oz/2 tbsp/15 g flour
1 lb/500 g tomatoes, peeled, seeded and chopped (p. 186)
16 fl oz/1 quart/1 litre water, more if needed
bouquet garni (p. 183)
12–18 toasted croûtes (p. 183)
pinch of cayenne

Heat the fat in a large saucepan and add the onions, garlic, salt and pepper. Press a piece of foil on top and cook gently until the onions are soft, 10–15 minutes. Note: do not let them brown. Stir in the flour, add the tomatoes and leave to cook for 2 minutes. Add the water, bouquet garni, salt and pepper, and simmer, uncovered, 25–30 minutes. Add more water if the soup evaporates too much.

Meanwhile toast the croûtes and put 2–3 in each soup bowl. Taste the soup for seasoning, adding cayenne, salt and pepper, spoon it into bowls and serve very hot.

Saumon et Celeris à l'Huile de Noix
— SALMON WITH CELERY AND WALNUT OIL —

This contemporary recipe calls for salmon, depicted in local prehistoric cave paintings and now reappearing in the Dordogne river, thanks to conservation efforts. The best walnut oil is expensive but you need only a little as the flavour is strong.

Serves 4
1¼ lb/625 g salmon fillet, or 4 salmon steaks
2 cloves garlic, finely chopped
4 tbsp chopped, mixed herbs
(chives, chervil, tarragon, parsley)
2 tbsp white wine
4 fl oz/½ cup/125 ml walnut oil
salt and pepper
small head celery (about 12 oz/375 g)
trimmed and cut in julienne (p. 184)
3 tbsp double/heavy cream
2 oz/¼ cup/60 g cold butter, cut in pieces
1 tsp lemon juice, or to taste

If using salmon fillet, cut it into 4 even diagonal slices about ½ inch/1.25 cm thick ('escalopes'); if using steaks, leave them whole. In a shallow dish, mix the garlic, herbs, wine, half of the oil, the salt and pepper. Lay the salmon escalopes on top, turning them so they are well coated. Cover and leave to marinate at room temperature ½–1 hour.

Meanwhile, preheat the oven to No 10/500°F/260°C. Blanch (p. 182) the celery, drain and rinse it under cold water.

Lightly oil a baking dish, lay the celery on top and sprinkle with salt and pepper. Top with the salmon escalopes or steaks (they should not overlap). Bake them in the oven until the salmon no longer looks transparent, 6–8 minutes. Note: the salmon should remain slightly transparent in the centre as it will continue cooking in its own heat. Transfer the fish to individual serving plates, arrange the celery beside it, and keep warm.

Meanwhile, put the marinade in a small saucepan; add the cream and boil until reduced to a glaze (p. 184), 2–3 minutes. Whisk in the butter a few pieces at a time, working on and off the heat so it softens creamily without melting to oil. Take the pan from the heat and whisk in the remaining oil in a slow, steady stream. Add the lemon juice and taste for seasoning. Spoon the sauce around the fish and serve immediately.

Périgord produces the finest goose fat, goose feathers and foie gras.

Rillettes d'Oie
GOOSE RILLETTES

The finest 'rillettes' consist of pure goose or duck, though they can be stretched by adding pork, preferably from the shoulder, in up to equal quantities. A high proportion of fat is essential (found naturally in fattened birds) and quality is important, as a minimum of seasoning is added so as not to disguise flavour. Any pork must be carefully trimmed so it can be simply pulled apart with two forks after cooking, producing the characteristically soft, rough texture of homemade rillettes.

Serves 12–16
2 lb/1 kg boneless pork shoulder
8–9 lb/3.6–4.1 kg whole goose, cut in 8 pieces (p. 183)
⅔ oz/1 tbsp/20 g salt
⅓ oz/1½ tsp/10 g ground pepper
1 tsp allspice
2 sprigs thyme
2 sprigs rosemary
3 bay leaves
16 fl oz/2 cups/500 ml water

Heat the oven to No ½/250°F/120°C. Cut the pork in 3 inch/7.5 cm cubes. Combine the goose and pork in a heavy pot, layering the pieces with the salt, pepper, allspice, thyme, rosemary and bay leaves and pouring on the water. Mix with your hands and press the meat down lightly. Cover tightly and cook in the oven, stirring occasionally, for 5–6 hours or until the meat is very tender and falling from the bones. The fat should be clear and all the water will have evaporated. Note: rillettes should cook very slowly – never let them boil.

Drain the meat, discarding the bay leaves. Reserve the fat and leave it to cool. Shred the meat with two forks, discarding bones and tough goose skin. When the fat is cool, mix half of it with the meat and taste the rillettes. Note: they should be quite highly seasoned. Pack the rillettes into glass jars or stone crocks and pour over enough of the fat to cover. If well sealed with fat, rillettes can be kept in the refrigerator for up to 4 weeks. Scrape or melt off excess fat before serving with country bread.

Magrets de Canard aux Cerises
DUCK BREASTS WITH CHERRIES

More and more markets are selling boneless duck breasts ('magrets'), or you can cut them yourself from a whole duck, reserving the legs for confit. I like to leave the skin, but if you prefer very lean meat, it can be removed before sautéing. Serve duck breasts rare, just like steak, as they are tough if well done. Sour cherries are classic for this dish, so if you use sweet ones omit the sugar and add a squeeze of lemon juice, or better still a handful of fresh redcurrants. Their acidity adds delicious bite to the sauce.

Serves 2
8 oz/250 g tart cherries
8 fl oz/1 cup/250 ml port wine
1 oz/2 tbsp/30 g sugar, more if needed
2 duck breasts
salt and pepper
1 tbsp butter
1 tbsp brown sugar
2 tbsp wine vinegar
4 fl oz/½ cup/125 ml duck or chicken stock (p. 186)
1 tsp arrowroot, dissolved (p. 182) in 1–2 tbsp water

Stone/pit the cherries and put them in a pan with the port and sugar. Stir, then leave 1–2 hours or until the juice runs.

To finish: simmer the cherries in their liquid until tender, 5–7 minutes. Score the skin on the duck breasts down to the meat and season both sides. Heat the butter in a heavy frying pan. Add the duck breasts skin side down and sauté briskly like a steak until most of the fat is rendered and the skin is crisp, 3–4 minutes, or 2–3 minutes if the skin has been discarded. Turn and brown the other side, allowing 2–3 minutes for rare meat. Remove the breasts and keep warm.

Discard fat from the pan. Stir in brown sugar and cook until it begins to caramelize. Add the vinegar, standing back as it will vaporize and sting your eyes. Stir to deglaze the pan juices, then add the liquid from the cherries and the stock. Bring the liquid to the boil and stir in the arrowroot paste, adding just enough to thicken the sauce lightly. Add the cherries to reheat them and taste the sauce for seasoning.

Cut each breast into thin diagonal slices and arrange them overlapping on warm serving plates. Spoon a little sauce on top, with the cherries at the side. Serve at once.

Confit de Canard

PRESERVED DUCK

'Confit' of duck or goose may be taken off the bone and used, like ham, to flavour soup and vegetable dishes, or a leg may be served alone, baked in the oven so the skin is temptingly crisp. 'Pommes Sarlardaises' – potatoes fried golden brown in goose fat and redolent with garlic – are the classic accompaniment. A galette of potatoes and wild mushrooms (below) or a purée of sorrel or spinach are alternatives.

Serves 4 as a main dish
a 4–5 lb/1.8–2.3 kg duck, cut into 4 pieces (p. 183)
3 tbsp coarse salt
1 tsp black pepper
2–3 sprigs fresh or dried thyme
2–3 bay leaves, crumbled
3 lb/1.4 kg lard, more if needed
salt and pepper

Rub each piece of duck with some of the salt and put the pieces in a bowl. Sprinkle with the remaining salt and pepper, and add the thyme and bay leaves. Cover and refrigerate, turning the pieces occasionally, for 12–24 hours, depending on how strong a flavour you want.

Wipe the duck pieces with paper towels. Heat the oven to No 2/300°F/150°C. Lay the duck pieces, skin side down, in a frying pan and fry gently for 15–20 minutes so that the fat runs and they brown evenly. Pack them in a small casserole and add enough melted lard to cover them. Cover with a lid and cook in the oven until the duck is very tender and has rendered all its fat, about 2 hours. The meat should be almost falling from the bone. Let it cool slightly.

To preserve the duck: pour a layer of the rendered fat into the base of a preserving jar or small terrine. Pack the pieces of duck on top and pour over enough fat to cover them completely, adding more melted lard if necessary. Cover and refrigerate for at least a week to allow the flavour to mellow. If sealed with a cloth sprinkled with salt and tightly covered, confit will keep for several months.

To serve the confit: heat the oven to No 6/400°F/200°C. Extract the pieces of duck, wiping off excess fat, and put them in a shallow baking dish. Bake them in the oven for 5 minutes, then pour off any melted fat. Continue baking until they are very hot and the skin is crisp, 10–15 minutes.

Salade de Chou Rouge au Confit de Canard

RED CABBAGE SALAD

The crispness of red cabbage and the melting richness of duck confit make an excellent marriage, a hearty appetizer for cold weather.

Serves 4–6 as an appetizer
4 pieces of duck confit (see recipe above)
1 small head (about 1 lb/500 g) red cabbage
2 fl oz/¼ cup/60 ml red wine vinegar, more if needed
3¼ pints/2 quarts/2 litres water
vinaigrette dressing (p. 187) made with 4 tbsp red wine vinegar, salt, pepper, 1 tbsp Dijon mustard, and 6 fl oz/¾ cup/175 ml walnut oil
4 oz/1 cup/125 g walnuts

Bake the confit in the oven until hot and crisp. Quarter the cabbage, and cut out the core. Very finely shred the leaves lengthwise with a knife to obtain long strips. Put the strips in a bowl. Bring the vinegar to the boil, pour it over the shredded cabbage and mix well. Bring the water to the boil and pour over the cabbage. Let soak until the cabbage is slightly softened, 1–2 minutes, then drain it. The cabbage can be prepared 3–4 hours ahead and kept covered at room temperature.

Make the vinaigrette dressing. Just before serving mix the cabbage with the walnuts and enough dressing to moisten well. Taste for seasoning, adding more vinegar if necessary. Pile the cabbage on individual plates. With two forks, pull the confit from the bones into coarse shreds. Scatter the shreds over the cabbage and serve while still warm.

Salade de Chou Rouge au Confit de Canard.

Galette de Pommes de Terre aux Champignons Sauvages

—————— POTATO GALETTE WITH WILD MUSHROOMS ——————

This galette was layered with fresh truffles in the days when they were cheap, but I've found other fungi, particularly cèpes, a quite acceptable substitute. Even cultivated mushrooms enliven an otherwise plain fried potato cake.

Serves 3

6 oz/175 g wild mushrooms, cleaned (p. 187)
2½ oz/⅓ cup/75 g goose fat or olive oil
salt and pepper
2–3 cloves garlic, chopped
2 shallots, chopped
2 tbsp parsley, chopped
1 lb/500 g potatoes, peeled
8 inch/20 cm heavy frying pan

Cut the mushrooms in large pieces. Heat 2 tablespoons of the fat or oil in a frying pan and add the mushrooms, salt and pepper. Sauté briskly, stirring, until the mushrooms are tender and all moisture has evaporated; cooking time varies with the type of mushroom. Stir in the garlic, shallots and parsley and taste for seasoning.

Preheat the oven to No 5/375°F/190°C. Cut the potatoes in ⅛ inch/3 mm slices, if possible using a mandolin slicer or a food processor. Heat 2 tablespoons of the fat or oil in the frying pan for 1 minute. Remove and arrange half the potato slices overlapping in circles. Sprinkle them with salt and pepper and spread the mushrooms on top. Cover the mushrooms with the remaining potatoes and spoon over the remaining fat. Press a piece of foil with a weight on top.

Cook the galette on top of the stove until the underside starts to brown, 5–8 minutes. Transfer it to the heated oven and continue cooking for 15–20 minutes until the potatoes are tender.

Remove the foil and weight and flip the galette in the pan. Alternatively, slide it on to a plate, then tip it back into the pan. Continue cooking it until the underside is brown. It is best served at once, though it can also be reheated.

Gâteau Frangipane

—————— ALMOND SPONGE CAKE ——————

Deliciously moist, this cake may be topped with a simple dusting of powdered sugar, or with glacé icing flavoured with ratafia. When the ratafia is based on red grape juice, the icing shades to a dusty designer pink.

Serves 4

8 oz/2 cups/250 g ground blanched almonds
6½ oz/1 cup/200 g sugar
4 eggs
2 egg whites
5 oz/⅔ cup/150 g unsalted butter, melted
2 tbsp cornflour/starch
1 tsp orange flower water, or few drops/½ tsp vanilla
For the icing
5 oz/1½ cups/150 g icing/confectioners' sugar,
more if needed
3 tbsp ratafia, or 3 tbsp water with a few drops/½ tsp vanilla
9 inch/23 cm springform pan or straight-sided cake tin/pan

Preheat the oven to No 3/325°F/160°C. Butter the cake tin/pan, line it with a round of greaseproof/wax paper and butter the paper.

In a food processor, work the almonds with the sugar until mixed. With motor running, add the whole eggs, one by one, then the egg whites. Work for 5 minutes, then transfer

the batter to a bowl. Fold in the melted butter with a wooden spatula, then fold in the cornflour/starch and orange flower water or vanilla.

Pour the batter into the prepared pan and bake in the heated oven 40–45 minutes until the cake is firm to the touch in the centre and shrinks slightly from the sides of the pan. Transfer it to a rack to cool. The cake can be stored in an airtight container up to a week.

For the icing: sift the sugar into a small bowl and stir in the ratafia or water and vanilla. Heat the bowl in a water bath (p. 187) until the icing is tepid. It should coat the back of a spoon. If too thick add a little more liquid; if too thin beat in more sifted sugar. Set the cooled cake on a rack, pour over the icing and spread it quickly with a palette knife so it drips down the sides. Leave it to cool and set, then transfer it to a serving plate.

Galette de Pommes de Terre aux Champignons Sauvages.

The imposing château at Grignan, a Provençal home to Madame de Sévigné.

PROVENCE

Through the mountains of the Lubéron to the 'explosive' food of the south, lavender honey, garrigues-fed lamb, and a profusion of garlic, wild herbs and fruity olive oil

If Normandy seems like home, Provence for me is high excitement. The sun, the smells, the flavours of the food bombard the senses. 'The partridges are all fed with thyme, marjoram and every ingredient that enters into the composition of our perfume bags,' wrote Madame de Sévigné in 1694. . . . 'As for the melons, figs, and muscadine grapes, it is really wonderful. If from any strange whim we should wish to find a *bad* melon we should be obliged to send for it from Paris for no such can be found here. There are sweet white figs, muscadine grapes like grains of amber which you may devour until they almost intoxicate you . . . What a life, my dear cousin!'

Madame de Sévigné wrote this letter from Grignan, which is on the very edge of Provence, just southeast of Mon-

Both green and black olives are inedible until cured.

Opposite: The landscape near Nyons – groves of fruit trees, olives and vines, interspersed with fields of wheat.

télimar. She spent many summers in the imposing château, which has changed little since her day. The panoramic view from the terrace of the château high above the town with its elegant stone façades gives you an idea of what's to come in this land of sun, stone and olive trees. The dairy land of milk and butter lies behind to the north; from now on olive oil is the characteristic cooking medium, the signature of the south.

Heading east from Grignan towards Nyons, already the crops are Provençal, with groves of fruit trees, olives and vines, interspersed with fields of wheat. These are four key products of the region. With a sharp eye you may spot a 'truffière' – a patch of stunted oaks standing in well-cleaned ground to encourage the growth of the treasured fungus. In the winter season, high quality black truffles, just as good as those of Périgord, adorn the market stalls of Nyons as well as such towns as Apt, Tricastin and Carpentras.

In Nyons, you can view local products at the Tourist Office, or better still a few steps away at the Moulin Jacques Ramade. This traditional olive oil mill, dating from the 1900s, is put to work each winter. After the first frost, the olives are picked by hand when black and ripe. The tree is shaken and the branches raked with combs so that the fruit falls into nets below. At the mill, a stone wheel layered with round mats called 'scortins' (once made of sisal, now of nylon) grinds them to a paste from which the oil is separated by centrifuge. This is the finest cold-pressed olive oil, known as 'vièrge' or 'extra vièrge' (terms are regrettably imprecise). Over 10 lbs of olives are needed to produce a litre. More can be extracted from the pulp through the application of heat and chemicals, but later pressings are inferior, producing a

bland oil that is sometimes harsh. The best extra vièrge is a dark gold green with a full, fruity flavour; in Provence food stores offer several vintages, and the chance to taste and compare as if it were wine. Virgin oil complements the robust Provençal ingredients, but a little goes a long way. Away from the Mediterranean it can be overwhelming.

Olives for eating may be picked ripe (black) or unripe (green) but either way they are are inedible until they are cured, as Racine learned the hard way in 1661: 'I hope to goodness I never taste anything so bitter again!' Nyons is best known for its green and black olives packed in jars, sometimes in brine, sometimes dry-packed with herbs after salting. The local 'tanche' variety is juicy and plump, in contrast to the famous little black olive from the coast around Nice. Niçois olives have little flesh but a particularly piquant taste, ideal for 'tapenade', the pungent Provençale purée of olives, anchovy, and capers that is served on bread, with hardboiled eggs, or with vegetable sticks. 'Anchoïade' is an equally strong concoction. Like tapenade, it dates back to Roman times and is basically a sauce of anchovy and garlic simmered in olive oil for dipping with sticks of celery or the local favourite, the thistle-like cardoon.

Heading south from Nyons to Carpentras the geography of Provence unfolds – in effect, a series of crested mountains running east to west like waves, with fertile valleys between. The first range is the Baronnies, then come the Dentelles de Montmirail dominated by the eerie peak of Mont Ventoux, visible for many miles. The summit is always white, whether with snow in winter or with barren rock, stripped of vegetation, in summer. The road passes through Vaison-la-Romaine, with its Roman ruins, and many an attractive fortified village to left and right.

At Carpentras itself the landscape widens to reveal the riches of Provence. You are in the centre of the former Comtat Venaissin, which was a papal possession until 1791. It was Pope Clement V, archbishop of Bordeaux around 1300, who saw to the planting of great vineyards like Châteauneuf-du-Pape. Today, production in the area includes full-bodied Tavel rosé, and rich red Gigondas and Cornas, now very much in vogue. Not to be missed is the languorous white muscat wine from Beaume de Venise, just north of Carpentras. Drunk as an aperitif, it is a treasure in the kitchen, excellent for sorbet, for marinating fruits, and for flavouring sabayon. One homemade speciality is 'vin cuit', reserved for family celebrations and festivals such as Christmas. This 'cooked wine' is made during the grape harvest by boiling down unfermented grape juice to concentrate the natural sugars, and then adding a little of the already fermenting new wine. The result is sweet and potent.

The stretch from Carpentras south to Cavaillon and beyond is one of the great fruit and vegetable gardens of France. Fancy irrigation systems and trim little villas, many surrounded by plastic greenhouses shielding lettuces and early vegetables, all suggest that money is in the making. The fertile soil has indeed brought profit to the region, but only since the advent of the railways, which revolutionized transport to Paris and the north. Before that, Provence was poor; vegetables were the staple diet, eaten boiled and dressed with vinaigrette, to be followed by a soup made with the vegetable water. Vegetables with hardboiled eggs are still eaten as a main course, accompanied by 'aïoli', garlic mayonnaise. At summer village fêtes centred around a bullfight or a donkey race, the platter is scaled up to an 'aïoli monstre' to serve a crowd. Other complete vegetable meals include 'tian', a mixture of vegetables often bound with egg custard and named after the deep terracotta dish in which they are baked. The locals also stuff artichokes with black olives 'à la barigoule' ('farigoule' is Provençal for thyme), and enjoy a tall aubergine/eggplant, tomato and onion mould called 'papeton', evoking the shape of a pope's tiara.

The town of Cavaillon is synonymous with melons, the best in the world in my opinion. Alexandre Dumas loved Cavaillon melons so much that when he heard the town library could not afford his books, he sent them a consignment in return for 12 melons a year. Small, sweet, orange-fleshed with a greenish yellow skin, a good Cavaillon melon is recognizable by its perfume and heaviness in the hand. Female melons, with a large round scar where the flower has fallen, are said to be sweeter than the smaller-scarred male. Some experts say that the best melons are like wine grapes, traceable to a particular slope or grove. The main enemy is the mistral, the north wind which whips furiously down the Rhône valley for days on end. Hence the characteristic windbreaks of cypress, reed and lime/linden which break up the Provençal farmscape.

Cavaillon itself is an undistinguished modern town. For true Provençal ambiance, you should branch east and cross the wide dusty bed of the Rhône to St Rémy de Provence.

Here the Saturday market is outstanding, spilling out from the main square into the surrounding streets. On the Place Péllissier are three handy shops: one for Provençal fabrics, another for pottery, and a third called Provence Gourmande, which has candied fruits and imaginative jams such as rhubarb with prunes or apricot with almonds, not to mention nectars and liqueurs of fruit like bilberry or quince.

It was Marie-Thérèse Bouterin who brought me to St Rémy. Cooking is in her family – I well remember when her son, Antoine, now in charge of one of New York's top restaurants, gave a cooking class in Paris. The colours, the intensity of flavours, the quantity of herbs he used – we were overwhelmed! I found Madame Bouterin hard at work on her intensive produce farm a few miles outside town. She wasted not a moment. Provençale cooking 'is like the light, red and yellow, explosive,' she told me. Despite the time of day – it was early morning – she insisted I try her vegetable soup served with basil-flavoured 'pistou' sauce, and her snails simmered in herb-flavoured broth, accompanied by aïoli, a glowing gold from the use of fruity olive oil. Madame Bouterin makes a notable 'ratatouille', a riot of zucchini, tomatoes, red and green peppers, and eggplant, all laced with olive oil and garlic. For me a crowning touch to ratatouille is the flavouring of musky coriander seeds suggested by Elizabeth David. I asked Madame Bouterin about 'bouillabaisse' and she sighed. 'The right fish are so expensive – you must have plenty of rascasse (scorpionfish), as well as eel and a good selection of white fish such as mullet and John Dory!' Instead she often makes a puréed fish soup (p. 84), serving it with the same rust-red 'rouille' as bouillabaisse, plus garlic-flavoured croûtes and grated Gruyère cheese. (Rouille is a chilli-flavoured mayonnaise.)

From St Rémy it is but a few minutes to Les Baux, hideout of the medieval rulers of Provence, the 'Wolves of Orange' who claimed kinship to the biblical Balthazar. Les Baux clings precariously to a ravine and boasts three Michelin-starred restaurants, surely a record for a village with only 433 inhabitants. The most famous is Oustau de Beaumanière. Its octogenarian proprietor retired recently, yielding the stoves to his grandson, Jean-André Charial, who serves such enlightened dishes as sautéed salmon in anchovy vinaigrette, and sweetbreads with black olives.

Next destination is Gordes, east of Cavaillon. The direct route, back through St Rémy and Cavaillon, is fast but dull,

Lex Baux clings precariously above a ravine and boasts three Michelin-starred restaurants, surely a record for a village with only 433 inhabitants.

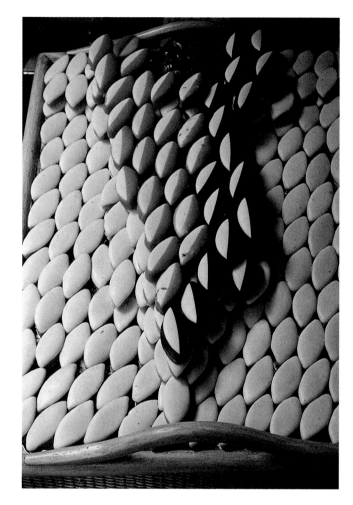

'Calissons' d'Aix.

ings constructed of flat stones. They have a remote, prehistoric air, though they were inhabited until quite recently.

Very much in the present at a couple of kilometres from Gordes is Le Mas Tourteron, a country inn run by Elisabeth Bourgeois, vice-president of ARC (Association des Restauratrices Cuisinières), a French association of women cooks. The day we were there we were almost alone and Elisabeth served us simple food of memorable finesse in her walled garden. We opened with a salad of spring vegetables – asparagus, baby haricots verts, broad/lima beans, each one carefully peeled, slivers of tomato, and crunchy slices of raw baby artichoke in a lemon dressing topped with a single chunk of fresh truffle. The main course was robust – a highly spiced, almost Asian, daube of lamb moulded inside thin slices of aubergine, a reminder of the cosmopolitan roots of Provence. Instead of cheese came a salty mélange of cheese and anchovy pâtés – very Provençal and too much for me. However dessert was once again perfect – 'nougat des Alpes' an almond and honey mould served with a fresh strawberry coulis. The meal was ample proof, if proof were needed, that modern cooking can be grafted successfully on to tradition.

Sweets in Provence are ultra-sweet. Nougat candy is a speciality of Montélimar and in Provence I found black nougat, a combination of caramelized honey packed with whole toasted almonds, at least double the amount you find in the familiar white version. Most towns have a special candy, such as the sugar-coated 'berlingots' of Carpentras, often flavoured with mint, and the 'calissons' of Aix-en-Provence, soft diamonds of ground almonds bound with candied melon and flavoured with orange flower water. A traditional Christmas feast features 'Les Treize Desserts'. True, several are just bowls of dried or candied fruits, but 13 desserts is prodigal nonetheless.

The most popular and versatile Provençale sweetmeat is candied fruit, for which the town of Apt is famous. Only a handful of artisan firms remain, struggling to outwit the marketing muscle of commercial enterprises. The height of the sales season is Christmas, when boxes of glistening pink, green and gold fruit are a traditional French gift. The actual dipping of fruit continues all year, for candying is an extended process. Fruits are selected for their perfect condition, then poached in ever more concentrated batches of syrup until completely saturated and preserved with a shiny sugar glaze. Apricots are most difficult, requiring as many as

so I'd suggest you continue south from Les Baux to Maussane-les-Alpilles, then eastwards to Mouriès and Eyguières, before heading north to Gordes. As so often, side-roads will amply repay the extra time as you travel into an area bisected by the mountain range of the Lubéron, the heart of Provence and now a national park. If possible, sidetrack to Oppède and Fontaine de Vaucluse, the one set on a rocky pinnacle like so many local towns, the other an ancient watering spot. Gordes is full of charm, although I'm not the first to have discovered it and the village is overrun with visitors for much of the year. The oldest olive press in France, dating from the 14th century, is to be found in a nearby museum. Its mighty beam, weighing 9 tonnes, is known affectionately as 'the sheep' because of its curious shape. Also close by is the village of Les Bories with its strange beehive-shaped dwell-

14 dippings, while a whole melon looks spectacular but can be cloying. My personal favourite is candied citrus peel, which can be made quite satisfactorily at home. The finished peel is tender and fragrant, worlds away from the commercial version.

You need a Provençale sweet tooth to enjoy candied fruits on their own, but I came across several ingenious ways of using them. One was to pack them in jars, then macerate them in cognac or eau-de-vie. After a few weeks they become agreeably alcoholic, excellent in breads and cakes, while the brandy is transformed to an after-dinner liqueur. Such treatment can be given to 'quatre mendiants', a 'four beggars' mixture of figs, unblanched almonds, hazelnuts and white raisins. Its colours are said to recall the robes of the four main monastic orders: Augustinian deep violet, Carmelite brown, Franciscan grey and Dominican white.

It was in Apt on the candied fruit trail that I stumbled on the Caizacs, whose family have been in the canning business for serveral generations. With truffles in such short supply, Vincent and Dominique now concentrate on terrines of game, including the traditional small birds. I was assured, however, that larks are no longer netted as in the old days, having been replaced in the commercial kitchen by the common starling or 'sansonnet'. After tasting a few samples I was taken next door to Madame Caizac, mère, in her little restaurant, La Terrine Gourmande. What she cooks 'depends on how I feel, on the ingredients from day to day', she explains. I was there at Easter, time for eggs – hardboiled eggs with tapenade or aïoli; scrambled eggs with fresh herbs; omelette with onion and tomato. Time, too, for baby lamb or beef, cooked 'en daube' in the classic pot-bellied 'daubière' of terracotta. As the pot cannot be heated strongly over the fire, the meat is simply layered with the other ingredients and doused with wine. Then the pot is sealed with a flour and water paste and left in the glowing ashes to cook very gently for six hours, until the meat is tender and soft enough to cut with a spoon.

South from Apt, the little route D943 winds over the Lubéron mountains to Bonnieux and Cadenet. This is 'garrigues' country, full of the wild herbs which give such savour to the animals which graze on them. Wild rabbits, pheasant and quail are abundant, while garrigues-fed lamb is renowned throughout France. The cheese from goats pastured here is also famous – ask for the cheeseboard in

The market at Cadenet.

Provence and you will be brought a platter of small rounds of goat cheese, each one flavoured with a different herb, or with garlic. The cheese from one flock is called 'sapeur pompier' or fireman's cheese, since the goats are employed to eat the underbrush as a break to the fires that can ravage the area in summer.

Bonnieux is a typical hill town strategically placed between the sheep country above and the richer valley land below. The houses rise tall to provide shade from the sun and shelter from the mistral wind. Nestling in one of the narrow streets is the Musée de la Boulangerie, just opposite an artisan baker who still uses the wood-fired oven indispensable to a really crisp crust. In Provence, bread ranges far beyond the standard baguette. Loaves of wholewheat and sourdough are part of the standard repertoire, while common

Beekeeper Joseph Bondin at work.

additions include walnuts and flavourings of onion or olive. 'Fouace', called 'gibassié' further south around Aix, is a soft egg bread, shaped flat and slashed to resemble a giant leaf. A wide variety of flavourings may be added, from lemon peel to orange flower water, herbs, or finely chopped olives, and the bread is sometimes also stuffed with cheese or anchovies.

From Cadenet we head south on the D973 towards the capital, Aix-en-Provence, stopping if you like at Pertuis and the Grégoire herb distillery. 'Thyme, rosemary, bay leaf and fennel are most common,' explained Madame Grégoire. All are part of the popular 'herbes de Provence' mix, with additions such as oregano, fennel, aniseed, and the coriander favoured by Madame. The best herbs grow in the mountains, she avers. They are gathered in the cool morning hours, then brought down to dry behind the dusty packing sheds. A few days of summer sun suffices to dry leaf herbs, but those on

the stem take several weeks, retaining superior flavour. Herb teas are taken seriously in France as a natural remedy. An infusion of the flowers of 'tilleul' (lime or linden), for instance, will ensure a good sleep, while 'verveine' (verbena) will cure headache, and mint is a digestive. Cowslip is known to be good for the chest, while lavender is not just a perfume, but also cures insomnia.

One of the most stunning sights in Provence is a field of lavender in bloom, seventh heaven for honey bees. Beekeeper Joseph Bondin is based in Lambesc, but he leads a nomad life, transporting his 500 hives from the rosemary flowers of early spring in the Lubéron to fields of colza near Lyon in May. Then it's a climb to the acacia and pines of the Jura mountains, with a return to Provence for the late-summer lavender. When I asked Joseph how he transported his bees, he said it was easy, 'I just wait until after dark, then load the hives and take the autoroute. It's not far, you know!' Indeed, a bee truck labelled 'transport d'abeilles' is not an uncommon sight in these parts.

Each crop of honey is different: pine honey is dark and strong, almost smoky; acacia stays liquid longer than any other, while mild colza honey thickens within a week or two. Rosemary and lavender honeys are pale and fragrant, pleasing to most tastes, though Joseph prefers the pine flavour. The more profuse the flowers, the harder the bees work and the more copious the crop. In parting, Monsieur Bondin tells me with pride that he has been to Texas and California to study American beekeeping methods. He was much impressed by the bees, bred to be less aggressive, and by the terrain. 'So much space,' he exclaimed.

Aix-en-Provence is a city of extraordinary charm and grace, noted for its annual arts festival and distinguished university. The central Cours Mirabeau sums it up – a wide boulevard shaded with plane trees, alive with promenading crowds and studded with cafés. Even the drinks epitomize the south – Pernod and its anise-flavoured cousins, pungent aperitifs like gentiane and Suze, refreshing mint syrup mixed with lemonade. By Aix standards the 17th- and 18th-century houses lining the Cours are young, for Aix was founded by the Romans, and the streets to the north are still medieval in atmosphere. Here you'll find attractions like Le Fournil des Augustins at 51 rue Espariat, with its artisan breads and great wheels of rustic fruit tarts. On the rue Boulegon there is a good source for the expensive but pretty potteries from Moustiers Ste Marie, fired in the mountain range to the northeast of Aix, along the Gorges de Verdon. A few doors along, L'Outil groups an outstanding collection of old household tools and country furniture, including the characteristic decorative salt boxes, dough trough and bread cabinets.

For Provençal food products, it is hard to beat La Taste – a chain to be found in most of the larger towns – and which takes its selection of olive oils, herbs, jams, candied fruits and wine very seriously. The famous Souleiado shops appear in many places, too, home of almost irresistible fabrics by the yard, table linens, shirts and dresses in the sun-slashed golds, sky blues, lavenders, rust-reds and muted greens of the surrounding countryside. For Provençal cuisine, the best cook in Aix, they say, is Jean Marc Banzo at Le Clos de la Violette, and I can attest personally to the

Fruits de Mer served in Aix-en-Provence.

excellence of his compote of rabbit. If you're near the Cours Mirabeau, you might drop in on the Bistro Latin, notable for its terrine of sea bass with tapenade, and leg of lamb with garlic purée.

Aix-en-Provence offers a fitting farewell to this most seductive province of France. At lunchtime you can shelter from the searing midday heat under parasols and plane trees, drinking cool rosé wine and sharing a plateful of raw vegetables and aïoli. The intoxicating light and shimmering colours have inspired many a painter – Renoir, Cézanne, Van Gogh, Matisse, Bonnard, Dufy. With its excellent climate and vibrant artisan heritage, Provence is prime ground for secondary residences of both French and foreigners. 'Very like the Côte d'Azur in the old days,' says my husband who can remember what Vence was like 40 years ago. Take advantage while the magic lasts!

RECIPES FROM
PROVENCE

Soupe au Pistou à la Minute
QUICK VEGETABLE SOUP WITH BASIL AND GARLIC SAUCE

This version of vegetable soup is so simple that it takes less than half an hour. Essential component is the 'pistou' sauce of garlic, parmesan cheese, olive oil and basil, the signature herb of Provence.

Serves 4
2 tbsp butter
2 medium leeks, cut in julienne strips (p. 184),
with some of the green
3 stalks celery, cut in julienne strips
2 medium carrots, cut in julienne strips
1 small head lettuce, cut in julienne strips
salt and pepper
1⅔ pints/1 quart/1 litre water
For the pistou
15 basil leaves
3 large cloves garlic, peeled
3½ oz/1 cup/100 g freshly grated Parmesan cheese
4 fl oz/½ cup/125 ml olive oil

Melt the butter in a large pan. Add the vegetables, seasoning the layers with salt and pepper. Press a piece of buttered wax paper on the vegetables and cover the pan. Cook the vegetables over very low heat until tender, stirring occasionally, 20–25 minutes. Note: do not allow them to brown. Add the water to the vegetables, bring to the boil, then simmer for 5–10 minutes.

Meanwhile make the pistou: chop the basil, garlic and cheese in a food processor or blender, then gradually work in the oil to form a pourable purée. Spoon the soup into bowls and pass the pistou separately. The soup is best freshly made.

Artichauts à la Barigoule
STUFFED ARTICHOKES WITH BLACK OLIVES

So popular are braised artichokes 'à la barigoule' in southern France that Escoffier, who was born near Nice, included them in his classic *Guide Culinaire*. In this recipe, anchovy and olive replace the more classic stuffing based on pork.

Serves 4
4 medium globe artichokes
½ lemon
1 carrot, sliced
1 onion, sliced
8 fl oz/1 cup/250 ml white wine
1¼ pints/3 cups/750 ml white veal stock (p. 186),
more if needed
salt and pepper
1 tbsp arrowroot or potato flour/starch, dissolved (p. 182) in
3 tbsp water
For the stuffing
1 tbsp butter
½ onion, finely chopped
2 cloves garlic, chopped
4 oz/125 g pork, minced/ground
1½ oz/½ cup/45 g fresh breadcrumbs
2 oz/60 g mushrooms, finely chopped
2 oz/60 g raw ham, finely diced
2 oz/60 g black olives, stoned/pitted, finely chopped
1 tbsp chopped basil
2 tbsp chopped parsley
1 tsp chopped fresh thyme
large pinch ground allspice
pepper

Preheat the oven to No 4/350°F/175°C. Break the stem off each artichoke and trim the base so it is flat. Cut off ¾ inch/2 cm from the top and trim the spiky tips from the leaves with scissors. Rub the cut surfaces with the lemon half. Parboil the artichokes in boiling salted water for 15–20 minutes and drain them. With a ball cutter or sharp teaspoon, remove the choke and inside leaves.

For the stuffing: melt the butter in a frying pan, add the onion and cook gently until soft but not brown. Add the chopped garlic and the pork and cook over medium heat until crumbling and browned, 5–7 minutes. Stir in the bread-

The fertile soil has brought prosperity to Provence, but only since the advent of railways, which revolutionized transport to Paris.

Papeton d'Aubergines

AUBERGINE/EGGPLANT MOULD

For the appropriate papal tiara shape, papeton is best cooked in a charlotte mould. The recipe is typical of the herb, oil and garlic-laden Provençal vegetable salads, at their best served at room temperature.

Serves 6–8
1 lb/500 g aubergines/eggplants
6½ oz/200 g courgettes/zucchini, sliced in thick rounds
salt and pepper
3 tbsp olive oil
2 medium onions, chopped
3 cloves garlic, finely chopped
1 large red pepper, cored, seeded and diced
1 large green pepper, cored, seeded and diced
1 egg, beaten to mix
1½ oz/½ cup/45 g breadcrumbs, more if needed
For the tomato coulis
1 lb/500 g tomatoes, peeled, seeded and chopped (p. 186)
bouquet garni (p. 183)
salt and pepper
2⅓ pint/1½ quart/1.5 litre charlotte mould

crumbs, mushrooms, ham and olives and leave to cool. Add the basil, parsley, thyme, allspice and pepper and mix thoroughly. Sauté a small piece of stuffing and taste for seasoning; salt may not be needed because the ham and olives are salty.

Fill the hollow of each artichoke with the stuffing and encircle the leaves with string. Put the carrot and onion in a casserole deep enough to contain the artichokes. Add the artichokes with the wine and boil for 5 minutes or until the wine is reduced by half. Pour enough stock over the artichokes to cover them by half, and add salt and pepper. Bring back to the boil, cover with buttered paper, and cook in the oven until tender, 40–50 minutes, basting with the juices occasionally and adding more stock if necessary to keep the artichokes moist. They can be kept in the refrigerator up to a day.

To finish: reheat the artichokes if necessary on top of the stove. Remove them and keep them warm. Strain the cooking liquid into a small saucepan and bring to the boil. Taste the liquid and reduce if necessary until the flavour is concentrated. Whisk in enough of the dissolved arrowroot or potato flour/starch to obtain a sauce the consistency of thin cream. Simmer for 2 minutes and taste for seasoning. Discard the strings from the artichokes and serve them on individual plates or shallow bowls. Pass the sauce separately.

Preheat the oven to No 7/425°F/220°C. Halve the aubergines/eggplants lengthwise, and score the flesh with a knife. Sprinkle the aubergines/eggplants and courgettes/zucchini with salt and let them stand for 30 minutes to draw out the juices. Rinse both vegetables with water and pat them dry with paper towels.

Put the aubergines/eggplants cut side down on an oiled pan and bake in the heated oven until the flesh is somewhat soft, 15–20 minutes. Remove the pulp with a spoon, being careful not to pierce the skin. Reserve the skins. In a skillet, heat 2 tablespoons of the oil and sauté the courgette/zucchini rounds until lightly browned on both sides.

For the tomato coulis: put the tomatoes, bouquet garni, salt and pepper in a heavy-based saucepan. Cover and cook over very low heat for 10 minutes. Uncover and simmer, stirring occasionally, until very thick, about 15 minutes.

In a large heavy pan, heat the remaining oil, add the onions and cook slowly until soft but not brown. Add the aubergine/eggplant pulp, courgettes/zucchini, garlic, red and green peppers, and half of the tomato coulis with the

Papeton d'Aubergines.

bouquet garni, salt and pepper. Taste the remaining coulis and reserve it. Cook the aubergine/eggplant mixture, uncovered in the oven, stirring occasionally, until the vegetables are tender and the mixture is thick, 25–30 minutes. Discard the bouquet garni. Remove the pan from the heat and let cool slightly. Stir in the egg and enough breadcrumbs to make the mixture stiff but not dry. Taste it for seasoning.

Preheat the oven to No 4/350°F/175°C. Oil the charlotte mould generously and line it with the aubergine/eggplant skins, purple sides outwards. Fill it with the vegetable mixture, folding any overlapping skins on top. Cover the papeton with oiled paper and set it in a water bath (p. 187). Bring it to the boil on top of the stove and bake in the oven until firm and a skewer inserted in the centre is hot to the touch when withdrawn, about 1 hour. Let the papeton cool. It can be refrigerated, with the tomato coulis, up to 2 days. Unmould it shortly before serving and serve it at room temperature, edged with the reserved tomato coulis.

Bouillabaisse

— PROVENÇAL FISH STEW —

For bouillabaisse, you need as wide a range of fish as possible, including white fish such as monkfish, mullet, bream, whiting, sea bass and John Dory, and rich fish such as conger eel and mackerel. The only bouillabaisse fish not commonly available away from the Mediterranean is scorpion-fish ('rascasse') and red gurnard ('rouget grondin'). Shellfish are not used in the traditional Provençal recipe. The soup is served with sauce rouille and garlic croûtes.

Serves 8–10
3 lb/1.5 kg white fish, scaled, cleaned, with their heads
2 lb/1 kg rich fish, scaled, cleaned, with their heads
2 large crabs, or 8–10 small spider crabs, optional
1 large spiny lobster, or 8–10 small lobster tails, optional
6 fl oz/¾ cup/175 ml olive oil
2 medium onions, sliced
2 leeks, trimmed, split and sliced
2 stalks celery, sliced
a bulb of fresh fennel, sliced, or 1 tsp dried fennel seed
1 lb/500 g tomatoes, peeled, seeded and chopped (p. 186)
3–4 cloves garlic, crushed
bouquet garni (p. 183)
thinly peeled strip of orange rind
pinch of saffron, soaked in 1–2 tbsp boiling water
salt and pepper
1 tbsp tomato paste
1 tbsp anise liquor
1 oz/30 g chopped parsley

For the marinade
3 tbsp olive oil
2 cloves garlic, finely chopped
pinch of saffron, soaked in 1–2 tbsp boiling water

For serving
sauce rouille (p. 84)
15–20 croûtes (p. 183) fried,
then rubbed with a cut garlic clove

Wash and pat dry the fish and cut them in chunks. Make a fish broth using the heads and tails: put them in a pan, barely cover with water, bring to the boil, cook for 15 minutes and strain. Meanwhile, marinate the fish chunks in a bowl by mixing them with the olive oil, garlic and saffron and its liquid.

If using shellfish, leave them in their shells. With a large cleaver, chop the large crabs and spiny lobster into pieces, discarding the stomach and intestinal veins of the lobster and the spongy finger-like gills of the large crabs. Chop small crabs in half and leave lobster tails whole.

Heat the olive oil in a large flameproof casserole. Add the onions, leeks, celery and fennel and sauté lightly until soft but not brown, 5–7 minutes. Add the tomatoes, garlic, bouquet garni and orange rind. Stir in the fish broth, saffron and its liquid and season with salt and pepper. Bring to the boil and simmer for 30–40 minutes. The liquid can be made up to 8 hours ahead and refrigerated.

Twenty minutes before serving, bring the liquid to the boil. Add the rich fish and shellfish and boil uncovered as hard as possible for 7 minutes. Don't stir, but shake the pan from time to time to prevent the mixture from sticking. Put the white fish on top and boil until the fish just flakes easily, 5–8 minutes, adding more water, if necessary, to cover all the pieces of fish. Note: keep the liquid boiling fast so that the oil emulsifies in the broth and does not float on the surface.

To serve: using a draining spoon, transfer the fish to a hot deep dish, arranging them so the different kinds are separated. Cover with foil and keep warm. Discard the bouquet garni and orange rind from the broth, then whisk in the tomato paste and anise liquor and taste for seasoning. Pour it into a bowl or soup tureen. Sprinkle the broth and fish with chopped parsley and serve both at the same time, leaving guests to help themselves to fish, broth, sauce rouille and croûtes.

Filets de Poisson en Tapenade
——————— FISH WITH BLACK OLIVE AND ANCHOVY SAUCE ———————

Usually served with hardboiled eggs or raw vegetables, tapenade is also delicious with a full-flavoured fish such as sea bass, bream, or John Dory. Tomatoes Provençale (see roast rabbit, p. 178) would make a colourful accompaniment.

Serves 8
3 lb/1.4 kg fish fillets
3–4 tbsp olive oil
juice of 1 lemon
salt and white pepper
For the tapenade
2½ oz/⅓ cup/75 g black olives, stoned/pitted
4 anchovy fillets
2 tbsp capers, drained
3 cloves garlic, peeled
2 fl oz/¼ cup/60 ml olive oil
black pepper

Prepare the tapenade: put the stoned/pitted olives, anchovy fillets, capers and garlic in a food processor or blender. Using the pulse button, gradually pour in the olive oil to form a coarse or finely chopped mixture, as you prefer. Season it to taste with pepper. Tapenade can be refrigerated, tightly covered, up to a week.

An hour or two before serving, marinate the fish: lay the fillets in a shallow dish and sprinkle them with half the olive oil, the lemon juice, salt and pepper. Cover and refrigerate them 1–2 hours, turning once or twice.

To finish: put the remaining oil in a heavy frying pan. Add the fish fillets and cover tightly. Cook over very low heat until the fish just flakes easily, 5–8 minutes, depending on thickness. Turn the fish once during cooking and do not allow it to brown. Transfer the fillets to a serving dish and spread the tapenade on top. The fish is good hot or at room temperature. (It can be kept for up to 2 hours at room temperature.)

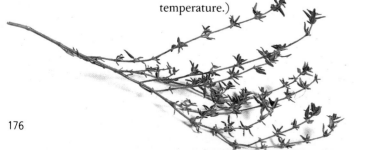

Cailles à la Camarguaise
——————— QUAIL WITH RICE PILAF ———————

Rice has been grown for centuries in the Camargue, the warm wet delta of the Rhône. Here it is cooked as a pilaf with quail, which thrive on the 'garrigues' terrain inland.

Serves 4
8 quail
8 quail livers or 2 chicken livers, cut in 8 pieces
salt and pepper
3 oz/6 tbsp/90 g butter
8 oz/250 g lean bacon or Canadian bacon,
cut in lardons (p. 184)
8 fl oz/1 cup/250 ml white wine
1 pint/2½ cups/600 ml chicken or veal stock (p. 186)
1¼ cups/225 g rice
bouquet garni (p. 183)
1 lb/500 g chipolata or baby frankfurter sausages
pinch of cayenne pepper
1–2 tbsp butter, to finish
string

Clean the quail and put the livers inside the bodies. Sprinkle with salt and pepper and tie them neatly with string. Heat the oven to No 4/350°F/175°C.

Heat one-third of the butter in a large casserole and fry the bacon until lightly browned. Remove the bacon, add the quail and brown them on all sides, 5–7 minutes. Remove them, drain off all the fat, add the wine and boil until reduced to 2 fl oz/¼ cup/60 ml. Add the stock and bring to the boil, then add the rice, bacon, bouquet garni, salt and pepper, spreading the rice so it is covered by the stock. Cover and bake in the oven 10 minutes.

Add the quail and continue cooking until all the stock is absorbed by the rice and no pink juice runs from the cavity of the quail when they are lifted with a fork, 8–10 minutes. If the rice is not tender, remove the quail, add a little more water to the rice and continue cooking it. The quail and rice can be cooked up to 48 hours ahead and kept covered in the refrigerator. Undercook them slightly to allow for reheating.

To finish: heat half the remaining butter in a saucepan and sauté the sausages. Reheat the quail and rice on top of the stove, if necessary. Remove the quail, discard the strings and keep them warm. Discard the bouquet garni and season the rice with the salt, pepper and cayenne. Stir to separate the grains and dot with the remaining butter. When it has melted, pile the rice on a platter and arrange the quail and sausages around them.

La Daube de Boeuf de Madame Caizac
—————— BEEF STEW WITH OLIVES ——————

Madame Caizac makes several changes to the traditional Provençal daube. She uses beef rather than lamb and likes to brown the meat before adding wine, so the sauce is more succulent. She also adds white rather than red wine, and does not bother with tomatoes. Fresh noodles (p. 91) are the best accompaniment.

Serves 6–8

3 lb/1.4 kg beef chuck or round roast,
cut in 2 inch/5 cm cubes
12 oz/375 g lean bacon, cut into lardons (p. 184)
12 oz/375 g lean salt pork, cut into lardons
4 tbsp olive oil
2 onions, sliced in thick rounds
2 carrots, sliced in thick rounds
6½ oz/1 cup/200 g black and/or green olives, stoned/pitted
1¼ pints/3 cups/750 ml brown stock (p. 186), more if needed
salt and pepper
8 oz/250 g mushrooms, sliced
kneaded butter (p. 184) made with 3 tbsp butter and 3 tbsp flour

For the marinade
2 bay leaves
2–3 sprigs of thyme
2–3 sprigs of rosemary
2 tsp juniper berries
3 sprigs of parsley
10 peppercorns
2 cloves garlic, peeled
1 bottle (3 cups/750 ml) dry white wine
2 tbsp olive oil
muslin/cheesecloth

In a bowl, combine the marinade ingredients except the oil. Add the beef, stir well, and pour the olive oil on top. Cover

The Moulin Jacques Ramade at Nyons, where olives are pressed by traditional methods.

and leave to marinate for 1–2 days in the refrigerator, turning the beef occasionally. Blanch (p. 182) the bacon and salt pork, drain, rinse under cold running water and drain thoroughly. Preheat the oven to No 2/300°F/150°C.

Remove the beef and strain the marinade. Chop the garlic and tie the herbs and peppercorns in a piece of muslin/cheesecloth. Pat the meat dry on paper towels. In a heavy casserole, heat half the oil and brown the meat very thoroughly on all sides over high heat. You may have to do this in several batches. Remove the meat, add the onions and brown them also. Add the reserved marinade to the casserole and stir to deglaze (p. 184) the pan. In layers, add the beef, bacon, salt pork, carrots and olives, with the garlic and the bag of herbs. Add enough stock to just cover the meat, with some pepper. Note: the bacon and olives will add salt. Cover and cook the daube in the heated oven until the beef is tender enough to crush in your fingers, 2–3 hours. Stir the daube from time to time and add more stock if it seems dry.

At the end of cooking, discard the herb bag. Sauté the mushrooms in the remaining oil until tender and stir into the daube. Add the kneaded butter in small pieces, shaking the pan so the butter melts into the sauce and thickens it. Simmer the sauce 2 minutes and taste it. Serve the daube from the casserole; it can be made up to 2 days ahead and kept covered in the refrigerator.

Lapin Roti à la Moutarde de Madame Bouterin

— ROAST RABBIT WITH MUSTARD AND TOMATOES PROVENÇALE —

Madame Bouterin's recipe for roast rabbit with mustard is very much in the vivid Provençale tradition, packed with herbs and garlic.

Serves 6
1 rabbit (about 3 lb/1.4 kg), cut into serving pieces (p. 186)
6–8 tbsp mustard
3 tbsp olive oil
2 tbsp chopped basil
1 tbsp chopped savory
1 tbsp chopped rosemary
bouquet garni (p. 183)
10 cloves garlic, unpeeled
2 medium onions, finely chopped
4 fl oz/½ cup/125 ml dry white wine
2 tbsp fresh parsley (for garnish)
For the tomatoes
3–4 large tomatoes
3 tbsp browned breadcrumbs
1 clove garlic, finely chopped
1 tbsp chopped parsley
salt and pepper
2 tbsp olive oil or melted butter

Preheat the oven to No 4/350°F/175°C. Generously oil a roasting pan. Brush the rabbit pieces evenly with mustard and set them in the pan. Sprinkle them with oil, basil, savory and rosemary and add the bouquet garni. Roast the rabbit in the oven until tender and golden brown, ¾–1 hour. During roasting, turn the pieces, brushing them with more mustard

and sprinkling them often with olive oil. Add the garlic after 15 minutes.

Cut the tomatoes in half crosswise, discarding the cores. Put them in a buttered baking dish. In a separate bowl, combine the breadcrumbs, garlic, parsley, salt, pepper and oil or melted butter, stirring to form a crumbly mixture. Spoon it on the tomatoes and bake them in the oven with the rabbit until just tender, 12–15 minutes.

After roasting, remove the rabbit pieces and garlic. Add the onions to the pan and cook, stirring, until they are golden brown, 3–5 minutes. Add the wine to deglaze (p. 184) the pan and simmer so it reduces well. Taste the onions for seasoning, spoon them over the rabbit, sprinkle with parsley and arrange the tomatoes around the dish. If reheated, the rabbit tends to be dry but on a hot day it is excellent cooked ahead to serve at room temperature.

Fouace

— FLAT YEAST BREAD —

Fouace contains a high proportion of yeast, so it rises quickly, forming a flat, oval loaf. The bread is its best eaten warm, broken into pieces at the table.

Makes 1 flat loaf to serve 4
⅓ oz/10 g compressed yeast, or ⅙ oz/5 g dry yeast
4 fl oz/½ cup/125 ml lukewarm milk
10 oz/2½ cups/300 g flour, more if needed
2 eggs
1 tsp salt
2 tsp sugar
4 tbsp finely chopped candied lemon peel (p. 180),
or stoned/pitted black olives, or 2 tbsp chopped fresh thyme,
oregano or rosemary
2½ oz/⅓ cup/75 g unsalted butter
1 egg, beaten with ½ tsp salt (for glaze)

In a small bowl, crumble or sprinkle the yeast over 3–4 tablespoons of the milk. Mix in enough of the flour to make a soft, sticky dough and let this starter rise in a warm place for 15–20 minutes. Sift the remaining flour on a board or marble slab and make a large well in the centre. Add the yeast starter, eggs, salt, sugar, candied lemon peel or other flavourings, and the remaining milk. Briefly mix the centre

Fouace.

ingredients, then gradually draw in the flour to form a dough. Knead the dough into a ball; it should be soft but not sticky, so add more flour if necessary.

Knead the dough by lifting it up and slapping it on the work surface for 5–10 minutes until very smooth and elastic. Pound the butter to soften it, then work it into the dough.

Knead the dough again to incorporate the butter thoroughly. Transfer the dough to a lightly floured bowl and sprinkle it with a little more flour. Cover with a damp cloth and let rise at room temperature for 1 hour or until nearly doubled in bulk.

Transfer the risen dough to a floured board or marble slab,

patting to knock out the air. Roll the dough into an oval about ¾ inch/2 cm thick on a lightly floured baking sheet. Slit it diagonally like the veins on a leaf, pulling the slits apart with your fingers. Let the dough rise until nearly doubled, 15–25 minutes. Preheat the oven to No 6/400°F/200°C. Brush the bread with the egg glaze and bake until golden brown, 10–12 minutes.

Les Oranges Confites
CANDIED ORANGE SLICES

Sliced pineapple can be candied like these sliced oranges. Other citrus fruits are too dense to absorb syrup and must be cut in strips (below).

Makes 12 oz/375 g candied fruit
1 lb/500 g navel oranges
2 lb/1 kg sugar
1⅔ pint/1 quart/1 litre water

Cut the oranges crosswise in ¼ inch/6 mm slices, including pith and peel. Discard the ends and any seeds. Heat the sugar with the water in a shallow pan until dissolved, then bring the syrup just to the boil. Arrange the orange slices loosely overlapping on a rack and lower it into the pan. Press a round of wax paper on top of the fruit so it is completely immersed and weigh it down with a plate.

Bring the syrup slowly to a simmer, taking 10–12 minutes. Continue poaching for another 15–18 minutes. Take the pan from the heat and let the fruit cool in the syrup. Leave it covered in the syrup at room temperature for 24 hours.

Lift out the fruit on the rack and leave it to drain for ½–1 hour. Transfer it to wax paper and leave in a cool airy place until dry, 3–5 hours. They may be stored, layered in wax paper, in an airtight container for up to a week.

Tarte aux Oranges Confites
CANDIED ORANGE TART

Candied orange slices are a spectacular filling for this simple tart. If you've no time to candy the slices at home, substitute commercial candied orange strips, or even prunes.

Serves 8
sweet pâte brisée (p. 184) made with 8 oz/2 cups/250 g flour,
4 oz/½ cup/125 g unsalted butter, 2 egg yolks, 2 tbsp sugar,
1 tsp salt, and 3–4 tbsp cold water
2 eggs, beaten to mix
8 fl oz/1 cup/250 ml double/heavy cream
12 oz/375 g candied orange slices (p. 180)
11 inch/28 cm tart tin/pan

Preheat the oven to No 5/375°F/190°C. Make the pâte brisée and chill it for 30 minutes. Roll out the dough and line the tart tin/pan. Blind bake the shell: cut a 13 inch/33 cm round of greaseproof paper and use it to line the shell, pressing it into the corners. Fill the shell three-quarters full with dried beans or rice to hold the dough in shape. Bake in the heated oven until the dough is set and the edges are brown, about 15 minutes. Remove the paper and beans or rice.

Whisk the eggs and cream until mixed. Arrange the orange slices overlapping in the shell and pour the cream mixture on top. Bake the tart in the heated oven until set and lightly browned, about 20 minutes. Note: if overcooked, the orange slices become tough. The tart is best served at room temperature, on the day of baking.

Écorces d'Agrumes Confites
CANDIED CITRUS PEEL

After candying, citrus strips may be chopped to use in cakes, or they may be rolled in sugar after draining and left to dry as a sweetmeat. Yet another alternative is to dip the strips in melted chocolate after drying them.

Makes 1½–2 lb/750 g–1 kg candied fruit
8 navel oranges, 6 grapefruit, or 16 lemons
2 lb/1 kg sugar
1⅔ pint/1 quart/1 litre water

Score the fruit in quarters with a sharp knife and strip away peel and pith with your fingers. Cut it in ¼ inch/6 mm strips. Follow the directions above for candied orange slices (a rack for cooking is not necessary). The peel is done when tender to the bite, 15–25 minutes, depending on the peel. (Grapefruit cooks the fastest and orange the slowest.) The candied peel will keep 2 weeks in an airtight container.

Opposite: Les Oranges Confites.

GLOSSARY OF COOKING TECHNIQUES

Arrowroot

Arrowroot (or potato starch) is used to thicken sauces lightly at the end of cooking. Mix the arrowroot in a cup with water, allowing about 1 tablespoon of water per teaspoon of arrowroot. It will make a thin, opaque mixture, which separates on standing but can easily be recombined. Whisk this mixture into a boiling liquid, adding just enough to thicken the sauce to the desired consistency. Do not boil the sauce for more than 2–3 minutes or it may become thin again.

Barding fat

Barding fat is thinly sliced pork fat available at most butchers. Barding fat is often wrapped around meat when it has little or no natural fat. It is also used for lining terrine moulds, where it is important to enclose meat to maintain a consistent level of moisture.

Blanching

Blanching is a preliminary to cooking. Generally, the food is put in cold unsalted water, brought slowly to the boil, skimmed, and then simmered for 3–5 minutes. Green vegetables, however, are blanched in water that is already boiling. The term 'to blanch' is misleading, for as well as whitening, it removes salt and other strong flavours, notably from bacon; it firms meats like sweetbreads and brains; it sets the brilliant colour of green vegetables and herbs, which often do not need further cooking; it loosens the skins of nuts and fruits like almonds and tomatoes; and it rids rice and potatoes of excess starch.

Blind baking

Pastry shells are blind baked (empty) before the filling is added. This procedure is used if the filling is not to be cooked in the shell, or if the filling is especially moist and might soak the pastry during baking. The dried beans or rice for blind baking can be kept and re-used.

For pies: heat the oven to 400°F/200°C/No 6. Crumple a round of parchment paper and line the chilled pastry shell, pressing the paper well into the corners; fill the shell with dried beans or rice. Bake the pastry in the oven for 15 minutes or until the edges are set and lightly browned. Remove the paper and beans or rice and continue baking until the base is firm and dry, for 4–5 minutes if the pie is to be baked again with the filling, or until well browned, 8–10 minutes, to bake the shell completely.

For tartelettes: heat the oven to 400°F/200°C/No 6. Line the chilled pastry shells with a round of crumpled parchment paper and fill with dried beans or rice. Alternatively, put a smaller tartelette pan inside each shell. Set the pans on a baking sheet and bake in the oven for 8–10 minutes. Remove the paper and beans or rice and continue baking until the pastry is firm and lightly browned, for 3–4 minutes if the tartelettes are to be baked again with the filling, or until well browned, 5–7 minutes, to bake the tartelettes completely.

Bouquet garni
A bundle of aromatic herbs used for flavouring braises, ragoûts and sauces. It should include a sprig of thyme, a bay leaf and several sprigs of parsley, tied together with string. Green leek and celery tops may also be included.

Brown stock, see stock, brown

Cèpes, to clean, see Wild mushrooms, to clean

Chestnuts, to peel
With a small knife make a slit at the end of each nut. Put them in a pan of cold water and bring just to the boil. Use a slotted spoon to lift out a few nuts at a time and peel them while still hot, removing both the thick outer skin and the thin inner skin. If the chestnuts cool and become difficult to peel, quickly reheat them. Do not allow them to heat too long, or the chestnuts will become soft and fall apart.

Chicken, to cut up, see Cutting up a raw bird

Chicken stock, see Stock, chicken

Crème Chantilly
For ingredient measurements, see individual recipes. Put the chilled cream in a bowl over ice and water and whisk until stiff. Note: if the cream is not cold it may curdle before it stiffens. Add sugar to taste, with vanilla or other flavouring, and continue whisking until the cream stiffens again. Note: do not over-beat or the cream will curdle. Crème Chantilly can be stored in the refrigerator for up to 12 hours. It will separate slightly on standing, but will recombine if stirred.

Crème fraîche
This French cream has a slightly tart flavour which is particularly good in sauces. To make 1¼ pints/3 cups/750 ml of crème fraîche, stir together in a saucepan 16 fl oz/2 cups/500 ml double/heavy cream and 8 fl oz/1 cup/250 ml buttermilk or sour cream. Heat gently until just below body temperature (25°C/75°F). Pour the cream into a container and partly cover it. Keep it at this temperature for 6–8 hours or until it has thickened and tastes slightly acid. The cream will thicken faster on a hot day. Stir it and store it in the refrigerator; it will keep for up to 2 weeks.

Croûtes
Croûtes are fried or toasted slices of bread used to add texture or to garnish dishes. If using French bread, cut the loaf into thin diagonal slices; if using sliced white bread, cut the bread in squares, triangles, rounds or hearts, discarding the crusts.

For toasted croûtes: bake the sliced bread in an oven heated to 350°F/175°C/No 4 for 10–15 minutes, turning the croûtes halfway through so they brown evenly on both sides. For a lightly fried effect, brush the sliced bread on both sides with melted butter before baking.

For fried croûtes: heat enough oil or butter, or a combination of the two, in a frying pan to coat the bottom generously. Add the slices of bread in a single layer, brown them on both sides over a brisk heat and drain them on paper towels.

Croûtons
Cut sliced white bread in cubes, discarding crusts. Fry as for croûtes, using enough fat for the croûtons to float. Stir briskly so they brown evenly.

Cutting up a raw bird
With a sharp knife, cut between leg and body, following the outline of the thigh until the leg joint is visible. Locate the 'oyster' piece of meat lying against the backbone, and cut around it so it remains attached to the thigh. Twist the leg sharply outwards to break the thigh joint. Cut forwards to detach each leg from the body, including the oyster meat. With a knife or poultry shears, cut away and remove the backbone. Cut along the breastbone to halve the carcass. Cut off the wingtips. The bird is now in 4 pieces.

To cut in 8 pieces, divide each breast in half, cutting diagonally through the meat, then through the breast and rib bones so a portion of breast meat is cut off with the wing. Trim the rib bones. Then, cut the legs in half through the joint, using the white line of fat on the underside as a guide. Trim the drumsticks and any protruding bones with poultry shears.

Deglaze

To deglaze a pan, boil the juices to a glaze (see separate entry) that sticks to the bottom of the pan (this may happen naturally during cooking). Pour off any fat, add liquid and boil, stirring to dissolve the glaze. Continue boiling until the liquid is reduced and has plenty of flavour.

Duck, to cut up, see Cutting up a raw bird

Eggs, to poach

Bring a large shallow pan of water to a rolling boil. Add 3 tablespoons vinegar per 1⅔ pints/1 quart/1 litre water. Break up to four eggs, one by one, into places where the liquid bubbles. Lower the heat and poach the eggs for 3–4 minutes until the yolk is fairly firm but still soft to the touch. Gently lift out the eggs with a slotted spoon and drain on paper towels. Trim the stringy edges with a pair of scissors. If the poached eggs are not to be used immediately, transfer them to a bowl of cold water. The eggs can then be reheated just before serving by soaking them in a bowl of hot water for 2 minutes and draining them.

Fish stock, see Stock, fish

Flaming

Food is flamed in spirit or in fortified wine with a high alcohol content. After flaming, only the essence remains and food is slightly toasted. To flame: heat the alcohol in a small pan, light it and pour over the hot food. Continue basting with liquid until the flame goes out. If the dish contains sugar, cooking should be continued until the sugar caramelizes.

Glaze, to reduce to a

When the cooking juices of meat or poultry are boiled down, they darken and caramelize to a shiny glaze which gives rich flavour to sauces and gravies. Glaze should be deep golden and of a sticky consistency. If cooked too far, it will burn.

Julienne strips

Julienne strips are matchstick length but more finely cut. For root vegetables, trim the sides of the vegetable to a square, then slice into 2 inch/5 cm lengths. Cut the lengths in thin vertical slices. Stack the slices and cut in thin strips. For celery, green pepper and similar vegetables, cut lengthwise in thin 2 inch/5 cm strips.

Kneaded butter

Kneaded butter is a paste made with butter and flour that is used to thicken a liquid at the end of cooking. It makes a richer, more traditional sauce than a starch thickener such as arrowroot. To make the kneaded butter, mash equal amounts of butter and flour together with your fingers or a fork until smooth. Add the kneaded butter gradually to boiling liquid, whisking constantly so that the butter melts and distributes the flour, thus thickening the sauce evenly. Continue boiling, adding the butter piece by piece until the sauce has thickened to the desired consistency. Kneaded butter can be made in large quantities and kept for several weeks in the refrigerator.

Lardons

Lardons are usually cut from bacon, but other fatty cuts of pork can also be used. To cut the lardons, trim the rind from the bacon and slice it ¼ inch/6 mm thick, then cut across the slices into short strips.

Morel mushrooms, to clean, see Wild mushrooms, to clean

Mussels, to clean

Wash the mussels under cold running water, scraping the shells clean with a knife and removing any weeds. Discard any shells which do not close when tapped, because this indicates that the mussel may be dead. The 'beard', or tough string dangling from inside the shell, should be removed only just before cooking the mussels.

Pastry Doughs

Pâte brisée: for ingredient measurements, see individual recipes. Sift flour onto a work surface and make a large well in the centre. Pound the butter with a rolling pin to soften it. Put the butter, eggs or egg yolks, salt and water in the well with flavourings such as sugar. Work together with your fingertips until partly mixed. Gradually draw in the flour with a pastry scraper or metal spatula, pulling the dough into large crumbs using the fingertips of both hands. If the crumbs are dry, sprinkle with another tablespoon of water. Press the dough together: it should be soft but not sticky. Work small portions of dough, pushing away from you on the work surface with the heel of your hand, then gathering it up with a scraper. Continue until the dough is smooth and pliable. Press the dough into a ball, wrap it and chill it for 30 minutes or until firm. Pâte brisée can be refrigerated overnight, or frozen.

Pâte à choux: for ingredient measurements, see individual recipes. Cut the butter into pieces. In a small saucepan, gently heat the water, salt and butter until the butter is melted. Meanwhile, sift the flour on to a piece of paper. Bring the butter mixture just to the boil (prolonged boiling evaporates the water and changes the proportions of the dough). Remove from the heat and immediately add all the flour. Beat vigorously with a wooden spoon for a few moments until the mixture pulls away from the sides of the pan to form a ball. Beat for ½–1 minute over a low heat to dry the dough. Beat one egg until mixed and set it aside. Beat the remaining eggs into the dough, one at a time, and beat thoroughly after each addition. Beat in enough of the reserved egg so that the dough is shiny and just falls from the spoon. If too much egg is added, the dough will be too soft and not hold its shape.

Pâte feuilletée: for ingredient measurements, see individual recipes. Melt or soften 1 tablespoon of the butter. Keep the rest of the butter cold. Sift the flour on to a cold marble slab or board, make a well in the centre and add the salt, water and the 1 tablespoon of butter. Work together with your fingertips until well mixed, then gradually work in the flour. If the dough is dry, add more water to form a soft but not sticky dough. Note: do not overwork the dough or it will become elastic. Press the dough into a ball, wrap it and chill it 15 minutes.

Lightly flour the butter, put it between two sheets of greaseproof/wax paper and flatten it with a rolling pin. Fold it, replace between the paper and continue pounding and folding it until

pliable but not sticky; it should be the same consistency as the dough. Shape the butter into a 6 inch/15 cm square and flour it lightly.

Roll out the dough on a floured marble slab or board to a 12 inch/30 cm square, thicker in the centre than at the sides. Set the butter in the centre and fold the dough around it like an envelope.

Make sure the working surface is well floured. Place the dough seam-side down and lightly pound it with a rolling pin to flatten it slightly. Roll it out to a rectangle about 7 inches/18 cm wide and 20 inches/50 cm long. Fold the rectangle into three, like a business letter. Seal the edges with the rolling pin and turn the dough a quarter turn (90°) to bring the closed seam to your left side so the dough opens like a book. This is called a turn. Roll out again and fold in

three. Wrap the dough and chill 15 minutes.

Repeat the rolling process until you have rolled and folded the dough 6 times, with a 15 minute rest in the refrigerator between every 2 turns. Chill the puff pastry at least 15 minutes before using it.

Pâte à pâté: follow the steps for making pâte brisée, adding the lard or butter and oil to the well with the eggs.

Pâte sucrée: for ingredient measurements, see individual recipes. Sift the flour on to a work surface and make a large well in the centre. (Note: in nut pastries, ground walnuts or hazelnuts may replace some of the flour.) Pound the butter with a rolling pin to soften. Put the butter, egg yolks, salt, sugar and vanilla into the well and work with your fingertips until they are well mixed and the sugar is partly dissolved. Draw in the flour, then work the dough and chill as when making pâte brisée.

Poaching eggs, see Eggs, poaching

Potato starch, see Arrowroot

Rabbit, to cut in pieces

Trim and discard flaps of skin, tips of forelegs and any excess bone. Using a heavy knife or cleaver, divide the rabbit crosswise into three sections: back legs, back, and forelegs including rib cage. Cut between the back legs to separate them; trim the end of backbone. Chop the front of the rabbit in 2 to separate forelegs. Cut the back crosswise into 2 or 3 pieces, depending on size, giving 6 or 7 pieces. Leave the kidneys attached to the ribs. For 8 or 9 pieces, cut each leg in two crosswise.

Spinach, preparing and cooking

Discard the stems from the spinach and wash the leaves well in several changes of water. Pack the wet leaves in a pan, cover and cook over medium heat, stirring once, until the leaves are wilted, about 5 minutes. Drain the spinach and leave to cool. Squeeze it by handfuls to extract as much water as possible.

Stock, brown

For about 4 pints/2½ quarts/2.5 litres stock, roast 5 lb/2.3 kg veal bones (you may use half veal bones and half beef bones, if you like) in a very hot oven for 20 minutes. Add 2 quartered carrots and 2 quartered onions and continue roasting until very brown, about 30 minutes longer. Transfer the bones and vegetables to a stock pot, discarding any fat. Add a bouquet garni (see separate entry), 1 teaspoon whole peppercorns, 1 tablespoon tomato purée/paste and about 4 quarts/5 quarts/5 litres water. Bring slowly to the boil, then simmer uncovered for 4–5 hours, skimming occasionally. Strain the stock, taste and, if the flavour is not concentrated, boil it until well reduced. Chill the stock and skim off any fat before using. Stock can be refrigerated for up to 3 days, or frozen.

Stock, chicken

Duck and other poultry bones can be substituted for the chicken. For about 4 pints/2½ quarts/2.5 litres of stock, in a large pan combine 3 lb/1.4 kg chicken backs, necks and bones; 1 onion, quartered; 1 carrot, quartered; 1 stalk celery, cut into pieces; a bouquet garni (see separate entry); 1 teaspoon peppercorns and about 6½ pints/4 quarts/4 litres water. Bring slowly to the boil, skimming often. Simmer uncovered, skimming occasionally, for 2–3 hours. Strain, taste, and if the stock is not concentrated, boil it until well reduced. Refrigerate it and, before using, skim any solidified fat from the surface. Stock can be kept for up to 3 days in the refrigerator, or frozen.

Stock, fish

For about 1⅔ pints/1 quart/1 litre stock, break 1½ lb/750 g fish bones into pieces and wash them thoroughly. In a pan cook 1 sliced onion in 1 tablespoon butter until soft but not brown. Add the fish bones, 1⅔ pints/1 quart/1 litre water, a bouquet garni (see separate entry), 10 peppercorns and 8 fl oz/1 cup/250 ml dry white

wine. Bring to the boil and simmer uncovered for 20 minutes, skimming often. Strain and cool.

Stock, white veal

Proceed as for brown stock, using only veal bones, but do not brown the bones and vegetables, and omit the tomato purée/paste. Blanch (see separate entry) the bones, then continue as for brown stock.

Tomatoes, to peel, seed and chop

Core the tomatoes and mark a small cross at the opposite end with the tip of a knife. Pour boiling water over the tomatoes and leave for 10 seconds or until the skin starts to peel at the cross. Drain the tomatoes and peel them. Halve them crosswise, squeeze them to remove the seeds, then chop them. The seeds can be sieved to extract the juice.

Trussing a bird

Trussing encloses any stuffing and keeps a bird in shape so it cooks evenly. Remove the wishbone to make carving easier: lift the neck skin and, with a small sharp knife, outline the wishbone and cut it free from the breastbone.

Set the bird breast up and push the legs back and down so the legs are sticking straight up in the air. Insert the trussing needle through one leg at the joint, then out through the other leg joint. Turn the bird over on to its other breast and push the needle through both sections of one wing and then into the neck skin, under the backbone of the bird, and out the other side. Now catch the second wing in the same way as the first. Pull the ends of the string from the leg and wing firmly together and tie securely.

Re-thread the trussing needle and turn the bird breast side up. Tuck the tail into the cavity of the bird. Insert the needle into the end of the drumstick, make a stitch through the skin, which should be overlapping to cover the cavity, and then push the needle through the end of the other drumstick. Turn the bird over and push the needle through the tail. Tie the string ends together.

Vanilla custard sauce

For ingredient measurements, see individual recipes. Scald the milk or milk and cream with the vanilla bean, splitting it to extract the seeds for more flavour. Cover and leave to infuse for 10–15 minutes. Beat the egg yolks with the sugar until thick and pale. Stir in the hot milk and return the mixture to the pan. Heat gently, stirring with a wooden spoon, until the custard thickens enough to leave a clear trail when you draw your finger across the back of a spoon (Note: do not boil or overcook the custard or it will curdle.) At once remove the custard from the heat and strain it into a bowl. The vanilla bean can be rinsed to use again.

Custard sauce can easily be flavoured. For coffee flavour, infuse the milk with coarsely ground coffee beans in place of the vanilla bean, straining the milk before mixing it with the egg yolk and sugar mixture. Or, you can add melted semi-sweet chocolate after the custard sauce has thickened and been removed from the heat.

Vinaigrette dressing

Vinaigrette dressing can be made with neutral vegetable oil, olive oil or nut oil. In France, red wine vinegar is most often used, but sometimes lemon juice is substituted (using roughly half of the quantity called for in vinegar). Other vinegars such as white wine, sherry, balsamic or fruit also make delicious vinaigrette dressings. Flavourings such as chopped onion, shallot, garlic or fresh herbs should be added to the dressing just before using.

For measurements and specification of ingredients, see individual recipes. In a small bowl whisk the vinegar with the salt, pepper and any other seasonings (such as Dijon mustard) until the salt dissolves. Gradually add the oil, whisking constantly so that the dressing emulsifies and thickens slightly. Vinaigrette can be made ahead and kept for several days at room temperature; it will separate but will re-emulsify when whisked.

Water bath

Water baths are used both for cooking and for keeping food warm. Water diffuses direct heat and ensures food keeps moist and not too hot.

To cook in a water bath, bring a deep roasting pan of water to the boil and set the mould or pan of food in it; the water should come at least halfway up the sides of the mould. Bring the water back to the boil and transfer to an oven heated to 375°F/190°C/No 5 or continue cooking on top of the stove, according to the recipe. Count the cooking time from the moment the water comes to the boil.

To keep foods hot in a water bath: set the mould or pan in a roasting pan of hot but not boiling water and leave over very low heat. The water should not boil.

White veal stock, see Stock, white veal

Wild mushrooms, to clean

All fresh wild mushrooms need the same preparation. Pick them over to remove twigs and grass then lightly trim the stems. Shake and gently brush to remove any earth; morels are the most gritty, so brush each one well, splitting the stem to remove any soil inside. Rinse with cold water, but never soak fresh mushrooms as they quickly soften to a pulp.

Soak dried mushrooms in warm water for 1–2 hours until fairly soft. Morels may need rinsing again, but liquid from other mushrooms adds flavour to a soup or sauce. The flavour of both fresh and dried mushrooms varies very much in strength, but 2 lb/1 kg of fresh mushrooms is the approximate equivalent of 3¼ oz/100 g of dried mushrooms.

RECIPE INDEX

Numbers in italics indicate illustrations.

INDEX